Eric Hoffer

The Longshoreman Philosopher

Eric Hoffer
The Longshoreman Philosopher

Tom Bethell

HOOVER INSTITUTION PRESS

STANFORD UNIVERSITY | STANFORD, CALIFORNIA

The Hoover Institution on War, Revolution and Peace, founded at Stanford University in 1919 by Herbert Hoover, who went on to become the thirty-first president of the United States, is an interdisciplinary research center for advanced study on domestic and international affairs. The views expressed in its publications are entirely those of the authors and do not necessarily reflect the views of the staff, officers, or Board of Overseers of the Hoover Institution.

www.hoover.org

Hoover Institution Press Publication No. 616

Hoover Institution at Leland Stanford Junior University, Stanford, California, 94305-6010

First printing 2012
17 16 15 14 13 12   9 8 7 6 5 4 3 2 1

Manufactured in the United States of America

⊗ The paper used in this publication meets the minimum Requirements of the American National Standard for Information Sciences—Permanence of Paper for Printed Library Materials, ANSI/NISO Z39.48-1992.

Library of Congress Cataloging-in-Publication Data

Bethell, Tom, 1936–
Eric Hoffer : The longshoreman philosopher / Tom Bethell.
    p.   cm. — (Hoover Institution Press publication series ; no. 616)
Includes bibliographical references and index.
ISBN 978-0-8179-1414-1 (cloth : alk. paper) –
ISBN 978-0-8179-1415-8 (pbk. : alk. paper) –
ISBN 978-0-8179-1416-5 (e-book)
1. Hoffer, Eric. 2. Social reformers—United States—Biography. 3. Philosophers—United States—Biography. I. Title. II. Series: Hoover Institution Press publication ; 616.
HN65.H54 B47 2012
303.48′4092—dc23   2011037057
[B]

CONTENTS

Photo section follows page 72, between Chapters Two and Three

ACKNOWLEDGMENTS

I am grateful to the ever-helpful staff of the Hoover Institution Archives, the main source of the information in this book. I also thank the late Lili Fabilli Osborne, with whom I had numerous conversations about Eric Hoffer; she died in September 2010, as the writing of the book was coming to an end. Thanks also to Lili's sons, Eric and Stephen, who shared their memories. In her blunt fashion, Lili's sister Mary Fabilli also told what she knew. My particular thanks go to Stacy Cole, who sat for several interviews and who probably knew Hoffer better than anyone beyond Lili and her family. Additional thanks are due to the late Joe Gladstone and his son, Rick; and to Tom Lorentzen, James T. Baker, Bill Fredlund, and John McGreevy. Thanks to those who answered letters, among them Richard Pipes and Calvin Tomkins.

The book would not have been possible without the generous support of John Raisian, the director of the Hoover Institution. My thanks also go to Barbara Egbert, whose editorial assistance greatly improved the manuscript.

INTRODUCTION

In 2000, the Hoover Institution acquired seventy-five linear feet of Eric Hoffer's papers from his longtime friend, Lili Osborne. She had accumulated them over many years; without her intervention they almost certainly would have been discarded. Hoffer himself died in 1983.

A few years after the papers were transferred, I had lunch with Thomas Sowell, a prolific author, columnist, and senior fellow at the Hoover Institution. He was interested in Hoffer, and with the help of an assistant had compiled a subject index to Hoffer's books, none of which had been published with an index.

Dr. Sowell told me he had heard I was working on a biography of Hoffer. I said that I had indeed been going through his papers but that a true biography would be a challenge. Not enough was known about the first half of his life. Three books about the man who became known as the Longshoreman Philosopher were published in his lifetime, all of them now out of print. All the facts about his early life in those books were drawn from interviews with Hoffer, conducted either by the authors or by other journalists. As far as I can tell, nothing that Hoffer said about his early years has ever been independently corroborated. Furthermore, little that I have been able to find in the Hoover Archives adds to our knowledge of Hoffer's early decades.

The watershed date is January 1934. In the first interview in which a reporter specifically inquired about his earlier life, Hoffer said that he "found himself broke in San Diego" in the year 1934. The rest of the article, about a thousand words long, included not one word about his life before he "found himself" in San Diego. It was published in a long-defunct newspaper, the *San Francisco Call-Bulletin,* in March 1951.

After 1934, Hoffer's whereabouts are well known. His account of his stay in a federal transient camp in El Centro, California (95 miles east of San Diego), is well documented by his own surviving and contemporaneous writings. He became a migrant worker and gold miner in California and his accounts of these activities in the latter half of the 1930s are plausible. His descriptions are numerous, credible, and consistent.

After Pearl Harbor, Hoffer moved permanently to San Francisco. His life in the 1940s is short on details, but we know where he was and what he was doing: he was working on the docks and writing his first book, *The True Believer.* After 1951 his life opens up. It becomes a matter of public record and, increasingly, is well known to the general public.

As to Hoffer's whereabouts before San Diego, I believe there is real uncertainty. I hasten to add that I do not have anything to replace his own sparse account. But there are questions and I raise them in this book. Nonetheless, mine is almost entirely a negative case and, as the saying goes, you can't beat something with nothing.

Hoffer's unpublished writings have been largely preserved—his notebooks in particular. The great majority date from the thirty-year period between 1950 and 1980. Entries are often polished. There are some earlier notebooks, usually not dated, but nothing seems to have been written much before 1936. No scrap of his writing before he arrived in El Centro is known to have survived. By then Hoffer was about thirty-five years old.

Going through Hoffer's papers, I became increasingly frustrated. I realized that to say anything at all about the first three-

and-a-half decades of his life I was entirely dependent on the books and articles that had already been published decades earlier. They in turn relied on Hoffer's oft-repeated but meager stories. Everything he said about his first twenty years in the Bronx, for example, can be written down in three or four paragraphs. He was pestered for more details, but this normally gifted storyteller was stubbornly reticent about those years.

If the first thirty-five years of a man's life are undocumented and depend exclusively on his own account—an account that is not fully convincing—then the resulting work is something less than a biography. This is especially true in the case of a man who became well known in later life. After 1965, Hoffer became a public figure. Before 1934, he is a mystery figure.

Will more information about Hoffer's background turn up? That's doubtful. There are signs that he was more than merely forgetful about his early years. In fact, I believe he was deliberately secretive. When pressed for more detail by journalists he would say he was confused or couldn't remember much of anything. About later events in his life he had an excellent memory. Were there things he didn't want us to know? One possibility that comes to mind is that he was an illegal immigrant to this country. But, again, I have no positive evidence. Did he really teach himself botany, chemistry, and Hebrew on skid row in Los Angeles? One can't help wondering.

Nonetheless, there is an abundance of new material available in the Archives. And after reviewing Hoffer's notebooks, this conclusion persists in my mind and will survive all doubts and questions: Hoffer was above all an original thinker and an outstanding writer. It is a precious combination. He subscribed to many journals and he followed current events. But he never followed any intellectual fashion.

He was free of the practical pressures that steer so many people of an intellectual disposition into conventional channels of thought. He lay beyond the peer pressure, grant-hunting, and cultural intimidation that stultify much of the academic world today.

He had talent in abundance and was conscious of Henrik Ibsen's claim that talent was more a duty than a property. In one of his later notebooks, Hoffer wrote:

> God has implanted in us the seeds of all greatness and it behooves us to see to it that the seeds germinate, grow and come to flower. We must see learning and growing as a sort of worship. For God has implanted capacities and talents in us, and it is our sacred duty to finish God's work.

In any consideration of his life, whether or not a used bookstore was his school or skid row his graduate school, these virtues will always shine through. He had the courage to stand alone.

A few years before his death—and long before I had considered writing this biography—I met Hoffer in San Francisco.

In 1980 I wrote to Hoffer, by now retired, asking him if we could meet in California. I had only read one of his books, *Before the Sabbath*. The dust jacket showed a man in his seventies, wearing a flat cloth cap and an olive-green workingman's jacket. He was looking out at the camera with a detached amusement. What impressed me about this slender volume was that it was so lucid, and not for a minute dull. Years later I read in one of his notebooks that a writer must above all entertain the reader—not a bad goal for any writer. He had certainly entertained me.

The book was in diary form, covering a six-month period from 1974 to 1975. His sentiments weren't what one might expect from a longshoreman. For over twenty years he had worked on the San Francisco docks under Harry Bridges, an influential labor leader who organized the West Coast longshoremen's strike in 1934. The U.S. government's attempt to deport Bridges as a Communist was overturned by the U.S. Supreme Court in 1945. Plainly Bridges was not a man to be trifled with.

But Hoffer's observations and comments didn't fit any union stereotype. Sometimes they were pro-capitalist, and always pro-American. If the subject came up, he was also anti-Soviet. I wrote to him in San Francisco, asking for an interview. Within a week I had his reply, written in an artless hand that was beginning to quaver with age. He was said to have been born in 1902, so that put his age at 78.

"Come any time," he wrote. "We shall eat, drink and talk."

The abbreviated story of Hoffer's life has almost a make-believe quality. He had grown up in the Bronx without any schooling, had gone blind for eight years, and then recovered his sight. He left New York for California, where (he had heard) orange trees grew by the roadside. He lived for a number of years on skid row in Los Angeles, studying botany and chemistry textbooks. Then he became a migrant worker in California's Central Valley. He went to San Francisco after Pearl Harbor, joined the longshoremen's union, rented a room, and wrote *The True Believer,* using a plank as a desk.

By the time I met Hoffer, he was living alone in a small apartment close to the Embarcadero, overlooking the waterfront. He had no telephone, then or at any time except for the last year of his life. To reach him by phone, one had to contact his longtime friend and companion, Lili Fabilli Osborne, who lived a few miles away.

On the day of our interview, I saw Hoffer for the first time sitting quietly in a corner chair in the Raphael Hotel lobby, wearing more or less the same outfit as in the photo, his cloth cap in place, a walking stick clasped between his knees.

By then, I had read several more of his books, but I was not prepared for the contrast between Hoffer on the page and Hoffer in person. It struck everyone who met him. He spoke with a strong German accent, often with vehemence. On the page, however, he was cool and detached. He was a critical observer rather than a participant.

I said right away how unexpected this was. It was as though his whole personality had changed.

"I am a vehement person, a passionate person," he said as we set off down Geary Street. "But when I write, I sublimate."

He walked as one who saw only indistinctly, and as though lost in thought. "It's not natural for a passionate person like myself to write as I write," he said. "I rewrite a hundred times, sometimes, so that it is moderate, controlled, sober. I need time to revise." He added that his accent was Bavarian and "it grows thicker as I grow older."

One of the complexities of Hoffer's personality became visible just during a short stroll to a coffee shop at Mason and Geary. A tourist couple recognized him and exchanged a greeting on the spot. Hoffer was pleased to be recognized and to know that he still had admirers. But it also bothered him that he couldn't be content with the fame he'd already received, including two CBS television interviews with Eric Sevareid in the 1960s and a dozen televised interviews by KQED in San Francisco.

Business was slow at the coffee shop at that hour, with three or four regulars at the counter. As we sat down at a Formica-topped table Eric told me that he "was never accepted by the San Francisco literary establishment."

I was surprised to hear that. "It is because I have praised America extravagantly," he said.

Herb Caen, the famous San Francisco columnist, seemed particularly ill-disposed, according to Hoffer. He in turn said of Caen that he had talent but that he had frittered it away writing gossip columns. It amused him that he had failed to impress the local literary establishment while Bertrand Russell had written a flattering review. But it bothered him that he was still hungry for praise.

Hoffer then took issue with something I had said about America possibly being in decline. He considered that a premature judgment.

"America is a fabulous country," he said, beginning to speak out in a booming voice. Soon he was shouting more than talking. Heads at the lunch counter craned around in our direction. (What was upsetting the old geezer?)

"It's not so conspicuous because the jetsam and the dirt are all on the surface," he said. "I remember when I first started to think about writing a book about America. I was going through my life writing down all the kindnesses done right from the beginning."

Pulling a pack of cigarettes from his pocket (while saying that he wasn't supposed to smoke but that he would anyway), he opened a theme to which he had devoted much thought: whether the pioneers who built America, especially the West, resembled the tramps he met in the thirties. "Consider the lengths people will go to come here. And who built this country? Really, nobodies. Nobodies. Tramps."

Another contradiction was Hoffer's stated disdain for "intellectuals." Yet it was his lifelong habit to write down quotations from people who would be almost universally regarded as intellectuals. He spent years collecting these quotations, mulling them over, and then writing books based to a great extent on his thoughts about them. The 1980 presidential election was three weeks off, and he was confident that Ronald Reagan would win it. "Well, we'll see what Reagan does," he said, lighting up. Just like America, the former California governor had always been underestimated, he thought.

"You see, it's easy to underestimate America. We underestimate America. Our friends underestimate us. Our enemies, thank God, underestimate us. But somehow there is a tremendous vigor in this country. It's true that our intellectuals are becoming more influential. They are shaping public opinion. But that won't last. There will be a reaction against it."

Hoffer's attitude toward religion was hard to pin down. He generally described himself as an atheist, yet during our interview he described religion as a significant source of leadership. "You have Pope John Paul, you have the Ayatollah Khomeini, you have them popping out all over. Reagan, too, is tapping into a religious strain."

He had long wondered: "When is the silent majority in America going to wake up?" And he wondered why he had failed to take religion into account. But if the rise of the "moral majority" were needed to restore America, he was all for it.

In *The True Believer*, Hoffer identified religion as a source of fanaticism and therefore danger. The main idea of the book was that true believers animate mass movements, whether religious, secular, or nationalistic. The true believer's mentality was such that he didn't much mind which movement he joined. Frustrated and disappointed, he above all wanted to be "rid of an unwanted self."

While talking about America he was pounding the table. I could see that he was a potential true believer himself. He had concealed this side of his character from his readers, but not from his viewers. He told Calvin Tomkins, who had profiled Hoffer for *The New Yorker:* "I have always had it in me to be a fanatic."

He told me that he was working on a book he would call *Conversations with Quotations.* "If you ever come to my room you'll see. I have just an enormous number of cards. All my life I used to write down anything that I wanted to remember. So I have got a thousand or maybe two thousand quotations. And every time, after that quotation, I am going to talk to that man."

Since moving to San Francisco, Hoffer lived in a succession of three small apartments, all downtown. The first, on McAllister Street, was where he wrote *The True Believer;* the second was a mile or so away, on Clay Street, in San Francisco's noisy Chinatown—too noisy for an author, in fact. In 1971 he moved to Davis Court.

A Room of His Own

Hoffer's Davis Court home was more a room than an apartment. His narrow bed folded up against the wall. He had a plain desk, a wooden chair for visitors, one bookcase, and some mounted shelves where he stored his cards with their quotations. That was about it. But from the seventeenth floor, he (just barely) had a view of the docks where he used to work. He liked to say that he could smell his own sweat.

The philosopher Baruch Spinoza had similar quarters. He, too, "occupied one room on the top floor, and slept in a bed that during the day could be folded into the wall."[1] Both worked for a living—Spinoza as a lens grinder, Hoffer as a longshoreman.

Reminding us of Immanuel Kant, Hoffer went on solitary walks, did not marry, had a stomach that often gave him trouble, and (after he moved to San Francisco) rarely traveled.[2] (Kant, it seems, never did.) Remarkably, we know more about Kant's early life than we do about Hoffer's. A professor of geography, Kant early on was more interested in science than in philosophy; Hoffer was the same. After moving to skid row in Los Angeles, he said, he taught himself chemistry and botany.

There were also profound differences. Hoffer's search for clarity shone forth in contrast to the obscurities of Kant, whose *Critique of Pure Reason* became famous for its difficulty. Spinoza's *Ethics,* with its definitions, axioms, and conclusions reached by deduction, turned truth into dust and was a universe apart from Hoffer's thoughts. Hoffer never believed that philosophical truths could be systematically established. A flash of insight conveyed more than any treatise; the polished aphorisms of the French essayist François de la Rochefoucauld were far more to his taste than the Germanic fogbanks of abstract nouns.

But Kant's remark that the origin of the cosmos would be explained sooner than the mechanism of a caterpillar appealed to Hoffer; even less likely, then, that mere intellect would ever "fathom man's soul."[3] He also agreed with Kant's opinion that no reward would induce him to re-live his life if he had to repeat it unchanged.

Spinoza, a free-thinking and excommunicated Jew, also came to conclusions in sharp contrast with Hoffer's. Spinoza was groping his way into the Enlightenment. Hoffer, it could be said, was seeking a way out of it. The equality of man was not a doctrine that greatly appealed to him. Spinoza, who rejected the notion of a providential

God, denied that the Mosaic law was binding on the Jews. Hoffer thought the Jews were distinct from other men. The rebirth of Israel filled him with hope and history with meaning.

It was struggle enough to express even one thought clearly, Hoffer would say, and if he could write a few decent sentences, well, the day wasn't wasted. He became publicly known as a philosopher, but he thought that modern philosophy was mostly faddish because its speculations were so short-lived.[4] "The purpose of philosophers," he said, "is to show people what is right under their noses."[5]

The few books on his shelves included his favorite writers: Fyodor Dostoyevsky, Michel de Montaigne, Blaise Pascal, the nineteenth-century French writer Ernest Renan, a few others. There were several Bibles, copies of his own books, and foreign translations of *The True Believer.*

For many years, when Hoffer was a migrant worker in California's Central Valley, public libraries provided the books he needed. In San Francisco, the main library was no more than a couple of blocks from his McAllister Street rooming house. He would buy books, but he rarely kept them. If they were heavy he sometimes broke them apart for easier handling and threw away the carcasses.

Hoffer's hundreds of three-by-five-inch index cards carried quotations from Aristotle, Bagehot, Clemenceau, Disraeli, Gandhi, Hobbes, Kant, Montaigne, Nietzsche, Pascal, Spinoza, and a hundred others, compiled over many years. Was there any precedent for this in the life of the nation? An apparently unschooled laborer who became a longshoreman and made an attempt to compile the wisdom of the ages on his own? He was filling them out by the 1940s and he continued adding to them until near the end of his life. The later dates are conspicuous because his handwriting becomes ever more shaky.

Hoffer kept quotations from people with whom he disagreed as well as those he admired. When I visited his room, I found him holding one of his cards, trying to fathom, as though for the hundredth time, what was written on it:

> "America is the most aggressive power in the world, the greatest threat to peace, to national self determination, and to international cooperation. What America needs is not dissent but denazification."—*Noam Chomsky.*

"Well, what do you do?" he said. "This was during the heat of the Vietnam thing, I suppose. What do you do? You try to understand. What is it that makes a man who is highly intelligent say such a thing? They call him a metaphysical grammarian. He was invited by Oxford to lecture. He is a very successful, prospering intellectual."

He paused to consider the man and then went on:

"What I know about Chomsky's past is that he grew up in an orthodox Jewish household. He says that all his ideas about grammar emerged from his familiarity with Hebrew grammar. He was born in this country. Somebody told me that he is good looking. I've been asking about him, you know. Not only does he side with our enemies, he sides with the enemies of Israel—Arabs, Palestinians, dissenters who live in Israel."

He reflected on a possible response. It seemed axiomatic to Hoffer that Chomsky's comment could not be explained by the facts of international relations or history. More likely the solution lay within Chomsky's psyche. As his notebooks would show, it was common for Hoffer to think along such lines. *The True Believer* was filled with arguments that were directed "at the man" (ad hominem).

Hoffer said he might respond with this:

> "Chomsky loves power. He is also convinced of his superiority over any politician or businessman alive in the United States. He sees the world being run by inferior people, by people who make

money, by people without principle or ideology. He thinks that capitalism is for low-brows, and that intelligent people should have a superior form of socialism."

He moved across the room to sit on his bed. He was still baffled. This combination of self-confidence, intelligence, and (as he saw it) error was a bone for him to chew on. It was also characteristic of Hoffer to look for illumination in abstractions of this kind.

"What gives people like Chomsky the confidence that they really know everything, that they are superior to everybody else?" he asked. "Just knowledge doesn't give confidence. If you went to school and you looked at your professors, you would see that the brighter they were, the less confident they were that they knew everything. There's something *else* here, something else . . ."

He searched, but evidently couldn't find what he was looking for.

He changed the subject, pondering the lack of gratitude among some of those who came to the United States and prospered. Some were grateful, others didn't see how much they owed to their adopted country. How easily we can take it for granted!

"Gratefulness is not a natural thing," he said. "There are two sorts of people coming to America. Both were nothing before they came, and both made good. One will say, I came as a barefoot boy and look where I am now. What a good country it is! The other will say, I came as a barefoot boy, and look where I am now. What a bunch of idiots they must be! He sees his own rise as evidence of others' inferiority."

He mentioned that there was a precedent for all this in Vienna. It brought him back to Chomsky and to one of his favorite topics—the alienated intellectual.

"Toward the end of the Hapsburg Empire, before World War I, there was a group of brilliant people, Jews and non-Jews, who were just glorying in the approaching doom. They knew that the end of the world was just around the corner. I could not figure out how intelligent people, who liked to eat the good food of Vienna, and sleep with the beautiful women of Vienna, should derive such tremendous pleasure from contemplating the approaching doom! And the answer is the same. They were so convinced that they were the fittest men to run the world that they wanted with all their hearts to wipe the floor and start from scratch. They would show us how the world should be run."

Hoffer put down his card, ready for something different.

"Maybe I should throw out Chomsky and have no business with him," he said. "But he needs explaining."

Toward the end of his life, Hoffer did compose a series of comments on his quotations (see appendix 1), but Chomsky was not included.

By the 1960s the disaffected intellectual had become a near-obsession for Hoffer and he planned a book on the subject. He wrestled with it for years but couldn't finish it. Some of his ideas on the subject were published as essays and reprinted in books.

But now his mood had changed. He directed me to another card, this one with a quotation by Arthur Bryant, the British historian. He had once written a column for the *Illustrated London News,* and that was where he had found the following. Hoffer asked me to read it aloud:

"There never has been a time in history when the Jews have not been news. And the periods during which the Jews have occupied and dominated Palestine have been the most exciting and significant in man's sojourn on this planet."

At this, Eric gave a sigh of pleasure. If Chomsky was the poison, Bryant was the antidote. "Here you have a Wasp, an Anglo-Saxon, with not a drop of Jewish blood in him, saying something that no Jewish chauvinist would dare say!"

He let out an odd whinnying sound that was half sigh and half laugh, almost like a horse neighing. "This is something I *can't* explain," he said, puzzled again. "The uniqueness of the Jews. I can describe their uniqueness, but why they became what they are I don't know. It's the greatest mystery in the world for me. I have been preoccupied with the Jews since 1929. It's a special thing to be a Jew, and this is what most Jews don't know. They think they are like others but they are not."

From 1968 to 1970 Hoffer wrote a newspaper column, which appeared in over a hundred newspapers. After the Six Day War he wrote three pro-Israel columns, widely circulated. (See appendix 3.) But his thoughts about the Jews and Israel appeared less frequently in his books.

Hoffer fell silent for a while and seemed exhausted. He lay down on his bed.

"The Jews have the atom bomb," he said eventually, staring at the ceiling. "They're going to use it if cornered."

At Home with Lili

Two days later, on a Sunday evening, Lili Osborne picked up Eric and then me at our separate locations and drove us to her house on Clayton Street. Eric sat next to Lili in her car and pointed out the Unitarian Church on Gough Street—a landmark, apparently, on Hoffer's Guided Tour of San Francisco.

"That's where all the radicals go who have lost faith in radicalism," he said. Catholicism then crossed his mind—Lili was Catholic—and he said that if he had a chance to meet the pope he knew exactly what he would tell him: "Go slow! The Church has lasted for so long. *Nothing* has lasted that long! It has discovered the secret of survival." Change was unpredictable so leaders should think twice before changing anything. He was thinking of the changes wrought by the Second Vatican Council in the mid-sixties.

He seemed far more sympathetic to religion than he had been in *The True Believer*. Later, when I studied his notebooks, I found that his thoughts about God were complex and that he could not be categorized as either a believer or an atheist.

Lili's house was large and decorated with her strong artistic flair. The routine was that Eric would go there on Sunday evenings. Other guests would come and Lili would cook. Eric would sit in his corner chair with a view of the Golden Gate if the fog hadn't come in. When I was there, after the meal was served someone said the Catholic grace, rattling it off as speedily as a courthouse oath. "Bless us O Lord . . ."

Eric immediately contrasted this way of saying grace with the "spontaneous" grace that one hears from Protestants: spontaneity, he concluded, so much admired in so many walks of life, was an overrated thing. He enjoined us more than once: "Count your blessings!" And in a way that was Hoffer's own grace.

He also launched into a diatribe. No one provoked him and he seemed to have brought it with him ready-made. He had been reading a book about Freud and he strongly disapproved of the Freudian message.

"We forgot all about the human condition," he said. "We forgot what evil is. With Burke there is still a whiff of evil, in his *Reflections*. But with Freud, all we need is a little screwing. The man was a pervert, I tell you! He admitted that he brainwashed little girls into saying that they wanted to play with him. He wanted to infect us with his own sickness and then offer psychoanalysis as a cure."

Later, Lili drove Eric back to his apartment, where she would make up his lunch for the next day, then leave him to contemplate his three-by-five-inch cards in his accustomed solitude.

When I first met her, Lili had three sisters and one brother living. The Fabilli family grew up in the Depression on a farm in Delano, California. Lili attended the University of California–Berkeley in the 1930s and in her twenties developed radical views. As a cannery worker in Monterey, she attempted to organize the workers into a union. It was through such activities that she met her husband, Selden Osborne. They were married in Arkansas in 1944.

Selden was a lifelong radical who played a role in Eric Hoffer's life right up to the end. He attended Stanford University, discovered a Socialist Party "local" in Palo Alto, and in the summer of 1932 organized a "Norman Thomas for President" club on campus. Then he shared an apartment in Palo Alto with Clark Kerr, who became chancellor at the University of California–Berkeley at the time of the sixties unrest. Kerr's career, too, intersected with Hoffer's.

Selden joined the longshoremen's union in San Francisco at the end of World War II. Eric Hoffer had joined three years earlier; they met on the docks in about 1949 or 1950.

Eventually Lili and Selden grew apart. She found that he was impractical to a fault; supporting his children seemed beyond his powers. Finally, they were divorced. She and Eric Hoffer became close, and he proposed marriage to her. But she declined. Her sister Mary, who lived in Berkeley until her death in 2011 at the age of 97, told me that Lili refused because she feared that Eric would try to separate her from the rest of her family, to whom she remained devoted.

Lili helped Hoffer in many ways and single-handedly saved his papers. When she died, on September 21, 2010, at the age of 93, her obituary notice said that "the love of her life was Eric Hoffer."

An Old Conflict Reenacted

April 1981: Six months had passed when I returned to see Eric Hoffer in his seventeenth-floor apartment. He had emphysema and had recently been released from the hospital. He wanted to know what people were saying about Ronald Reagan (now president). There had been a lot of criticism, I said. He was regarded as simplistic. *The Washington Post* seemed unhappy that he was in the White House.

Hoffer groaned, and repeated what he had told me earlier: that Reagan had always been underestimated. In fact, Hoffer himself had misjudged him. He told Eric Sevareid in 1967 that Reagan, then the governor of California, had been a B-movie actor who wanted to turn California into a B-movie state. But he changed his mind about Reagan.

Hoffer was disappointed that I had not yet written my article about him. He wanted me to entertain him, so he asked me to read from one of his favorite books. His father had called him an idiot when he was a child, and this had inspired his curiosity about the novel by Dostoyevsky. He had read *The Idiot* many times. Now he handed me the book and instructed me to read aloud from a certain section.

After about two pages he had heard enough. Had I read the book myself? I confessed that I had not. Now he was doubly disappointed in me—neither writer nor reader! He gave the impression that I was wasting his time and I saw in that moment how unforgiving he could be. His health was poor, he was tired, and plainly he didn't want to waste any more time with me.

I was saved at that instant by the buzzer ringing from the lobby. Over an intercom, the doorman announced that an old friend had come to see Eric. His name was Selden Osborne.

Hoffer had been drooping over with boredom, but now he sprang to life. He let me know that here indeed was an interesting fellow—a "true believer," he said. They had known one another for many years.

I asked Hoffer if Selden had been the real-life model for *The True Believer*. Hoffer shook his head, no. But he acknowledged that Selden may have later helped him to arrive at a better understanding of the "true believer" type.

"He's a doctrinaire socialist," said Eric. Then Selden came into the room.

Sixty-nine years old, slim, and well preserved, Selden was of medium height, with a trimmed white beard. He was wearing a light khaki safari outfit.

Lili's son Stephen Osborne told me that in the old days Selden and Eric would have "bitter disagreements" over Lili's dining room table. They were political, not personal, and they would end amicably. For me, it was a stroke of luck. If they were to recapitulate their old disputes I would be on hand as a recording secretary. I sensed that both welcomed having an audience.

"I was an active participant in the union," Selden told me by way of background. "Eric was more of an observer. He always said that the table was laid for him."

"I appreciated it," Hoffer said. He was sitting on his bed, still subdued but girding himself for combat.

In one of his notebooks, Hoffer wrote that as a longshoreman he had enjoyed "millennial working conditions." He saw no reason to tell Harry Bridges how to do his job. He was content to do his work and leave. Selden, on the other hand, was a born activist who wanted to participate in the union leadership. At times he was incautious enough to oppose Bridges directly—to Lili's dismay.

"Eric was violently anti-Communist but he gave credit to Bridges," said Selden. In contrast, Bridges "was afraid of educated longshoremen."

"No!" said Eric, who had obviously given the matter plenty of thought over the years. "He was afraid of longshoremen he couldn't use."

Now he was beginning to recover his old energy, and Selden changed the topic more directly to Hoffer himself.

"Eric always said that America is the country of the common man. I disagree. It's the most imperialistic country of all. Also, take the union under Bridges. I favored democracy in the union. But Eric said democracy wasn't so important. Do you remember that, Eric? You said you never grew up with a sense of democracy because you never went to school."

Eric was leaning forward on his bed, paying close attention to what his old adversary was saying. Through the open window I could see two sailboats on San Francisco Bay, leaning over in the wind, their masts parallel with Eric's tilting body.

"Repeat what you said," he demanded. It was as though the years and decades had fallen away. It pleased them to have this opportunity to lock horns once more.

Selden repeated it, and added: "I think the leadership of this country is hell-bent to rule the world."

"His antagonism to this country is because it doesn't give him a role in leadership," Hoffer said, addressing an audience of one. His argument repeated a central claim of *The True Believer*. True believers are disappointed men—disappointed in their own lives. But instead of recognizing this they seek to reform the world.

"It's very difficult to become a leader," Eric said.

"Unless you have a lot of money."

"Nooooo-o-o."

Eric was shouting now, and his shout somehow turned into a boo. He knew that Selden had erred with that comment.

"Bridges didn't have no money. You're not a democrat, Selden. You're an exclusivist. You resent any set-up where an ignorant son of a bitch can run for office and get elected."

In a profile of Hoffer published in 1967, Hoffer had mentioned an "ordinary longshoreman" called Sanchez who ran for vice president of the union. When he won, the intellectuals in the union—Selden Osborne among them—"nearly had a nervous breakdown."[6]

Hoffer's new outburst had exhausted him and he lay back on his bed, coughing. He lay quiet for a minute.

"Take Truman," he said, recovering his breath. "He was an ignoramus and yet he made a good president. To me these things are all miracles."

He challenged Selden to name a better country.

"Better country? I couldn't say. I might have said Australia or New Zealand. There is some advantage to a parliamentary form of government."

"I learn from Selden all the time," said Eric, changing the subject and handing me a summary of their relationship. "I classified him as a fanatic."

Fanatics are often important, Hoffer added. "If you have a battle to fight you had better have some fanatics on your side. You won't win without them."

"In those days I was a dissident Trotskyite," said Selden. "I remember I once took Eric to hear the Socialist writer and theorist Max Schachtman. Most of the educated longshoremen were followers of Bridges. Bridges was a Communist and Eric was an anti-Communist. The union paper never acknowledged Eric's existence, even after *The True Believer* came out."

"I never spoke a word to Bridges," Eric said, looking up at the ceiling from his bed.

Finally he sat up. He wanted to correct something that Selden had said earlier, about the table having been laid for him.

"I don't want to be nitpicking, but in my case it was not Bridges but America that set the table for me. I asked Lili to put on my tombstone: 'The good that came to him was undeserved.' Many times I had ignorant people correct me. I never found a common man who would agree with Henry Adams that America was created by a bunch of crooks. It was always axiomatic for the common man: America was the last stop. If you couldn't make it here, you couldn't make it nowhere. It's a sort of treason to complain about America. Selden's disagreement was crucial. But I love him."

There was some amicable talk, and eventually I left with Selden. We went down together in the elevator. He was glad to talk and conveyed that he wanted to be my friend.

Selden's story was unexpected. He told me that he had joined the longshoremen because he believed that the revolution was coming and would start with the working class. So he would be in the vanguard—the equivalent of an early investor in some great enterprise. In one of his notebooks, Hoffer put a slightly different spin on this, but essentially he agreed. He said that Selden had joined the union because he thought he could use his position within it to rise to a leadership position.

Now, however, Selden knew that in consciously attempting to join the working class in preparation for the revolution he had greatly misjudged events. I admired his candor. Without any necessity or embarrassment, he disclosed an error of judgment that must have affected his entire life. He could easily have avoided the subject entirely.

As we walked downtown, he told me that he was going down the Peninsula to a place called Pescadero, near Santa Cruz, where an old friend named Joe Gladstone owned eighty acres. Selden had his own room and had lived there for a while.

A fellow radical, Gladstone had known Selden since the 1930s. Often, in earlier decades, Selden and Lili would go there together and sometimes Eric Hoffer would join them and go on long walks.

Tonia Osborne, Lili and Selden's only daughter, died from an epileptic seizure in Manhattan in her early twenties and her ashes were buried at Pescadero. And when Selden himself died, in 1994, his ashes were buried there, too.

Now, however, Selden was planning to meet there with some peace activists. "My whole concern today is disarmament," he said.

As for Hoffer, Selden said: "All his conclusions are wrong—every one of them. But he writes beautifully and he asks the right questions." They remained on good terms, and when Eric Hoffer died two years later, in the room where we had met, Selden was with him.

On the Road Again

That evening I was in the car again with Lili and Eric. Eric mentioned the impasse of all his arguments with Selden. Neither one could ever persuade the other of anything, and so it had been for more than thirty years.

"Selden is so anti-American that it frightens you," he said. "Born and raised in America. If anyone is for America it should be him." It was interesting that Hoffer had seen it as anomalous that both Noam Chomsky and Selden were "born in America" and yet neither had been able to see the gift that they had been given.

There was a silence, and Eric turned to me with a surprising question: "Do you think he likes me, deep down?"

I hesitated. I didn't know it at the time, but Selden had never seemed to mind the close relationship that developed between Lili and Eric. He may even have welcomed it. Lili also told me that Selden and Eric were always on good terms; Selden retained a key to her house after their divorce.

If I had known that, I would not have hesitated. Despite their disagreements across the board, Selden liked Eric. He also knew that friendship does not depend on political agreement. In fact, he knew that better than Hoffer, for whom personal relations, especially with men, often tended to be difficult.

At the moment when I hesitated, Lili turned the wheel and changed the topic of conversation. She said we should never forget that Selden was a man of strong convictions. "He has gone to jail for what he believes," she said.

"Of course, ready to sacrifice himself for the cause," Eric said, returning to his old vehemence. Selden conformed to the stereotype of the true believer—always ready for self-sacrifice.

Hoffer was staring resolutely ahead, once again his stick between his knees and his trusty old cap in place.

"Not many people are willing to die for what they believe," Lili said.

"Lili, I have told you a hundred times," Hoffer said, his reply polished and immediate. "It is easy to die for what you believe. What is hard is to live for what you believe."

CHAPTER ONE

The Enigma of Eric Hoffer

My life is not important. It's not even very interesting.
Ideas are all that's important.

—ERIC HOFFER
Interview with biographer James Koerner

Eric Hoffer was unknown to the public in 1951 when he published his first book, *The True Believer*. Almost overnight, the San Francisco dockworker became a public figure. Recognized as a highly original thinker, he became known as the Longshoreman Philosopher. A 1956 profile in *Look* magazine identified Hoffer as "Ike's Favorite Author," elevating this blue-collar working man to the level of President Eisenhower's bedside table.

It wasn't just Eisenhower who appreciated Hoffer's intelligence and wit. Public figures, ranging from the author and historian Arthur Schlesinger Jr. to the philosopher and social critic Bertrand Russell, praised his work. Since September 11, 2001, some commentators have noted that Hoffer's analysis of "the true believer" and mass movements in general—although written with Hitler's and Stalin's followers in mind—applied equally well to Islamic fundamentalists.

Hoffer worked on the San Francisco waterfront for almost a quarter-century. After *The True Believer*, he published ten more books; later in life he often (although not always) said that his first book was his best. Then, in one of those only-in-America stories that

Hoffer himself so loved, this self-made man, this unashamed patriot and fan of Ronald Reagan, became an adjunct professor at the University of California–Berkeley during the Free Speech movement.

Hoffer's place in American politics and intellectual thought is an enigmatic one. Much of his writing was in the form of aphorisms, short, pithy remarks that touched on eternal truths. But he was also capable of the sustained thought and expression that went into *The True Believer* and his other books and newspaper columns. Hoffer was interested in probing the depths of human behavior and discovering the motivations behind the twentieth century's wars and revolutions. Wary of public praise, he resembled the prophets of the Old Testament, free to make people of high and low estate uncomfortable with his insights.

Little is known about Hoffer's early years. Hoffer offered interviewers a rough outline of his first four decades, but his various versions contradicted each other. His date of birth is uncertain, often given as 1902 but more likely 1898. He claimed his German accent came from Alsatian immigrant parents, but it was often described as Bavarian. And the account he often gave of losing his sight at an early age and then regaining it several years later doesn't fit with some of his other versions or with medical probability. The man who startled readers with his insight into the truths of revolutionary movements took particular trouble to conceal the truth about his own background. Quite possibly, he was born in Germany and never became a legal resident of the United States.

Eric Hoffer's life divides into two roughly equal parts. The first part is from birth to his move to San Francisco after Pearl Harbor. The second is his life in San Francisco. Before Pearl Harbor, without exception, Hoffer's life is documented only by what he said or wrote. It is the same with the research and interviews of others. Hoffer was their sole source. His best friend, Lili Osborne, summarized the difficulty: "All we know about Eric's early life is what he told us."

She didn't mean just the first few years either, but the first thirty-five years. He described his life in those decades many times. But nothing can be corroborated. After he moved to San Francisco, his life is well known from the recollections of those who knew him, from press coverage, magazine articles, televised interviews, and public appearances. The first half is barely documented at all.

It's as though he stepped out of the San Francisco fog in the 1940s with stories to tell about his past, but nothing that can be verified. He died in 1983, still in San Francisco.

Lili Osborne first met Hoffer in 1950, perhaps six months before *The True Believer* was published. Over the next thirty-three years she knew him better than anyone in the world. But, she said: "I never met anyone who knew Eric in his earlier life."

For a twentieth-century American to have such an utterly untraceable past is beyond remarkable. It's bound to raise the question: was Hoffer born and reared in this country? Despite considerable publicity surrounding publication of *The True Believer*—along with reviews, Hoffer's photograph was printed in newspapers around the country—no one is known to have come forward to say that he and Hoffer had once been friends. No one has claimed him as a childhood companion. No one volunteered that he and Hoffer had been associated in any way. Nor did his national television appearances in the 1960s prompt any such claims or reminiscences.

A sharp dividing line does occur in January 1934, when Hoffer joined a federal homeless shelter in El Centro, California. Thereafter, and throughout his time as a migrant worker, he provides us with a wealth of detail that is absent from his account of life in the Bronx and Los Angeles. He still provides no names, but the flood of detail marks an abrupt change that is not otherwise explained.

The Canonical Life

In summary, this is Hoffer's early life as he described it to journalists, biographers, and historians who interviewed him in the decades after he became a public figure through publication of *The True Believer*:

He was born in New York City, his parents having come to the United States from Alsace-Lorraine at the turn of the century. A German woman called Martha Bauer accompanied his parents and all four lived in the Bronx. Hoffer never gave the address. His taciturn father, Knut, a "methodical, serious, German cabinet maker" or "self educated carpenter," brought books with him from Europe, but Eric had "hardly any conversation with my father all my life."[1] Once, Knut took the 11-year-old Eric to a concert in New York and they heard Beethoven's Ninth Symphony, but no other details are given.[2]

A "village atheist," according to his son, Knut Hoffer had "all the paraphernalia, all the books that a German intellectual ought to have. Encyclopedias, dictionaries, books on medicine, the works."[3]

These books were kept in a cupboard with glass doors, and Hoffer remembers pulling out the books and classifying them according to size, color, and language. He spoke German in the home and he taught himself "to read both English and German at the age of five."[4]

His mother, Elsa (a small woman), was in the habit of carrying Eric (a large child) around the house. One day, when he was six, she fell down a flight of stairs while she was carrying him. Two years later, she died and Hoffer went blind. His blindness lasted for eight years. When asked, "Did the fall cause those things?" he responded, "I don't know."[5] Hoffer also didn't remember the fall itself, nor could he recall whether his sight returned suddenly or gradually. In an early account he said that he went "practically blind," followed by a "gradual improvement."

His father had no money for doctors, and Eric's blindness meant that he "never attended school or received any sort of formal education."[6]

Martha Bauer was a "Bavarian peasant" and his German accent came from her.[7] Young Eric slept in her bed. "We always slept together, always." As to the restoration of his sight, he doubted at times whether he welcomed it. Before, he had been fed, cared for, and loved by Martha. "Then I got my sight back and there was—separation."[8] She also told him that all his family was short-lived and that he would die at age forty. "I believed her absolutely," he said.[9]

Hoffer's biographers, Calvin Tomkins and James Koerner, describe only one scene outside the family house. It was a second-hand bookstore on the same block in the Bronx. It had acquired a library from an estate, and in the years after his sight returned Hoffer treated it as his library. There, he became "something of an expert in botany."[10] His father would leave him a little pocket money on a shelf and sometimes, to keep the bookstore owner happy, Hoffer would buy the book he was reading.

He was "seized with an enormous hunger for the printed word," and developed "the bad habit of swallowing any book I liked in one gulp instead of savoring it slowly." He was reading ten or twelve hours a day, in a hurry because he didn't know if he would go blind again.

> "Reading was my only occupation and pastime. I was not a normal American youth—no friends, no games, no interest in machines, no plans and ambitions, no sense of money, no grasp of the practical."[11]

In the bookstore, he saw Dostoyevsky's *The Idiot*. The word was familiar because his father had once said within earshot: "What can you do with an idiot child?"[12] It is the sole comment that Eric attributed to his father. Hoffer said he later read the novel a dozen times.

Martha Bauer returned to Germany in 1919 and Hoffer's father died in 1920. His death remained "rather hazy in my mind." But Eric received $300 from Knut's fraternal society, and he decided to move to California. He had heard that it was a good place for poor people. When he left, according to Koerner, he took along "a huge basket of books that he had bought at the second hand bookstore." In a letter to Margaret Anderson, to whom he dedicated *The True Believer*, he said that he brought with him "several trunks full of books."

He made his way to skid row in Los Angeles, where he "lived life as a tourist." Because he believed Martha's claim that he would die at forty, any plans were pointless.

His life was books, blindness, recovered sight, more books, and nothing but books. Except for his parents, the only person identified is Martha Bauer. Outside the house, no one at all is identified. His mother is not described or quoted. As to the father-son relationship, the only comment each made about the other, in Hoffer's account, seems to have been "idiot child" and "village atheist."

Los Angeles in the 1920s

Hoffer said he stayed in Los Angeles for ten years. He took a cheap room near the public library, paid rent in advance, and began to read.[13] In fact, he spent "every minute reading."[14] Hoffer knew how to live frugally, but when the money was gone he sold his books and a leather jacket. Then he "began to go hungry."[15]

His hunger episode appears in every account of his life. He is on Main Street, staring through a pet shop window. Two pigeons engage in a courtship ritual and Hoffer becomes so absorbed that he forgets his hunger. Then he is aware that he had forgotten it, and this inspires him.[16] "Hunger wasn't so terrible. It wasn't so mysterious after all." He enters a nearby restaurant where he offers to scrub pots and pans in exchange for a meal. The owner accepts, and a fellow dishwasher tells him where he can get a job.

The State Free Employment Agency is Hoffer's next snapshot. He repeated the story often. It was a big hall with maybe five hundred men sitting on benches; in a booth was the dispatcher. His phone would ring and he would call out:

"A man to move furniture."

"A man to rake leaves."

Hands would shoot up, and someone would get the job. How did the dispatcher make his choice? Hoffer approached the problem scientifically and by trial and error found ways to improve his odds. If he sat not in the front row but in the sixth, looked as though he didn't have a care in the world, and carried a book with a red cover, his chances improved.[17] That way he could get enough jobs to sustain his solitary, bookish life.

"I lived that way for nearly ten years, reading and thinking and making a living on skid row," he told Tomkins.[18]

He immersed himself not just in books but in textbooks. He studied Hebrew. He read chemistry, zoology, and botany. Why should the stem of a plant grow upward and the roots downward? He came across *Strasburger's Textbook of Botany*, a classic published in thirty editions, and by chance he also discovered a slim botanical dictionary, in German, written "as a special aid to the study of Strasburger's textbook. It never failed me. To master this material I had to take notes."

Hoffer also studied chemistry, using an eminent textbook by Joel Hildebrand, *Principles of Chemistry* (first published in 1918). Hildebrand, a scholar of international renown, lived to be 101. He even had a chemistry lab at UC–Berkeley when Hoffer himself, years later, had an adjunct position there.

By coincidence, James Koerner knew Professor Hildebrand. He arranged for Hoffer to meet him at Berkeley. So it seems likely that Hoffer really had studied Hildebrand's textbook. Koerner photographed their encounter, but he did not report any of their conversation.[19]

Returning to the Los Angeles of the 1920s, Hoffer reappears as an orange salesman. His boss drove him to the suburb of Westwood and told him to knock on doors. His commission was 25 percent. At first tongue-tied, Hoffer became an exceptional salesman. The housewives could not resist his pitch. But he was tempted to lie, claiming, for example, that he had grown the oranges on his own farm, with needy wife and children to feed. He was hooked by this deception, so he quit. The owner "blew his top," Hoffer said later, when told that his best orange salesman was leaving. [20]

We come now to a man whom Hoffer identified as Farbstein in early accounts and Shapiro later. Hoffer said that he worked in his "pipe yard" for two years and proved to be a good worker—"quick, conscientious and quiet," in Hoffer's self-evaluation. Farbstein or Shapiro, the only person whom Hoffer identifies in his ten years in Los Angeles, was attentive to Hoffer, solicitous of his diet and his reading, and paid him well.[21] Hoffer admired him.

In *Truth Imagined*, published in 1983, Hoffer adds more details about this man's Jewishness (by now he is Shapiro) and Hoffer's own interest in the Jews and in the Old Testament. Shapiro, said Hoffer, owned Ernest Renan's *History of the People of Israel*, and recommended it to Hoffer. The work (in five volumes) was "hard to get but Shapiro had it in his library."[22] Years later, Hoffer himself acquired these rare volumes, and they were in his bookcase when he died. An oft-quoted source in Hoffer's books, Renan was a major influence on Hoffer's intellectual life.

Hoffer experienced Shapiro's death in 1929 as a liberation. He appreciated the man's solicitousness; but now that Hoffer had some savings he wanted to resume his solitary life.

He decided to "spend a few months of leisure, and then commit suicide. Just like that!" He regularly ate supper at a cafeteria on Hill Street.[23] By now he was studying the Bible and this odd routine continued for weeks. But the thought that once his money ran out he would have to return to work, "day in day out till death," filled him with weariness.[24]

He read up on poisons in the Encyclopaedia Britannica and resolved to take a fatal dose of oxalic acid. After a final day spent "rereading for hours the tales of Jacob and his sons, chuckling over the vivid details" in the Bible, he set forth along Figueroa Street until "oil derricks like gibbets suddenly loomed ahead."[25] He removed the stopper from his bottle of poison and took a mouthful.

"It was as if a million needles pricked the inside of my mouth. In a blaze of anger I spat the oxalic acid out, continued spitting and coughing, and while wiping my lips I let the bottle fly and heard its thud in the dark."[26]

Thereupon he "rejoined the human race." Bells and street cars were ringing in his ears. Now, all "the handiwork of man seemed part of my flesh and bone." He entered a cafeteria with a ravenous appetite. Recovered now, he had reached a turning point. He knew he must get onto the open road.

On that day "a workingman died and a tramp was born."[27]

He packed some things in a knapsack and walked south out of Los Angeles. His heart was light. A German in a shiny new car en route to Anaheim gave him a lift. Asked where he was going, Hoffer didn't know. The German gave him a lecture on the need for a purpose in life.[28]

"A man must have a goal," he said. "It is not good to live without hope." He quoted Goethe (in German) as saying: "Hope lost, all is lost; it were better not to have been born."[29]

Hoffer didn't believe Goethe could have said that, so he checked the quotation at the Anaheim library. He found that the correct quote was "courage lost," not "hope lost." That was a very different proposition; to Hoffer it sounded more like Goethe.

A sign nearby said: "Dishwasher wanted." Hoffer got the job, stayed on for several weeks, and became acquainted with some of the customers. Among them was the German driver who had misquoted Goethe; Hoffer told him of his error. The customers liked Hoffer and called him "Happy" because of his "good cheer under all conditions."[30]

Abruptly, we now come to a new phase in his life. Hoffer tells us that he "walked to San Diego," and from there he "plunged into the world of the migratory workers." In the early 1930s, San Diego was "a small stale town populated by sailors and whores," he wrote.[31] There were no jobs, and "of begging there was no thought." Or so he wrote in his earliest known account of these years.

> I had lived so long alone that even a casual contact with strangers was a muddled affair of stuttering and confusion; let alone the act

of soliciting favors under fear of rebuff. I tried to obtain a meal in exchange for work in restaurants and failed.

He went two days without food. On the evening of the second day he drifted toward the wholesale vegetable market where a truck was unloading a mountain of cabbage. He edged in, helped the driver unload the truck, "and was soon devouring cabbage cow-fashion." The truck driver agreed to take Hoffer on his return journey, back to a small town called El Centro in the Imperial Valley. It is only a few miles from the Mexican border.

It was nighttime, and Hoffer had "glimpses of a white road winding between pale brown mountains and gray precipices." The driver dropped him off on the outskirts of El Centro. Hoffer gave the date as January 1934.

For the first time, Hoffer's story of his life begins to include a wealth of convincing detail. What had been a dreamlike account turns abruptly into a realistic one. Perhaps some real change had occurred once he arrived in San Diego and was driven to El Centro.

If so, what was that change?

Lili Osborne thought it possible that Eric Hoffer was not born in New York at all, but may have come to the United States as an immigrant. She had no proof. But from the moment she first heard his foreign-accented voice on the telephone—her husband, Selden Osborne, had met him on the docks, told Lili about him, and she invited Eric to dinner—she thought of him as an immigrant. Her impression that he was not born in America stayed with her all his life, even after she had grown to know him better than anyone.

One of many clues that Hoffer wasn't a native-born American was revealed when foreign travel was discussed. Hoffer was one of Israel's biggest boosters, but he never visited the country, despite invitations. Once, Lili said, "Why don't you go to Israel? I think you would love it."

"If you can find my birth certificate," Hoffer replied, implying that with the right papers, he would be happy to go, but that they might not be easy to find.

His birth certificate never was found, despite a search. He had no passport, and he never left the United States, except for a brief, cross-border excursion at Tijuana. Then he hastily returned north, fearful that he might not be allowed back into the country.

Man Without a Past

Eventually, Hoffer became a well-known public figure, seen coast to coast on network television. He was given tremendous publicity by President Johnson, who invited him to the White House; press photographers recorded the event. Hoffer was appointed to the President's National Commission on the Causes of Violence, where he became a polarizing figure.

It seems extraordinary, then, that no one from Hoffer's early life should ever have shown up. Possibly—just possibly—he actually came to America for the first time across the Mexican border in 1934, the year after the El Centro camp was opened. Perhaps he walked to San Diego and was by then every bit as hungry as he said he was, ate some cabbage "cow fashion," and found the truck driver who took him to El Centro.

Only one earlier acquaintance from Hoffer's migrant worker days has been identified by name. Four letters to Hoffer from a Bill Dale of Santa Cruz have survived. Lili wrote this note on one such letter: "Eric's only correspondent from his past—pre-T. Believer."

"The highlight of the year is your visit, which always stays in my memory for a long time," Dale wrote to Hoffer in 1959. In another letter (August 1960) he wrote: At "this time of year I am looking for your annual visit which I always enjoy so much." Dale describes his roses and petunias, and promises "some fresh apple cider when you come." (Apparently Dale lived in a house that he had built himself.)

But there is no description of their earlier times together—telling when or how they met.

In a late notebook, Hoffer describes a fleeting encounter with an old acquaintance from the 1930s. This former companion appears in San Francisco, greets Hoffer, and as quickly disappears:

> I remember one migratory worker whose name I did not know. Like the other workers I traveled with he used to listen when I told stories about the things that had happened to me. He seemed unmoved, never joined the laughter. Later when I published books and settled in San Francisco I came upon him and he greeted me warmly. He said: "We are all proud of you." My elation at his praise left me speechless. He said: "You are probably a busy man and I must not keep you." We parted and I kick myself for not asking his name and address.

Like Bill Dale, however, this person dated from Hoffer's days as a migrant farm worker, and gives no clue to where he lived before about 1934.

Journalists and historians received varying versions of the canonical life, but none was able to persuade Hoffer to reveal more details, or resolve the contradictions some of them noticed.

Three books about Hoffer were published, all in his lifetime. Again, Hoffer is the sole source of all the information about his pre-*True Believer* days. The first and most influential was *Eric Hoffer: An American Odyssey*, by Calvin Tomkins (New York: E.P. Dutton, 1968), based on an extensive profile he wrote for *The New Yorker*, where he still works. The book included photographs by San Franciscan George Knight, many of them taken on the docks. Next was *Hoffer's America*, by James D. Koerner, a program officer and then vice president of the Alfred P. Sloan Foundation in New York (Open Court Publishing, 1973). The photographs were Koerner's. Finally

James T. Baker of Western Kentucky University published *Eric Hoffer* (Boston: Twayne Publishers, 1982). Baker was introduced to Hoffer by Stacy Cole, who provided most of the previously unpublished information in the book.

Other than Lili and her family, the man who may have known Eric Hoffer better than anyone was Cole, who taught American history at a community college in Fremont, across the Bay from San Francisco. Now retired, Cole attended Hoffer's weekly seminars at UC–Berkeley and became his general factotum, secretary, and companion. Their friendship lasted from 1968 until Hoffer's death, and during those fifteen years Cole saw Hoffer almost every week. His account coincides with Lili's: "I never met a single person who knew him before he worked on the waterfront."

Asked about Hoffer's family background, Cole also remarked, "It puzzled me that I never got from him any definitive information about his parents. He never talked about his father except in the most general way. And not at all about his mother." Stacy reckoned that he had more conversations with Hoffer "than anyone alive other than Lili."

It's understandable that Hoffer might have concealed his background if he were indeed undocumented. If born abroad he was not an American citizen, for he never went through any naturalization ceremony. Congress severely restricted immigration to the United States in 1924 and by the 1930s, when jobs were scarce, U.S. residents found to be here illegally were deported without due process. Some were minor children born in the United States. In one report, "between 1929 and 1935 some 164,000 people were deported for being here illegally, about 20 percent of them Mexican."[32] Others estimate that between 1929 and 1939 as many as a million people were unceremoniously repatriated, many of them to Mexico. If

Hoffer himself was in the United States illegally, he was wise to keep quiet about it.

Intimations of Germany

An examination of the contradictions among Hoffer's various versions of his biography opens a window into the America of the first third of the twentieth century, and—even more interesting—a window into Hoffer's ideas and how they evolved. Even while claiming to have been born in this country, Hoffer's statements and even his accent revealed an identification with immigrants and a familiarity with German history.

Immigrants' children who are born in the United States almost always speak with an American accent, no matter what they hear at home. But Hoffer spoke with a German accent, which (he said) became more pronounced as he grew older. In rare cases, if a child grows up with immigrant parents, and is sufficiently isolated, he may speak with the accent he hears at home—the only accent he ever does hear. Hoffer does claim that his upbringing was isolated, so his accent does not prove the case against American birth. But if accent were all they had to go by, most listeners would guess that Hoffer was born in Germany.

Hoffer also spoke German and did so fluently. Stacy Cole related this tale: Late in life, Hoffer came out of his apartment building and encountered a group of tourists who seemed lost. Hoffer recognized them as German and immediately engaged them in conversation—speaking in German. Cole had lagged behind and when he caught up the tourists had moved away. Hoffer turned to Cole and said that this had been the first conversation he had had in German in decades. Clearly, Hoffer spoke German as a child. If he had learned it as an adult, he would have forgotten it after those many years without practice. Did Hoffer learn German in the Bronx? He said he hardly spoke to his father at all, but his mother might have spoken to him in German.

Hoffer also studied textbooks written in German, including Strasburger's. He noted his good fortune in coming across a German dictionary tailored to Strasburger's text.

When the trucker gave Hoffer a ride from San Diego to El Centro, he came to a federal shelter or encampment where he stayed for a few months. While there he helped produce a performance, and the archives include a skit written out longhand. Headed "1934 El Centro," it seems to be his earliest surviving piece of writing.

It takes the form of a comic discourse by a German professor, Professor Koch, who makes fun of the migrants (watching the skit). The professor has an assistant, Fritz, "who accompanied me to the U.S. because of his skill in laboratory manipulations." Phrases are written out in German.[33]

In other accounts there are several intimations of life in Germany and references to the ominous prospect of Hitler. In one account Hoffer recalled a time when he was in a lumber camp, probably in California in the mid- to late 1930s.

> Then came Hitler. It's incredible for young people to realize how it hit us. I remember I was in a lumber camp when Hitler came to power and they had a radio there. I heard Goebbels say, 'Hitler is Germany and Germany is Hitler.' And I had a fit of laughter. It seemed incredible that anyone could say that. . . . I don't think I would have started to write if it weren't for Hitler.[34]

"Hitler is Germany" is usually attributed to Rudolf Hess, who said it at the Nuremberg Rally in September 1934. Nonetheless this remark reveals a deep interest in German politics.

Hoffer said many times that "the Hitler decade" had changed his life; sometimes he specified the 1930s. He must have been one of the few migrant workers in California who paid close attention to these events. For someone to think at the time that the claim "Hitler is Germany" was laughable implies a considerable background knowledge of that nation.

Hoffer also wrote a few unpublished pieces of fiction. One, "Chance and Mr. Kunze," was handwritten in 1939 and is among his earliest literary endeavors. It concerns a fictitious character called Arthur Kunze, who went to California in 1882 at the age of seventeen, became a successful businessman, and over forty years later retired as a millionaire. Then he makes a "hurried visit to Germany," and there sees "the devastating effects of a depreciating currency."

> The thousand-mark banknotes, once precious and treasured, were barely buying a loaf of bread. These banknotes were once the depository of dreams, ardent wishes, and a power that knew no resistance. Now they were little better than paper. People were utterly bewildered. And from day to day the German mark sank lower. In Mr. Kunze's eyes this was the greatest catastrophe the world had seen; greater than the world war and the Bolshevik revolution. There was a sickening ugliness, and something akin to obscenity, about this vanishing of money into thin air.[35]

In one of his last speeches, in 1979, Hoffer discussed inflation, which had destabilized Germany and facilitated Hitler's rise to power. Inflation was unusually high in the United States at the time.

Charles M. Kittrell, the executive vice president of the Phillips Petroleum Company and a great Hoffer admirer, had arranged for him to make several speeches in Bartlesville, Oklahoma, in the late 1970s. In Hoffer's last appearance outside San Francisco he said:

> Anybody who lives the long life I've lived knows that it was inflation that produced Hitler. Here was a nation, the Germans, they had a strict society. They had absolute values. Suddenly the beautiful mark, a thousand mark—a bill—looked so beautiful, white with beautiful writing, a thousand marks that before that could

buy all the [inaudible] and now it couldn't buy a loaf of bread. And once the value of money is destroyed, all values are destroyed . . . [Hitler] was born of that breakdown of values due to inflation. So all my life I was primed to recognize inflation as the real, as the only danger, really . . . [36]

One can't help wondering how Hoffer, either on skid row or working in the fields, knew about thousand-mark banknotes in Germany. It was the highest denomination note in pre-war Germany, originally worth about $240. The hyperinflation came in 1922–23.

On his return to California, Kunze wants to learn about life in the fields. Since he was known as a wealthy man, he adopts a new identity. He leads a double life as a migrant worker in California. Did Hoffer himself adopt a new identity when *he* came to California?

One more bit of indirect evidence comes in an article in the September 1976 issue of *Reader's Digest*. Hoffer remarks, "For more than 20 years, until I landed on the San Francisco waterfront in the early 1940s, I lived a life of hardship, of self-education and of teaching myself to write. I wanted to be left alone to do what I was doing. That is what the millions of immigrants who came to this country also looked for: a chance to do what they wanted to do. Many failed, but there were more chances here than anywhere else."

Although writing about others, Hoffer seems to be thinking of himself as though he, too, were an immigrant.

His Blindness

Hoffer's description of his temporary blindness evolved through the telling, and the character of Martha Bauer came and went. Hoffer repeatedly said that he went blind at the age of seven or eight and then recovered his sight at sixteen. In that time he was looked after by Martha Bauer.

Hoffer's blindness has functioned in all accounts as an alibi, explaining why he didn't go to school, didn't have friends, spoke with a German accent, had "shadowy" recollections, and so on. How reliable is his blindness story?

Suddenly going blind as a child would have been the most shocking event of his early life, rivaled only by the sudden recovery of his sight. Both events would have been memorable, to say the least. But Hoffer's accounts are inconsistent. Tomkins relates in his book: "His mother died when the boy was seven years old and later that same year Hoffer suddenly and inexplicably went blind. As a result of his affliction, he never attended school or received any sort of formal education. At the age of fifteen, having recovered his sight as mysteriously as he had lost it, he experienced what he has described as 'a terrific hunger for the printed word.' "[37]

Hoffer told Tomkins a few pages later: "I don't know how my sight came back—whether it was slow or fast. We were poor, and we had no money for doctors. I have a feeling that it must have been a blockage of some kind."[38]

He was often pressed for more details. "I've been asked these questions over and over, and it's all the vaguest, the most blurred thing in the world to me," Hoffer said.

Hoffer added something new in 1974 when interviewed by John McGreevy for the Canadian Broadcasting Corporation. He said that when he went blind "at the age of seven, I lost my memory for a while, for a short while. . . . I actually forgot my own name. I forgot the words. And I went through life believing that I have no memory, which is very important."[39]

Koerner wrote in 1973 that for years he had been "fascinated by the fact that Eric Hoffer existed—a common laborer who had been blind in childhood, who had then recovered his eyesight and proceeded to educate himself entirely by his own efforts; whose reading had been broader and deeper than that of many leading intellectuals in the United States and Europe . . . ."[40]

Koerner added that "Hoffer's eyesight returned as suddenly as his blindness had come."[41]

Koerner went to San Francisco often and talked to Hoffer "over many years." Hoffer trusted him. Yet he found that "Hoffer is ill at ease talking about his personal life." Once when he was probing further, Hoffer responded that his life was "not even very interesting." Koerner found that he "plainly dislikes talking about" his early life.[42] He quoted Hoffer as making this familiar and oft-repeated comment, listed among his aphorisms:

"We can remember minutely and precisely only the things that didn't happen to us. When you hear somebody describing something from his childhood in great detail, he is making it up or somebody told it to him."[43]

For most people, of course, this is not true at all. Detailed descriptions of childhood events tend to be particularly convincing.

An important source is the early correspondence between Hoffer and Margaret Anderson. His letters were written before *The True Believer* was published. As to his blindness, Hoffer wrote:

"Between 1910 and 1916 I was practically blind. Then came a gradual improvement. . . . I had no schooling. I was practically blind up to the age of fifteen . . ."[44]

There is a big difference between being blind and being practically blind, and between a gradual improvement in vision and its sudden return. A young person would remember if it were one or the other. His claim that there was "no money for doctors," explained why, if he was slowly losing his vision—much more likely than sudden blindness—he was not taken to see a doctor.

But there's a dissent from Selden Osborne's friend, Joe Gladstone, who first met Hoffer in the 1950s. Gladstone, who lived into his nineties and died in 2011, grew up in New York with serious eye problems of his own. His family, too, had "no money for doctors." In the 1930s he "spent a lot of time running around to clinics that were practically free," he said in 2010. One such clinic still functions to this day. When Gladstone told Hoffer about these free clinics, Hoffer "never commented and changed the subject."[45]

What do modern eye doctors say?

Stephen Ryan, an expert in macular degeneration at the Doheny Eye Center in Los Angeles and a professor of ophthalmology at the University of Southern California, said that he had "not heard of such a case" as Hoffer's. But it "would fit the world of neuro-ophthalmology," he said, so he forwarded the query to an expert in that field, also a professor at USC.

"I've given some thought to this scenario and I admit it's hard to find a biological basis for trauma leading to complete blindness two years later, much less a complete recovery eight years after that," wrote Alfredo Sadun. "The best I can do is to mention that rarely, following head trauma, there will be a small cerebral bleed that blocks the ventricle cerebral spinal-fluid system. This can lead to diminished vision or memory (but not total loss) that might infrequently reverse spontaneously years later."

One magazine grew curious. In 1976, when the *Reader's Digest* was one of the most thoroughly fact-checked magazines in print, a *Digest* researcher wrote to Hoffer: "One of our editors has asked a question to which I cannot locate the answer. How did you regain your sight after eight years of being blind? I wonder if you would mind answering this question for me."

There is no evidence that she received an answer. The published article quotes Hoffer as saying he "fell off a flight of stairs at the age of five, and two years later lost my eyesight. I remained blind until the age of 15."

Martha Bauer

Other than Hoffer's parents, Martha Bauer is the only person identified from those New York decades. In later years he spoke of her with growing love, tenderness, and fondness: how she had cared for him, cooked for him, and was always so cheerful. He spoke with eloquent regrets about her return to Germany after the Armistice in 1918 and her abrupt departure from his life.

"How utterly callous can adolescence be?" he told Tomkins. "I never wrote to her. I don't even know what happened to her."[46]

He was interviewed several times in the 1950s, and before that had written to Anderson about his earlier life. But in his earliest accounts there is no mention of Martha Bauer.

The best evidence is an article that appeared in *The Reporter*, a magazine of the post-war period edited by an Italian immigrant named Max Ascoli. *The Reporter* published several articles either by Hoffer or about him in the 1950s. One was written by Eugene Burdick, who went on to co-author two best-selling books, *The Ugly American* and *Fail-Safe*. But the most interesting article, "Migrant with Message," was by Richard A. Donovan, who lived in Los Angeles.

Published on October 30, 1951, his article was inspired by the recent publication of *The True Believer*. Donovan's was one of the first magazine articles—perhaps *the* first—by a writer who made a special trip to San Francisco to interview Hoffer, evidently at Ascoli's behest. *Time, Life, Newsweek, Look*, and other magazines, including *The New Yorker*, came in their turn, but *The Reporter* was there ahead of them all. (By some oversight, this *Reporter* piece is never listed in Hoffer bibliographies.)

Donovan's article contains a bombshell, although no one seems to have noticed it. Donovan wrote that Hoffer's life began "in 1902, in a cold-water walk-up" and he learned to read before he was six, but before he was eight he was blinded; his mother was injured so badly she died two years later, in a household accident in which both of them fell down a flight of stairs.

So far, it's the standard account. Donovan continues with this direct quotation from Hoffer:

"From my seventh to my sixteenth year, I groped helplessly about my room," Hoffer has written. "Except for my mind, I was inert—I had no friends, no games, no ambitions, no grasp of reality. I had no contact with my father, who was a rigidly silent Alsatian cabinetmaker. Once, in another room, I heard him call me the 'blind idiot.'

"When I was sixteen my eyesight began to return, gradually, although in retrospect it seems to have been sudden. I began to read indiscriminately, not to catch up but in dread I would go blind again. . . . I was not a normal American youth."

No Martha. And his claim that he "groped helplessly" about his room seems to rule her out. It strongly implies that there was no one there to help him. In later accounts Martha was not just a friend but his *only* friend, and yet Hoffer here says that he had no friends.

There is something else. The above passage has Hoffer *writing* this. "Hoffer has written," said Donovan. To whom did he write it?

In the Hoover Archives, there is one piece of correspondence from Donovan. It is a letter that he wrote from Los Angeles to "Miss Anderson," on June 25, 1951, four months before his article was published in *The Reporter*. He told Anderson that he had recently interviewed Hoffer for a profile to appear in *The Reporter* and had accumulated a "staggering sheaf of notes." But he needed some reviews of *The True Believer* to help get "Mr. Hoffer launched properly in the narrow and standardized confines of a magazine." In his final paragraph Donovan added: "Mr. Hoffer suggested I write you instead of the Harper's editors. If you will send me the necessary clips, or have Harper's do it, I'll be much obliged to you. I plan to start writing the piece as soon as the clips arrive . . . Sincerely, Richard Donovan"

Margaret Anderson probably sent some of her material to Donovan, and not just reviews of *The True Believer*. She may also have sent copies of the letters that Hoffer had written to her earlier. Donovan is probably referring to such letters when he says that Hoffer had "written" these things.

Portions of these early autobiographical letters have survived. What do these early Hoffer letters to Anderson say about Martha Bauer? Again, nothing. In a letter that Hoffer wrote in May 1941, he said:

"In 1920 my father died. I lived a year with an aunt (an old girl, and my only relative). In 1922 I scraped together a few dollars and crossed the continent to Los Angeles."

There is no Martha, and in this account he clearly lived with this aunt for a year *after* his father died, thus accounting for the gap between his father's 1920 death and his 1922 departure for Los Angeles. Hoffer's later and oft-repeated account of a $300 legacy from his father's guild is also contradicted.

Anderson typed out copies of the relevant parts of Hoffer's originals—he wrote everything by hand—and kept the originals. The one known recipient of at least some of this material was *The New Yorker* magazine.

In a later letter, dated December 24, 1949, Hoffer wrote to Anderson: "And now about your questions: I had no schooling. I was practically blind up to the age of fifteen, and racked by monstrous headaches. My childhood was a nightmare and its shadow still hovers in the back of my mind."

Starting with the word "racked," above, a further section of about 150 words was published in *The New Yorker* in April 1951. And here again, there is no Martha. The letter then continues with additional material, which wasn't published but is contained in the Hoover Archives:

"When my father died I realized that I would have to fend for myself. As far as I knew I was the only Hoffer left in the world.

All my people were short-lived, and I considered it axiomatic that I won't live to be forty. It was a simple question of spending the remaining twenty years or so in the least troublesome manner."

Martha Bauer has still not put in an appearance. The one comment consistently attributed to her in later interviews was the claim that his people were short-lived and that he wouldn't live past forty. Now it is Hoffer himself who considered this to be "axiomatic."

When *The True Believer* was published, Anderson diligently kept a scrap book with every bit of news she could find about Hoffer. Later she sent it to Hoffer; it includes the Donovan article in *The Reporter*. Lili Osborne retrieved the scrap book later and it is among the Hoover materials today.

When did Martha first appear in the Hoffer saga? Eugene Burdick's account may have been the first.

Then a member of the Political Science Department at UC–Berkeley, Burdick interviewed Hoffer in 1956. They became friends. Shortly before his sudden death at the age of forty-six, Burdick hailed Hoffer's appointment to an adjunct faculty position at that university.

His *Reporter* article was published February 21, 1957, with the title, "Eric Hoffer: Epigrammatist on the Waterfront." Here at last a "German housekeeper named Martha" appears and plays her now-familiar role: taking care of Eric between the ages of eight and sixteen. The lines attributed to her would become familiar in the years to come:

"Martha had often consoled him with the advice: 'Don't worry Eric. You come from a short-lived family. You will die before you are forty. Your troubles will not last long.'"

These thoughts were earlier attributed to Hoffer himself.

Why should portents of an early death have been thought "consoling"? Maybe Hoffer inserted a short time-horizon into his own story to explain why so obviously talented a young man should have set off for Los Angeles and then become, by his own account, a drifter and a migrant worker.

The New York Void

New York City was *the* major American city in the first half of the twentieth century. By his account, Hoffer's first twenty years were spent in the Bronx. What does he say about his most impressionable years in this most dramatic urban environment? He lived in an apartment on an unnamed street. He was blind for eight years and recovered his sight. His father took him to a concert. He frequented an unnamed bookstore. And that was it. All attempts to locate Hoffer or his parents, Knut and Elsa, in the Bronx, either through census data or Ancestry.com, have drawn a blank.

Lili Osborne's son Eric remarked in 2010, after his mother's death, that he "tried looking through some of that Ellis Island stuff and I could never find a Knut Hoffer." The Hoffers supposedly came from Alsace-Lorraine. Young Eric, who went to Europe in the 1970s, lived and worked in Alsace-Lorraine. He found the residents have a "beautiful mix of French and German—a very light German. It isn't the accent he [Hoffer] had. His accent was real Bavarian."

Young Eric once said to Hoffer: "I feel like hiring a genealogist in New York to look up your father." Hoffer replied, "Are you sure? Are you sure you really want to know?" Describing this conversation, Eric Osborne said it was "like there was some dark stuff. Maybe when the mother fell down the stairs his dad went to prison. I don't know. There's stuff happened that he didn't want anybody to know. He had a real casual and dreadful way of letting something slip. 'Are you *sure* you want to know?' I remember that. That was when I was about fifteen."[47]

At any rate, all Eric Hoffer could say about the city of his youth fills two or three sentences. He was almost forty years old before he acquired a definite street address. A highly observant and intelligent man, Hoffer was interviewed by some of the best known journalists in the United States, who pressed him for more details. Yet he was unable or unwilling to oblige.

Tomkins asked Hoffer if he had ever returned to New York City. As quoted in Tomkins' article in *The New Yorker*, Hoffer replied:

> "Just once," he said, holding up a finger. "All those years I had a certain landscape in my mind from that street in the Bronx—the church, the bookstore, the little square, the flight of stairs. But gradually it became a bit confused. So one day a few years ago, I decided to go back and see if I could find the place. Mrs. Osborne took me out to the airport on a Saturday morning. I'm sure she thought she was never going to see me again. I'm still a mysterious person to her. Well, I got to New York, and I didn't find anything. Maybe I found the church—I'm not sure. But nothing else. So I turned right around and flew back the same day, and Mrs. Osborne met me at the airport."[48]

"There was no reason to go back," Hoffer added. "There was nobody there who knew me."

But he would have known that before he left. So why did he make so arduous a journey? San Francisco to New York and back on the same day, with a scouting expedition to the Bronx squeezed in, would be a considerable ordeal for the most hardened business traveler today. It was almost unthinkable for Hoffer, sunk as he was in his daily routine and frequently disclaiming any interest in his early life.

Lili Osborne said Hoffer decided to make his special trip to the Bronx only after he learned that a journalist from *The New Yorker* was coming to town to write a profile. Perhaps Hoffer felt as a matter of some urgency that he had to establish a few basic facts about the lay of the land in the famous city that he may not have ever seen.

Hoffer concluded his exchange with Tomkins on a familiar note: "All my memories of that time are so vague."[49] What may be more likely is that Hoffer came to America as a teenager or young adult and never did live in New York.

He once told Koerner that in his New York years he had never been Americanized, adding this provocative comment: "Actually, I came to America in 1920 when I went to California." That was not meant literally, but as a way of saying that he encountered America for the first time when he went to California. Possibly, however, his arrival in California really was his first experience of America.

Crossing the Continent

The next memorable event about which Hoffer had curiously little to say was his cross-country journey from New York to Los Angeles. He was twenty-two years old (if his father died in 1920), and by then the young Hoffer still had not left New York City. Then he goes to Los Angeles. By the conventional account, it was the first journey he made anywhere.

So how did he travel? In several accounts he was noncommittal. "I made my way" to the West Coast, he would say.

In *The New Yorker*, Tomkins quotes Hoffer: "So I bought a bus ticket to Los Angeles and I landed on Skid Row, and I stayed there for the next ten years. You might say I went straight from the nursery to the gutter."[50]

Five or six years later, Hoffer gave a different account of the journey to Koerner:

"So he told the burial society [after his father died] that he wanted to go to California. The society presented him with a one-way train ticket and a patrimony of $300 with which to begin his new life.

"'So I was transferred,' said Hoffer, 'from the nursery to the world, almost overnight.'"[51]

The conflict between bus and train cannot easily be reconciled. If Hoffer made the journey at all, he would have to have remembered it. It is the only time he is known to have crossed the continent overland. Not until the 1960s, and then by air, did he do so again. The disagreement between his accounts raises a red flag.

Crossing the country by train was far more likely. There's a question whether cross-country bus service even existed at the time. It might have been possible to complete such a journey by taking a large number of short bus trips—arduous but maybe not impossible. But doing so while loaded down with "trunks" of books, as Hoffer once said, is inconceivable.

Koerner adds one or two details about the train ride. Looking for a cool drink, Hoffer went into the dining car. The waiter was boiling tea, which he poured over ice. "It seemed to me the craziest thing in the world—to boil tea and then pour it over ice," Hoffer said. It was then that he added the provocative comment about coming to America "when I went to California." On the train journey he also experienced hotcakes for the first time. "Everything was new and strange to me."[52]

All this would be easier to believe if he really had come "from the nursery." But he was already in his twenties (eighteen if we accept his later birth date). A person born in America, even if blind for a number of years, is fully Americanized by the age of eighteen.

He spent ten years in Los Angeles, by his account, and then another eight in the fields. But he told us far, far more about the fields than he did about Los Angeles. He provided no details about that most colorful of cities, the city immortalized by Raymond Chandler. His decade there seems to have made as dim an impression on him as his twenty years in New York. His reminiscences amounted to a few set pieces that could have happened anywhere. He notes his own hunger at a pet shop window; finds work in a hiring hall; works in a pipe-yard for a solicitous boss; sells oranges to housewives; comes close to suicide; corrects a German motorist who misquotes Goethe.

Undoubtedly he was in Los Angeles in the 1930s, but more likely he was in and out. When he rented his room in San Francisco, perhaps in 1942 (the exact date is not known), he said it was the first time he had a fixed address in California. At no time did he say what his address in Los Angeles had been, just as he never mentioned a Bronx address. When he visited Los Angeles in 1953, he told a correspondent that he "could not identify" the places where he had lived.

The Entertainer

It's easy to understand why Hoffer would make up an American background if he was eager to avoid questions about his citizenship, but why so elaborate a ruse?

Hoffer was a great storyteller, and he insisted that a writer should entertain as well as inform his audience. He was also a master at diverting attention from his own background. Finally, he did provide a few hints that his story shouldn't be taken too seriously.

Calvin Tomkins, still working at *The New Yorker* forty-five years after he met Hoffer in 1966, interviewed the longshoreman philosopher at length. Asked in 2009 whether he had any unpublished recollections to add to Hoffer's story as he published it, he replied, "I'm afraid I can't shed any light on your questions about Eric Hoffer and his early life. I did no research on the subject, relying simply on what he told me at the time. The things he said about his early life did sound quite shadowy, but he was a great talker and he made it all seem authentic."[53]

Hoffer's own *Truth Imagined*, published a few months after his death, covers precisely the missing early years, ending in 1942. But, as the title suggests, it cannot be relied upon as a factual record. Some things Hoffer said were certainly true, and much was imagined. But as we have no other sources to turn to, the great problem with *Truth Imagined* is to distinguish truth from imagination. The book was primarily based on stories that Hoffer told about his earlier life to Gemma Kabitzke, a court reporter who knew Stacy Cole and who had been engaged to type up Hoffer's quotations and notebooks. (The book is dedicated "To Gemma.") Hoffer told her at the time that his stories were often imagined.

The author of a doctoral thesis at the University of Illinois at Urbana-Champaign, Paul Wesley Batty, wrote to Hoffer in 1970. Batty asked for his verdict on a chapter he had written, giving familiar information about Hoffer's life. Hoffer's unsatisfactory reply: "Your guesses and interpretations are as good as any I might have. Nearing seventy, I am uninterested in my distant past. I have probably told everything worth telling."[54]

CHAPTER TWO

The Migrant Worker

America set the table for me.

—ERIC HOFFER, *1981*

Homeless in El Centro

Near the beginning of Hoffer's lengthy account of his stay in El Centro, he wrote: "Late in January 1934 I found myself in San Diego, California, penniless and with no job in sight."[1] He hitched a ride to El Centro in the Imperial Valley, only a few miles north of the Mexican border.

In the account that followed, Hoffer described his experience of the early New Deal. Hundreds of thousands of unemployed men, known as transients or vagrants, roamed the country. For some time they had been "considered a menace to the health, wealth and morals of the respectable citizens, and treated accordingly." But by early 1934, he wrote, there was a change. The Roosevelt administration was setting up federal camps. And any transient who was considered a danger by one of those respectable communities "was actually longing for the sight of a uniformed cop."

If he saw one, "he made a beeline for this once dreaded arm of the law." With luck he would then be directed, "and sometimes even given a lift," to one of these new camps.

The trucker Hoffer had accompanied on his return journey from San Diego dropped Hoffer off on the outskirts of El Centro and suggested that he go to "the unemployed headquarters." Hoffer had barely walked a block when a motorcycle policeman directed him to the federal shelter, then recently opened. It was a converted garage, "dimly lighted and packed with cots, all occupied. The air was vibrating with heavy breathing."

Hoffer was signed in by a middle-aged clerk who asked him many questions. "It's a lot of bull but it got to be done." He apologized for not having a vacant cot and gave Hoffer three blankets. He stretched out on the cement floor near the door.

The camp had been created in 1933 by the Federal Emergency Relief Administration, an early New Deal program and predecessor of the Works Progress Administration, the WPA. Its "transient" division was established in July 1933. Hoffer consistently said that he enrolled in the camp in January 1934, so the dates fit. He moved into what today would be called a homeless shelter. In fact, it was one of the first such shelters that the federal government established.

Hoffer's lengthy, handwritten account was transformed several times over the years. An abbreviated version of his original account was typed (Hoffer never did his own typing) and titled "Tramps and Pioneers." Atop the first page was written "Eric Hoffer, c/o Margaret Anderson," with her address in Mayville, New York. He may have sent it to her in 1941. A new version, further abbreviated and titled "The Role of the Undesirables," was published in *Harper's* magazine in December 1952. It was reprinted in Hoffer's first published collection of essays, *The Ordeal of Change.*[2] Finally, at the end of his life, Hoffer reworked some of this old material and published it as sections 10 and 11 of *Truth Imagined.*[3]

The Hoover Archives has the original handwritten version (with four pages missing). It dealt with Hoffer's life in 1934, first in El Centro and then farther north, in San Bernardino. It was not written until 1938. As Hoffer wrote toward the end of this piece:

"Four years have passed since. During the brief prosperity of 1936 the camps were curtailed. Now, with the recession, they are again in full operation. There are changes. The camps consist of spick and span standardized barracks. Food and sanitation are excellent. There are compulsory blood tests. Some camps have sizable libraries. Work is planned in advance. In many cases the men work on W.P.A. projects at a wage of from 40–60 dollars a month, of which they pay twenty dollars to the camp for bed and food."

The later account published in *Harper's* and then in *The Ordeal of Change* differs considerably from the original piece, which was more factual and less sparing of his fellow transients. In *Truth Imagined*, published just before he died, Hoffer wrote that no one could have predicted that "my stay in El Centro's transient camp would color all my thinking and would furnish the seed of all I was going to write during the next 50 years."[4]

The initial account was more prosaic, and Hoffer even provided a footnote or two. For example, he ascribed the claim that "the migrant population of Calif. has increased to more than 300,000 men, women and children" to: "Dr. Omer Mills, regional economist of the Farm Security Administration in Calif. in a talk given at the annual convention of the Calif. league of Municipalities at Santa Barbara, Sept. 8 1938."

Much later, Hoffer decided that "the social scientist is no more a scientist than a Christian scientist is a scientist." But in 1938 he was influenced by social science and felt obliged to throw in some figures. For example, he listed the percentage of the men in the camp who were "cripples," confirmed drunkards, elderly, and so on.

Although he was at El Centro's camp for three months, Hoffer gives no account of the dramatic developments taking place on the streets outside. Kevin Starr relates in his multi-volume history of California that exactly when Hoffer was present, a three-month agricultural workers' strike was organized to gain 35 cents an hour for lettuce workers in the Imperial Valley. There was violence, with union organizers very much on the defensive. On January 23, 1934, an ACLU lawyer helping the strikers was kidnapped from his El Centro hotel, "beaten by members of the American Legion and left in the desert eleven miles outside the town of Calipatria, barefoot and stripped of his money and personal belongings." Two hundred vigilantes milled about in the street outside the hotel.[5]

Hoffer says nothing about this drama, which surely must have been discussed in his camp. When he joined the longshoremen's union in San Francisco eight years later, he said it was the first and only union he joined. His employment by growers in rural California in the 1930s was always non-union.

In April 1934 he hitchhiked north and joined a second camp in San Bernardino. He was assigned to a work crew at a ranger station in the San Bernardino Mountains. Supervised by rangers, the crew worked regular hours for pay, clearing firebreaks and building rock walls. The government was now finding useful work for the men, as did not seem to have been the case at El Centro. His original article, closing on an upbeat and almost bureaucratic note, was as close as Hoffer came to admiring the New Deal:

> "There is work to be done in the national forests and the counties, provided it can be accomplished at a reasonable expense. There are firebreaks to be cleared, trails to be built, roads to be improved, and noxious weeds (such as Johnson grass and the wild artichoke) to be eradicated. Here is where the transient camps come in. With careful planning, and with flexibility in expansion and contraction during the slack and busy agricultural seasons, the camps can employ the transients in useful work and manage to be, almost, self-sustaining.

At El Centro the men were paid a stipend of $4 a month, much of it being spent on drink the same day. "That night about three fourths of the men were in various stages of intoxication." There were fights, and several men landed in the county jail. "Some who sobered up and found that they had wasted their pay to the last penny bundled their things in disgust and took to the freights."

Hoffer's writing, in his earliest surviving non-fiction work, was remarkably judicious and detached:

> It is probable that opinion will always be divided concerning the merits of the present Roosevelt Administration. But on one point there is bound to be considerable agreement, namely, that there was no ailment of the national body—slight or serious—which this administration has not noticed, probed and finally prescribed for . . . In the following pages I record the little I have seen of one attempted cure. It concerns a minor ailment, a mere rash on the national [body], namely, the transient problem.

Here, in contrast to his sparse and unconvincing accounts of his first three decades, he provides detailed and realistic descriptions of events. True, as before, he fails to mention a single name. But his account is lifelike. Some passages are reminiscent of George Orwell's *Down and Out in Paris and London*—and written in a detached and lucid style that is not unlike Orwell's.

> Games were my first step in the acquisition of sociability. I learned to play checkers, dominoes and chess. The men took their games seriously. . . Sometimes, when a man lost several rounds in succession, he would sweep the board and pieces off the table and get up with a curse. It was also the common opinion that, to beat your opponent, you have to undermine his morale by taunting and overbearing. This was known as playing with psychology. There were very few who won or lost with good grace, and in each case I found it an indication of an innate gentleness. . . .

> The men on the whole were friendly. The young bucks were inclined to be boisterous, but fights were rare. Many seemed to have something on their mind. You saw men who were sitting on the benches reading, or were strolling quietly about the yard, burst out suddenly in oaths, or talk loudly to themselves. One man who played checkers in a dogged manner and rarely talked

would invariably fall into a rage whenever the oversweet voice of a woman came over the radio. He would turn around and address the radio with a torrent of obscenity, then abruptly turn back and [resume] pushing his checkers.

Arguments were heated and conducive of bad feelings. Statements were handed down dogmatically and stuck to. It was like rubbing two pieces of hard metal against each other; it produced heat and noise. Of reasoning, which is the life blood of an argument, there was none. When on rare occasions a man was found who, by a series of obvious questions and answers forced his opponent to recede from his original statement, the results were disappointing. He was considered as taking unfair advantage of his opponent by employing "lawyers tricks."

Tramps as Pioneers?

When Hoffer hitchhiked north from El Centro in April 1934 to join the federal shelter in San Bernardino, he passed through the town of Indio. As he left, lush date groves and grapefruit orchards abruptly gave way to a desert of white sand. The sharp line between garden and desert gave the impression of a job cut short, said Hoffer, who described it as resembling a stretch of cloth embroidered on one edge while the rest of it remained untouched. Completing the work—turning desert into orchards—was a job "one would jump at," he thought. It would surely appeal to the transients "segregated in their camps, wasting away their lives. They have the skill and the ability of the average American," and they, too, had the potential to build and create. But their energies would be quickened only by some spectacular task; making the desert bloom would qualify.

He considered: "Transients as pioneers?" This later became "tramps as pioneers" and Hoffer became enamored of the idea. He later wrote that the original pioneers who settled the West were probably men who "had not made good" in their hometowns: "men who went broke or never amounted to much," men of ability who were "too impulsive to stand the daily grind," and so on.

"Tramps as pioneers?" he reflected. "It seemed absurd." Everyone in California knew that the pioneers had been giants, men of boundless courage and indomitable spirit. But as he strode on across the white sand, he "kept mulling over the idea."

He talked to old-timers in the state capital of Sacramento, the Central Valley agricultural city of Fresno, and the Sierra foothills settlement of Placerville; they told him that, as far as they could recall, the pioneers even looked like the present-day "Okies and fruit tramps."[6]

It was a bold flight of imagination, characteristic of Hoffer. He referred to it several times, and again at the end of his life. The family likeness between tramps and pioneers took "a firm hold on my mind," he wrote. "It kept intertwining itself with a mass of observations which on the surface had no relation to either tramps or pioneers." This moved him to speculate on ever-more remote topics.[7]

In 1951, Hoffer showed a copy of "Tramps and Pioneers," then still unpublished, to an early correspondent named Bob O'Brien, who had come to see him in San Francisco. He wrote to Hoffer saying that he had read the essay with great interest and it read like "a voyage of discovery." But one comment he did not accept. When Hoffer had asked people what group in California most closely resembled the pioneers, the answer was always: "The Okies and the fruit tramps." Bob O'Brien responded that that didn't ring true: "No one who knows the native Californian's regard for the pioneers and his contempt for the Okies and fruit tramps would find it credible . . . It represents too pat a confirmation of the theory you had formulated . . ."[8]

A similar criticism was made by a reviewer for the *San Francisco Chronicle* when the essay was published by *Harper's* in 1952. At El Centro, Hoffer had counted his fellow transients in different categories, finding 15 percent to be crippled, 30 percent "confirmed drunkards," 25 percent fifty-five and over and only 5 percent too young to vote.

The *Chronicle's* Joseph Henry Jackson commented in 1952 that a much higher percentage of the pioneers must have been young, sober, and sound of body.[9] O'Brien recommended to Hoffer further reading on the California Gold Rush—the works of H.H. Bancroft, for example. (He also revealed in this letter that Hoffer was then planning a book "on Enthusiasm.")

In his account of the Great Depression in California, historian and former state librarian Kevin Starr reports that attitudes toward the 1930s migrants were often hostile. Although they were white Anglo-Americans, Starr writes, and often fleeing from the Dustbowl in Oklahoma, Texas, and elsewhere, they were regarded as a despised racial minority by much of white California. The same charges leveled against blacks, Mexicans, and Filipinos—laziness, shiftlessness, promiscuity, and a predilection for squalor—were "now lodged against the white migrants."[10]

There's no evidence, incidentally, that Hoffer ever did study books on the California pioneers. Stacy Cole, who taught American history, commented on Hoffer's surprising lack of interest in the country's history. "Eric knew American history in general," he said, "but he was not interested enough in the specifics to do much in the way of reading." He was far more interested in European writers. "He did read biographies occasionally, but had little to say about American writers and thinkers, relegating them to a permanent inferior station. I would have thought that he would have delighted in Benjamin Franklin, but, to my recall, he almost never referred to him. Lincoln, the quintessential American, hardly interested him either. Hoffer should have found much in common with these self-made men, whose sharp intellects were more practical than purely theoretical, but they seemed almost alien to him."[11]

Small interest in American history is quite often a characteristic of immigrants. They take U.S. history as a given—something they and their ancestors were not responsible for. And because they have something alien to compare it to, they are often more disposed to appreciate America's merits than do the native-born. Hoffer certainly did. "America set the table for me," he said. It is an immigrant's sentiment.

The poor experienced considerable hardship in the Depression years in California, but Hoffer almost always sounded upbeat about his life. This is particularly so in *Truth Imagined*, where he often seems to treat life as a lark. Today we are apt to forget how difficult things could be. In the nation as a whole, unemployment hit 25 percent and crop prices fell by 60 percent. For much of the country, conditions were improving by 1934, when Hoffer "found himself" in San Diego. But the flood of Dust Bowl refugees—the largest migration in American history—prolonged the hardship in California. This was particularly so in the Central Valley, where Hoffer spent much of his time.

Kevin Starr writes that the Depression didn't arrive in earnest in California until 1933. By June 1934 "some 1,225,000 Californians out of a population approaching six million were dependent on some form of public assistance." In 1935 California had 4.7 percent of the nation's population but triple that percentage of its dependent transients. Police departments opened shelters for transients; female transients sometimes requested lodgings in jails. In a single month, the Southern Pacific Railroad evicted an estimated 80,000 transients from its boxcars—Hoffer's frequent mode of travel.[12]

San Bernardino National Forest

After registering at the San Bernardino camp, Hoffer was sent to a work camp at a ranger station seven miles northeast of San Bernardino. The crew's job was to cut firebreaks and build rock walls in the rugged San Bernardino National Forest.

At first all went well. Loafing was not tolerated; two manicured dandies from Los Angeles "did not take friendly" to brush-clearing and were gone the next day. Hoffer joined a crew of masons who broke rocks and fitted the pieces together into walls. It was satisfying work. In the evening the men would look over their handiwork and were in no hurry to quit. "It was fun to straighten one's back after placing a particularly difficult rock."

The purposeful work contributed to a general satisfaction. Men would point up to a steep slope on the mountain range and boast that they had cleared that particular firebreak.

"Living conditions were barely adequate, the food was poor, there were no books, the work was hard, the pay was only $4 per month," Hoffer wrote, "and yet the men were on the whole satisfied." He gave much credit to the camp superintendent, an ex-plumber who was both friendly and strict. Grumblers were promptly sent away, so there was "a constant weeding out of the disaffected."

All this changed with the fire season. Superintendents from the region selected men for their good conduct and nimbleness—"the cream of the transient camps." Hoffer was selected and placed in a ten-man crew sent up over 7,000 feet to Big Bear Lake. Rangers welcomed them and treated them as equals. They were supplied with good living quarters, a shower bath, and a well-furnished kitchen. They even had their own cook, a supply of books, tickets to a local theater and dance hall. As to fires, they "were few and more play than work."

Then "something unpredictable happened." It raised doubts as to whether the transients really were "average Americans."

> "Our group of select transients was seized with a senseless fury of wrecking. Plates and bowls were crushed and stamped upon. Kitchen utensils were thrown into the brush and left there. The kitchen door was torn off its hinges and the wooden floor bashed in with an ax. Books from the library were thrown about and damaged."

The living quarters were in constant disorder, the ground around the tent became filthy with excrement—the men were too lazy to climb up the hill to the toilets. The truck that took them to Pine Knot was wrecked several times. At last this was too much for the rangers, who packed the whole crew into a truck and hauled them back to San Bernardino before the fire season was over.

"The fire-fighting crew at Lake Arrowhead (half way up to Big Bear) behaved similarly," Hoffer added. But there "the rangers took a hand early and put the fear of God into the men."

Hoffer wondered: "How explain this lust for wrecking?" It was not madness, nor did he hear anyone justify it as an act of vengeance.

> Was it an assertion of manhood? Or had years of prosperity developed in these men a passion for wasting, which, now that they had no release in spending, found an outlet in a fury of destruction? It is beyond my understanding. I have discussed the subject with several intelligent transients and they agreed that the rage for destruction is strong among us, but that it was not wholly lacking in the other layers of population in this land.

He never resolved the issue, nor did he again mention what he had observed.

In a newspaper column in the 1960s, he described being part of a team sent from "skid row" to build a road "on the side of a hill in the San Bernardino Mountains," and in this account they did a wonderful job. "If we had to write a constitution, we probably would have had someone who knew all the whereases and wherefores," he wrote. They "could have built America."[13]

Following his Forest Service work, Hoffer began his career as a migrant farm worker—briefly interrupted by a spell of gold-panning. He traced the beginning of his life as a migrant farm worker to his time in El Centro, which is in the reclaimed desert known as the Imperial Valley. His first stay in that heavily agricultural region "was the beginning of my full life as a migratory worker," Hoffer wrote.

Here began my freight riding life from one end of California to another, and the establishment of a routine as repetitive and monotonous as the steadiest job one could think of. Beginning with sugar beet thinning in the spring, I followed the unalterable cycle of fruit and vegetable harvesting until I saved enough for a grub stake for [gold] prospecting from July to October. The spongy lump of gold (button) when sold in Sacramento, made it possible for me to spend four months of reading, writing and studying.[14]

Gold Country

Hoffer provided few dates, but after El Centro they do begin to appear. "In 1936," he wrote, he spent "a good part of the year picking peas." Starting out in January in the Imperial Valley he "drifted northward picking peas as they ripened," until he picked "the last peas of the season in June, around Tracy." The town of Tracy is more than 500 miles from El Centro. Then he shifted even farther north to Lake County, where he would turn to string beans. He remembered how "hesitant and anxious" he was that first morning. "Would I be able to pick string beans? Even the change from peas to string beans had in it elements of fear."[15]

In another newspaper column,[16] Hoffer described being in San Francisco in 1936 when the Golden Gate Bridge was under construction. That same year, he tried prospecting for gold and, more importantly for his future career as a writer, discovered the sixteenth-century French writer Michel de Montaigne. According to Hoffer, he was on his way to the gold country in the Sierra Nevada when he stopped in a bookstore in San Francisco looking for something to outlast his stay in the hills, "perhaps a scientific volume." He bought the thickest book he saw—the *Essays of Montaigne*. He was indeed trapped by snow so he read the book at least twice. He "also formed the habit of taking notes."

Montaigne "gave me a taste for the good sentence," he said. "I never had the urge to write until after I read Montaigne."[17] Montaigne's skeptical, open-minded inquiry seemed to come from a later century, and he "never wearied of expatiating on the inconstancy, lack of uniformity, involuteness and unpredictability of human manifestations."[18]

One of his early notebooks is filled with quotations from Montaigne, copied in November-December 1936. One notebook entry quotes from *The Atlantic Monthly*'s May 1936 issue. Hoffer noted that Montaigne began writing his essays at the age of 39—close to Hoffer's own age at the time. He also found the French mathematician and philosopher Blaise Pascal's *Pensées* in a Monterey bookstore at about the same time.

In a 1963 notebook, Hoffer wrote that his style came from "biographical accident—an acquaintance with Montaigne, the Old Testament and botanical textbooks." His subject matter, he said, derived largely from the events of the Hitler decade. The shaping influence on his ideas came from Alexis de Tocqueville and Ernest Renan.

"I developed my thoughts in relative intellectual isolation," he wrote. "Though I have lived my life in America I am probably not largely American in my tastes, thinking and mode of expression."

As to the gold mining:

> It was all placer. It is hard work, shoveling dirt into a sluice box for ten hours a day. I never hit it rich. Still, after a four months' stay in the hills I used to come down with two or three hundred dollars worth of gold.

"In those years women were important to him for sexual release," James Koerner wrote, "but he preferred to keep them at the same distance he did the men with whom he worked." He described Hoffer as a natural loner; in fact, all his life he wanted to be left alone. For many years his relations with women were therefore confined, with one exception, to prostitutes.[19] Koerner adds that Hoffer was "terrifically lusty":

"I had an eye for women all the time. I was full of juices that got bottled up in the camps. Your imagination burns you up there in the woods, so you get up out of your bunk and walk to the nearest whorehouse—it is maybe thirty miles away! . . . I must say that somewhat took the edge off it."

Many times he was simply abstinent for long periods, either for lack of money or opportunity. At the end of such periods "the procedure," he recalls, "was always the same. When I got out of the woods and back to town, I had money. First I bought all new clothes and threw the old ones away. Then I went to the Japanese barber . . . Then I got myself a room halfway between the library and the whorehouse."

Hoffer knew whorehouses the length and breadth of California. The girls liked him, he remembers, because he was kind to them. "I treated them like human beings," he says. "I brought them candy and sometimes a little vial of gold when I had been prospecting."[20]

Just as he knew the whorehouses, Hoffer knew the libraries in the state and had a card for many of them. When he was not working, his life alternated between the two establishments.

Helen

Hoffer said that he had "one love affair." The woman was named Helen, and was five years his senior. Forty years after the event he recalled that she was the most beautiful woman he had ever seen.

He was working as a busboy in a twenty-four-hour cafeteria on Shattuck Avenue in Berkeley. It was summer, probably in 1937 or thereabouts. Early one morning, as he was leaving the cafeteria, he saw the "red train," the electric street car, pull up on Shattuck. Two women got off with a suitcase. They looked around, obvious newcomers. He bought them breakfast in the cafeteria and then found them a room farther up in the hills, with a view of San Francisco Bay.

One was Helen. She and Eric became close friends, he said. She enrolled at Boalt Hall, the university's law school. Impressed by his mind and his gift for theorizing, she tried to persuade Eric to audit classes "in higher mathematics and advanced physics."

The owner of the rooming house where they stayed would join them for dinner and lectured Eric one evening about the need for a goal, saying that people must feel that they are going somewhere. "It was a sin to waste my great talents," Hoffer summarized their exchange.

Helen told him, "It would be wonderful if you could spend a whole year with us in Berkeley. Later if you feel like it, you could return to harvesting and mining. We have been so happy these months."[21]

"She had things all worked out," Hoffer told Koerner. "She was going to educate me. She wanted me to become a professor of physics and mathematics. She wanted to throw a rope around me." So, Koerner wrote, Hoffer "took his departure. It was not yet time, if it would ever be, for him to get married. He made no effort to keep track of Helen and has no idea of what became of her."[22] But he never forgot her.

Was Helen a real person? Both Stacy Cole and Koerner believe she was.

"I am reasonably certain that she was real," said Cole. "He talked to me about her too many times, and never without a sort of passion that struck me as genuine." Hoffer also wondered if the other woman, who apparently disliked Eric, had a "lesbian connection" with Helen. Anyway, Hoffer kept her memory fresh. Here is a late entry, from a 1977 notebook:

> She was five years older than he so that now that he was 75 she would be eighty. And he has not seen her for 50 years. Yet she remained alive in his mind all through the years. His old heart and his shriveled mind clung to the memory of her.

A few months later, Hoffer referred back to the unnamed Helen once again, in a longer entry:

She would be near eighty now. She was vivid in his mind—as vivid as the day he saw her fifty years ago. It seemed to him that her face was engraved on every thought he had during the fifty years. And her name, he still called it out whenever he remembered something unpleasant, for it was like a cry for help. Yet not once during the fifty years did he have an impulse to go and find her and see her again. She was near him all the time and it seemed enough. But yesterday on his 75th birthday it suddenly came to him that he could not live in peace unless he knew where she was. He needed a purpose. It might take him the remaining few years to track her. Was she still alive?

A final detail that Stacy Cole recalled from his conversations with Hoffer: Helen's "radical posture" and her admiration for what she believed the Russian Revolution had achieved led Hoffer to suspect that "she might have gone to Russia in the 1930s, and perished there."

The earliest documentary record of Hoffer's existence is a photostat of his application for a Social Security account, filled out on June 10, 1937. He said at the time that he was thirty-eight years old, having been born in New York City on July 25, 1898. If so, of course, he was four years older than he claimed at other times.

He identified himself as the son of Knut Hoffer and Elsa Goebel, and gave his address as 101 Eye Street, Sacramento. His employer at the time was the U.S. Forest Service in Placerville, California. It is the only documentary evidence of his life to be found in the archives before he moved permanently to San Francisco. It is confirmed by a Waterfront Employers Identification card, issued in 1943 and retained by Lili Osborne in her possession. Hoffer was photographed at that time, and his date of birth is again given as 1898.[23]

By this time Hoffer had library cards in a dozen towns along the railroad. He was reading all the time, and his years "as a migratory worker developed whatever ability I have to write." He had indeed become a polished writer, as his 1938 description of El Centro showed. He didn't move to San Francisco until probably 1942, so his time as a migratory worker lasted for perhaps eight years. It was an eventful time. In addition to his manual labor, he found plenty of time to study, read, and write. He also made contact with the outside world.

Common Ground

A journal called *Common Ground*, addressed to the foreign-born "and those who ought to know more about them," published its first issue in September 1940. It was funded by the Carnegie Corporation and it is likely that Hoffer came across it during one of his frequent visits to one of the Carnegie libraries—named for Andrew Carnegie, the Scottish-American steel magnate and philanthropist who built almost 1,700 libraries in the United States. Hoffer liked what he saw in this journal, assembled some of his written material, and mailed it off as an article. The editor, Louis Adamic, was himself an immigrant and had come to the United States from Slovenia in 1913. The magazine lasted for thirty-seven issues before closing in late 1949 after the Carnegie funding was discontinued.

Hoffer's exact contemporary, Adamic promoted "diversity" long before it was fashionable and was later recognized as a founding father of ethnic studies. The idea of America as a melting pot did not appeal to him. Later he became a keen supporter of Yugoslavian leader Marshal Tito and was accused of Communist sympathies. It's safe to say that he would have disagreed with the later Eric Hoffer about almost everything. Gerald Meyer reported in *Socialism and Democracy* that in September 1951 "Adamic set ablaze his own home—which included his library and research—and then shot himself." Others say he was murdered.[24]

Eventually Hoffer heard back, not from Adamic but from Margaret Anderson, who by 1942 had become the editor of *Common Ground*. They couldn't publish his submission, she wrote, but she urged him to continue writing. Her continuing interest and support sustained Hoffer throughout his solitary years struggling to write *The True Believer.*

The draft of a letter that he wrote to Margaret Anderson at this time is of particular interest. Hoffer rarely kept copies of his own letters, but he was in the habit of writing rough drafts in his notebooks. The following has been pieced together from an early notebook, probably from 1941. Evidently by then he had already sent some of his writings to Anderson, and he is curious to hear her opinion.

Lili Osborne called the following letter "a very special record of who the early Eric was."

Dear Miss Anderson:

Please forgive the delay in answering your letter. I have been away picking peaches and apricots. Tonight I'm off to Fresno for alfalfa haying. Until the rains come I shall be continually on the move, with occasional stopovers in Monterey as I shuttle back and forth between Northern and Southern California.

Right now I feel stale, everything seems very old stuff. My honest opinion is that I'm not worth bothering with and that I'm wasting your time and sympathy. The fact that I have not deliberately planned this waste gives me little comfort. However, you are the one to decide one way or the other. And the moment you realize that there is not much in me you can wash your hands of the mess and no real harm done.

The piece "Oranges" is as you have guessed the middle part of an essay on business. I enclose it as I wrote it in 1936. I wrote it in a speech-making mood.

In some parts of California a man can walk along the highway and shout to his heart's content and wave his hands and do practically anything he pleases without making a spectacle of himself. You are not likely to meet anyone except occasional cars whizzing by at a mile a minute, and that intrude no more than a passing fly. You have the highway and the landscape all to yourself. Vigorous walking seems to ease the flow of words; and speech-making in its turn gives [rise to] the effortlessness of gesture.

The speeches were addressed to "you of the future"—people living two hundred years from now and in a world completely unlike our own. I have only a very vague idea of what these children of the future would be like. I imagined my audience to consist of people not unlike the fine children I had met while selling oranges, and this world as completely regulated in its economics but free in its intellectual ferment. The important part was that to my imaginary audience the familiar details of our everyday life seemed outlandish and fantastic, and my speeches were therefore about familiar things: work, business, money, hunger, suicide, the Bible, nations, food and clothes, freight trains and highways, prospecting, advertising; everything, in short, of which I had some first-hand knowledge.

The whole performance, though somewhat absurd and affected, suited my inclinations. The feeling of being a stranger in this world is probably the result of some organic disorder. It is strongest in me when I'm hungry or tired. But even when nothing is wrong I sometimes find it easy to look at the world around me as if I saw it for the first time. After six or eight weeks in fields picking fruit or in the hills chopping wood a return to civilization is like the opening act in a fairy tale. And as in a fairy tale the strangeness which assails the senses is not confusing but seems to emanate from a simple, symmetric design.

I don't know whether the essays have any merit. But they undoubtedly strengthened in me a habit of detached observance. This habit may not be good for a writer, as you imply in your letter, but it suits my nature and I feel almost downgraded whenever it is momentarily swept aside by bursts of passion. Only then [in maintaining detachment] can I retain my tolerance, love of humanity and the awareness of the marvel of life on this earth. It is therefore that I must lead an insecure existence. I have to guard against fear, self-righteousness, cynicism and wishful thinking;

for these blunt the mind and the senses, and more than cancel out all the advantages of an insecure existence. This is not difficult, one needs only a little courage, a little intelligence and the inclination not to take oneself too seriously.

I want to answer all your questions. All my people were short-lived. My mother died at 26, my father at 42, and an aunt at a little over fifty. None of my grandparents reached fifty. At my age I'm a finished product: stomach ulcers, asthma.

My eyes are good. But now and then when I sleep in a windowless hotel room I wake up and find I have to strike a match to make sure that I have not lost my eyesight.

I send the short novel "Four Years in Hank's Young Life." It cost a fortune to have it typed. It should tell, if you have the patience to plow through the 170 pages, whether I can write. Frankly, I don't know whether it is good, even in part. I can't judge my own writing. But though it is not autobiographical, it necessarily tells more about me than I can do in a dozen long letters.

At present I have no address. I might manage later in the season to spend some weeks in Santa Rosa, during hop picking, and to receive there my copy of Common Ground.

Very thankfully yours, Eric Hoffer

Eric Hoffer, 1973.

Publicity photograph for
The True Believer, *1951.*
This was the earliest photo
of Hoffer of which Lili Fabilli
Osborne was aware.

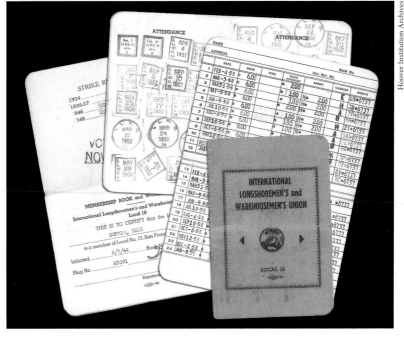

Eric Hoffer's membership books from ILWU, 1950s.

Eric and Lili at home, 1960s.

Hoffer with Eric and Stephen Osborne, early 1960s.

*"With love to Lili, Eric.
July 1967."*

*Lili with her sons, Stephen (l.) and Eric Osborne (r.), at home, during
mid-1960s.*

Hoffer had love and respect for his fellow dockworkers, and it was mutual. Some called him "the one who writes books."

While a ship's rigging is changed, the dockhands could take a break; Hoffer reads a pocket-sized book, with British paper, The Statesman, *tucked underarm.*

At work on the docks: The then 62-year-old Hoffer and his partner labor to roll a full oil drum into its assigned position, and then tip it up with one great heave.

One of the few known photographs of Hoffer speaking to students at Barrows Hall, University of California at Berkeley, 1967–68.

Hoffer speaking at the Stanford University student union. (See text, p. 147, for a description of this event.)

A gift from Lyndon Johnson, during visit to The White House in 1967; the photograph was autographed, "To Eric Hoffer, from his friend Lyndon B. Johnson."

Hoffer at the inauguration of San Francisco Mayor Joseph Alioto in 1968. Hoffer was as demonstrative in person as he was self-controlled in his writing. He called Mayor Alioto a "renaissance man."

Hoffer studies rare volume held in display case in library.

Hoffer at Lili's, 1971.

A recent photo of Eric Osborne in Alaska.

Hoffer in his Davis Court apartment, 1974, showing his desk and book case.

Eric Hoffer at his desk in his Davis Court apartment in San Francisco.

Hoffer smoking pipe at his desk (showing writing paraphernalia and file drawers containing the quotations he collected).

Stacy Cole at Lili's, November 1978.

Eric Hoffer and Stacy Cole, 1978. Eric is in his customary place by Lili's rear window. From his position, the Golden Gate is visible on a clear day.

Photo by Mary Fabilli

Selden Osborne, November 1992.

Hoover Institution Archives; photo by Ara Guler

Hoffer at Lili's house.

CHAPTER THREE

On the Waterfront

*In the morning it occurred to me that the waterfront
is the only place where I have felt at home. All my life,
wherever I went, I felt an outsider. Here I have a strong
feeling of belonging. One of the reasons is of course that I
have tarried here long enough to take root. Yet it seems to
me that I have felt at home here from the first month.*

—ERIC HOFFER

Working and Thinking on the Waterfront, *February 21, 1959*

"Not a single human achievement was conceived or realized in the
bracing atmosphere of steppes, forests and mountaintops," Hoffer
once wrote. Everything was achieved "in the crowded stinking
little cities of Jerusalem, Athens, Florence, Shakespeare's London,
Rembrandt's Amsterdam . . ."[1]

There are many such panegyrics to city life in Hoffer's writings.
It's not hard to understand why he moved to San Francisco. It's
harder to understand why he didn't do so earlier, or why he moved
away from Los Angeles ten years before that. There was always work
for an able-bodied man with initiative and ability, and Hoffer qualified on both counts.

Once in San Francisco, he moved near the public library. He said
it was the first time he had a fixed address in California. It may
also have been his first fixed address anywhere: a rooming house at

1438 McAllister Street. His rent was $20 a month, at least for the first few years, and he stayed there for seventeen years.[2]

Pearl Harbor spurred his move. By 1942 he had registered for the draft at a local board in San Francisco, and within months was turned down by the U.S. Army because of a hernia. His selective service card, dated July 1943, shows that he was classified 4A.

An employment agency in San Francisco dispatched him to the longshoremen's union — "sheer luck," he wrote.[3] The war, the nationwide draft, and a labor shortage on the docks made it possible for him to become a longshoreman at the age of forty-five. In a form he filled out, Hoffer claimed that over the preceding fifteen months he had been employed by the U.S. Army Supply Base in Oakland, and for the four months before that as a trucker with the Southern Pacific Company. (However, both Lili and Stephen Osborne believed that Hoffer never learned to drive.)

"It was only during the war that the union opened its doors to newcomers," Hoffer wrote. "In normal times entrance into the Longshoreman's Union is more difficult than entrance into an exclusive aristocratic club."[4] In peacetime it would not have been possible for a forty-five-year-old man with no union connections to be hired as a longshoreman.

The union which Hoffer joined was led by a legendary figure in West Coast labor circles: Harry Bridges. In a violent three-month strike at San Francisco's Embarcadero in the early summer of 1934, Bridges succeeded in displacing the then-president of the local branch of the International Longshoremen's Association, Joseph Ryan, who was seen by longshoremen as a sellout to business interests. Two strikers were killed. In 1937 Bridges organized West Coast dockworkers into the International Longshoremen's and Warehousemen's Union. An incorrupt labor leader who lived modestly, Bridges became a major force in the union movement. "In the very depths of the Depression, labor had organized, virtually overnight, a major American industry, West Coast shipping, using agreements that in one form or another would last for the rest of the century."[5]

Born in Australia in 1901, Bridges had encouraged Communist participation in the strike and later became well-known in the newspapers as a Communist. In 1940 the House of Representatives passed a bill to deport him as an alien—he had failed to become a U.S. citizen—but the U.S. Supreme Court came to his rescue a few years later.

Bridges' main adversary in the San Francisco strike was Roger Dearborn Lapham, the president of the American Hawaiian Steamship Company and a wealthy bon vivant who became mayor of San Francisco from 1944–48. His father had been a founder of Texaco. Lapham contrasted sharply with Bridges—thin, sharp-featured, tense, and sardonic, in Kevin Starr's description. Bridges, from an Irish Catholic background, thoroughly out-maneuvered Lapham, who was said to have squandered the family fortune, often betting large sums at poker without looking at his cards.

In 1976 his grandson Lewis Lapham became editor of *Harper's* magazine, where some of Hoffer's best-known articles (including "The Role of the Undesirables") had appeared. In the late 1970s Cowles Communications decided to sell *Harper's*, which by then was losing money. Lewis Lapham recalled that one day in about 1980 Harry Bridges came to see him in New York and offered to buy the magazine.[6] But he was unable to do so, and eventually it was acquired by the MacArthur Foundation. Bridges, who had retired from the union presidency in 1977, died in 1990.

In public, Hoffer preserved a discreet silence about Bridges. Later he said that he never once had a conversation with him. His notebooks contain criticism of Bridges' Communist sympathies, but in most respects he admired the labor leader. Toward the end of his life he wrote that, like America, "the union was founded by a leader. Harry Bridges is a sort of Jefferson. And like Jefferson, he created an organization that functioned well without leaders."[7]

Hoffer had high praise for the union's work rules, which were much to his advantage. A longshoreman could stay home if he didn't want to work on a given day, and was paid only for the days that he did work.

When Hoffer joined the union—it was his only union job—the San Francisco docks were working at full capacity. "They used to pile on the work and we went at it as though we were going into battle," Hoffer told Calvin Tomkins. There were many accidents. In 1943 a five-ton crate crashed to the wharf and just missed him, but it destroyed his right thumb. He was in the hospital for months as a new one was reconstructed from his own thigh. It was little more than a stump.

A rare pre-*True Believer* anecdote about Eric Hoffer comes from Peter Duignan, who worked on the docks as a student in the summer of 1944 and later became a senior fellow at the Hoover Institution. One day he partnered with Hoffer. Two men lifting a 130-pound sack of coffee must lift simultaneously, or the one who lifts first will tip the weight down onto the other—which the inexperienced Duignan did. Hoffer cried out: "Don't give me that Portagee lift!"[8]

Interviewed by Eric Sevareid of CBS, Hoffer referred to "the tremendous trust" that Americans repose in their fellow men, a trust that offended the Communists on the waterfront. Newspaper stands at the entrance to the docks used an honor system. Everyone was trusted to put in a nickel and nothing stopped anyone from taking a paper if he didn't. To disrupt this arrangement, the Communists would steal the papers:

> Not because they wanted a paper, but to destroy that trust. It offended them that a capitalist, self-seeking society should have so much trust![9]

Hoffer's notebooks included comments on Harry Bridges that were at times admiring and at times critical. In August 1950, Hoffer wrote:

There is a fantastic roundabout way by which men reach their goal. Men reject the faith of their fathers and mothers, yet in the end realize the aspiration of their parents in a bizarre and extravagant manner. A man like Harry Bridges has a pious Catholic, Irish mother. He rejects his mother's faith and nationalist prejudice. Yet his aspiration is a combination of anti-Anglo-Saxonism and a craving for sainthood. His dream is of ending up as a saint in the new faith of Communism and being buried in a niche in Lenin's mausoleum.

He also thought Bridges was a cynic and that "his cynicism dates from 1939–41" (during which time the Nazis and Soviets maintained a non-aggression pact). He wrote in 1951:

The somersault he had to perform on the Soviet-Nazi pact has irremediably tainted his soul. Having played the role of a puppet himself, he has been behaving since as if the members of ILWU were mere puppets to be manipulated at will.

Hoffer said the attitude of Bridges and his clique could partly be explained "by the line laid down in Moscow." At the same time, "by watching B. perform" one could get some clue as to the intentions of "the gang in Moscow." Hoffer compared Bridges to the French minister Charles Talleyrand, who "before departing on a mission received instructions of which he was himself the author."

Nonetheless, Hoffer admired the way the union had been organized. "I have not as yet overcome my surprise at the almost millennial conditions realized on the waterfront," he wrote. Hoffer "never spoke up at union meetings" and had no inclination to give advice "to people who had achieved so much."

This letter from Hoffer to an unknown correspondent, "Henry," was drafted in 1949:

Things here are as usual. The Hawaiian strike drags on and the waterfront is fairly dead. The apartment house owners among our longshoremen are crying their eyes out. In my case conditions seem ideal. I average about 40 hours a week, which is more than enough to live on. And all I have to do is put in 20 hours of actual work. It's a racket and I love it.

Last week I had an interesting experience. We discharged a small Norwegian ship at pier 39. The cargo was newsprint in rolls of 1500 pounds each. Usually such a ship means hard work for us dockmen. You work yourself to death, and if your partner is a chiseler it is the easiest thing in the world to rupture yourself. This time however I was in the midst of a miracle. The work has been completely mechanized and it was a beautiful thing to watch. For two days I did no more work than if I would be sunning myself on the beach. Indeed I managed to get a fine sun tan.

The machinery is extremely simple and believe it or not it was invented by two longshoremen working as gear-men. I am told that the two said longshoremen are not particularly bright, which goes to show you never know how smart a guy is by looking at him or listening to his talk. The two inventors have patented their device and are now manufacturing it in a machine shop here in 'Frisco.

Intrigued by the true believer Selden Osborne, Hoffer noticed that he was "siding with Bridges" in opposing the U.S. intervention in Korea. Selden also opposed any loyalty screening. At one meeting, Hoffer watched Bridges "while Osborne was defending him. It seemed to me that I saw a flicker of contempt."

Selden became a "diet faddist," and Hoffer noticed that, too. How true is it, he wondered, "that true believers have an affinity for diet cults? You attain immortality either by embracing an eternal cause or by living forever." Selden told Eric that when he ate, he methodically chewed so many times on one side, so many times on the other.

When a group of longshoremen was driven in a bus across San Francisco Bay to discharge a ship in Oakland on September 2, 1950, Hoffer talked to his neighbor, unnamed, and was content to play the role of reporter:

> The fellow looked sharp-faced, reserved, though with a ready smile. We assisted each other in closing the window of the bus as we crossed the Bay Bridge. A number of ships could be seen anchored in the bay waiting for berth or cargo. He counted 14. I recounted and found 15. I asked him whether he had seen them all lighted up the night before while we were discharging paper at Pier 40. He said he was too busy with the paper lift he was driving to notice anything. It made him dizzy and jittery. I said practice makes perfect. If he worked on the lift for a month he might not need to concentrate on anything. . . .
>
> We reminisced about the hundreds of ships which crowded the Bay at the end of the Second World War. We agreed that once we get enough men and material into Korea we will clean up the mess in one sweep. I suggested that the American soldier had to be surrounded by gadgets in order to feel confident. He said it shows that we are spoiled and made soft by luxuries. I disagreed. We are not weak, though it is true we cannot match the fanatic's ability to fight stubbornly and enthusiastically with a minimum of material. Stalin's secret weapon, I said, was his ability to inspire fanaticism in all masses of people.

What did his fellow longshoremen think of Hoffer? Accompanying him to the docks in 1966, Tomkins met one or two workers who referred to Hoffer as "the professor." An official from the union said that he was considered an "odd duck."

Hoffer later told of an encounter with a retired longshoreman he had known in the 1940s. The man by then owned a five-acre apple orchard in Northern California and was prospering. "His warmth was tangible and pleasant." He told Hoffer that he bragged to neighbors about their association and even "gives away my books." Hoffer was flattered and pleased that at least some of his fellow workers regarded "the professor" with admiration and even a certain amount of awe.

Hoffer was considered to be a vigorous worker and never sought any job other than that of ordinary dock worker. He consistently said that he enjoyed the work. He could earn enough by working two or three days a week, leaving him free to stay home and write. During a three-month strike in 1946, and another in 1948, he was able to make good progress with *The True Believer*. But excepting these union-imposed breaks, he apparently never took time off to write.

"It would be hard to find another occupation with so suitable a combination of freedom, exercise, leisure and income," he wrote to Margaret Anderson in 1949. "By working only Saturday and Sunday (eighteen hours at pay and a half) I can earn 40–50 dollars a week. This to me is rolling in dough."[10] But in a 1944 notebook he recorded that creative thought was incompatible with hard physical work.

> Long hours of hard work undoubtedly stifle intellectual activity. They have a doping effect. A hard working community cannot be possessed of marked intelligence or taste. It's true that leisure as such does not automatically stimulate intellectual creativeness. It often leads to dissipation or stagnation or senseless tinkering. Nevertheless, leisure is one of the essential prerequisites of any creativeness.

In 1963, he addressed the same question: Was physical labor conducive to thought, or did it leave workers too tired to think?

> Work has been draining energy away from thought and imagination. People who work eight hours a day cannot pursue truth, cannot even grope for it, cannot even see the goal they are supposed to grope for. Now with the coming of automation there is an enormous release of human energies—millions of brains are

ready for a full time pursuit of truth and beauty. We must assume that the grown generation is a generation of the desert. It is the new generation that must be equipped with the new skills and the new set of values.

A different picture of Hoffer's mental life on the docks is to be found in *Working and Thinking on the Waterfront,* which Harper & Row published in 1969. It is the most readable and in some ways the most informative of all his books.

By now he found work conducive to mental stimulation. It left him free to think of other things and even work out problems with his own writing. He could talk with his partners and compose sentences in the back of his mind at the same time. Automation surely helped. An ideal environment for him, he said, was one in which he was surrounded by people and yet not part of them.

"Chances are that had my work been of absorbing interest, I could not have done any thinking and composing on the company's time, or even on my own time after returning from work." But routine work was compatible with an active mind. On the other hand a highly eventful life could be mentally exhausting and drain all creative energy. He cited John Milton, who wrote political pamphlets throughout the Puritan agitation, and postponed *Paradise Lost* until his life was more peaceful.

Hoffer once reconstructed one of his mental flights. He had drawn a partner known to be a poor worker. Partners are expected to build their side of the load equally, but this man was always wandering off—"giving foreign aid to somebody else." Hoffer began "a beautiful train of thought," and was soon "in orbit" thinking about it. Clumsiness, he concluded, is inconspicuous for those who are not on their home turf. Similarly, the cultural avant-garde attracts people without real talent, "whether as writers or artists." Why? Because everybody expects innovators to be clumsy. "They are probably people without real talent," he decided. But those who experiment with a new form have a built-in excuse.[11]

Union rules contributed to Hoffer's mental freedom. The dispatching system spread the work fairly and prevented workers from monopolizing the best jobs. If unloading delays meant that longshoremen didn't have any work at a given moment, they didn't have to pretend otherwise. They could sit down and read if they preferred. When Tomkins went to the docks, Hoffer brought along with him an issue of the quarterly *Partisan Review*. It was just the right size, he said.

Over the years, several photographers took pictures of Hoffer at work. Sometimes he is shown sitting on a pallet and reading a book. In the mid-1950s *Time* magazine published this perfect thumbnail sketch:

"Eric Hoffer is a pink-faced, horny-handed San Francisco dock worker who pays his dues to Harry Bridges' longshoremen's union and preaches self-reliance more stalwartly than Emerson. He gets up at 4:45 in the morning and spends his days working on the piers of San Francisco's Embarcadero. Evenings he spends in his room in a shabby McAllister Street lodging house, bent over a plank desk, writing."[12]

By 1963, Hoffer had become worried about automation. Once a hundred men would take a week to unload a ship; now it took only a few hours. The ship might sail the same day. It was a key moment for Hoffer. Later he changed his mind about automation, but while his fears lasted they unleashed a burst of activism that changed his life. He became a public speaker and an advocate. But it wasn't his own job that he was concerned about. The union had accepted automation and management had contributed millions of dollars to offset the displacement of workers. Their own paychecks were safe. It was the consequences for America that worried Hoffer.

His thinking went like this: Unlike Europe, America owed little to elites. In fact, "America was not America until masses took over." The U.S. workforce was "the most skillful and competent the world has ever known."[13] But if the masses were to be put out of work by machinery they would be destroyed and America itself would not survive. Those were his premonitions. Later he saw that his fears had been greatly exaggerated. But by then his career as the advocate of America was launched, and it began with this issue.

The union "was run by nobodies," just like America, Hoffer said. He liked to talk about a Mr. Sanchez who ran for vice president of the local to the dismay of "the intellectuals." They wondered if he could even sign his name. Sanchez won the election and did a good job, despite his lack of qualifications. When he wrote the union bulletins, Sanchez even illustrated them with his own drawings.[14]

"It did not occur to the intellectuals," Hoffer commented, "that in this country nobodies perform tasks which in other countries are reserved for elites." It was one of his favorite reflections.

In the privacy of his notebook, he wondered what life on the docks would be like if the longshoremen's union owned the ships they discharged. "What a serious business would our daily life then become!" he concluded. "To relax would be to slack, casualness would be sabotage, to sample the cargo—a legitimate practice now—would be treason."

His more conventional thoughts on this topic were published in *Harper's* at about the same time.[15] He rejected the doctrine of the fascists and the communists: that management and labor should be unified by the state. This device—nationalization—was a plan to extract "the maximum performance from an underpaid labor force" and was "more a threat than a promise." He supported private ownership of production and an independent labor force (by which he meant a unionized one). True, the cleavage between labor and management created strife, but tranquility wasn't necessarily the best policy, he thought.

But his unpublished comment on how life would change if labor and management were unified under private ownership was a more interesting speculation. In his public remarks, Hoffer was always tactful about unionization, never so much as hinting that it might have drawbacks, such as increased unemployment. He evidently recognized the ability of a labor union to raise wages above the market rate, judging from his observation on the last page of *Working and Thinking on the Waterfront*:[16]

"The union has taken in five hundred new longshoremen. They have been sifted out of several thousand applicants, and make an excellent impression." Perhaps as many as ten applicants for every vacancy showed just how desirable the job was.

When Tomkins interviewed Hoffer, close to the end of his time on the waterfront, he was working three days and taking home $80 a week. "I'll be working there until the day I die, you can be sure of that," he said at the time. Lili Osborne said that Hoffer "wants to die on the job."[17]

Financial records show that Hoffer made $4,100 as a longshoreman and $1,095 in *True Believer* royalties in 1953. By 1956 he was reporting to work three or four times a week and earning over $5,000 as a longshoreman.

From June 1958 to May 1959, Hoffer kept a diary, later published as *Working and Thinking on the Waterfront*. He kept an additional notebook, also in diary form, in the summer of 1961. It concentrates on his work on the waterfront and on the men he worked with. At times, he deliberately played a reportorial role. Extracts from that unpublished diary, reproduced below, reveal a great deal about the work of a longshoreman and about Hoffer and his co-workers, many of whom were from Central Europe.

Waterfront Vignettes—1961

June 18, 1961

2:30 p.m.: Made four hours on the Lurline at Pier 35. This is the first time in three weeks that I'll make a decent check—about $95 take-home pay. As baggage man I hustled without any eagerness or greed but also without dignity. This lack of "dignity" has been with me most of my life. The reason is probably that I have no real concern about what people think of me. After all I am up in years, and a writer, and so I should be dignified. The total lack of any sense of belonging is undoubtedly a factor.

June 30

3:30 p.m.: I am so unused to meeting people that the fact that I am going to meet the Ceylonese parliamentarians this evening bothers me considerably. They are probably a group of posturing pseudo-intellectuals. I doubt very much whether they have any interest in Americans. They are interested first and last in themselves. It is also a safe bet that they came to us not to learn how to build and run a modern society but to teach us and particularly lecture us about our crude materialism. I could easily make hash of the whole bunch—but what's the use.

I am taking Selden with me. For him it'll be a real treat. He has a naïve craving for foreign lands. Why? I can't put my finger on it. He is through and through a typical American with the soul of a Rotarian, with faith in education and the educational value of foreign travel. How he lost his way and ended up a radical is beyond me. Joining the workers was a short-cut to leadership. To become a great man by following traditional paths is a slow and arduous process.

The examples of Lenin, Mussolini and Hitler, where intellectually undistinguished men made themselves through faith and single-minded dedication into shapers of history is a challenge to every mediocrity hungering for power and capable of self delusion.

10 p.m.: The man we met, a Dr. Pereira who is the head of the Ceylonese Federation of Labor, turned out to be an intelligent and civilized human being. Though darkish in color he looked not unlike an American congressman. He had seen Bridges this afternoon and we talked about this meeting first and then about the Negroes in the Union and the operation of the Union.

What I shall remember most, however, is Selden's performance. I knew long ago that if ever he should go to a foreign country and write a book about America it would be a most dishonest monstrosity. Now I discovered that the picture he gives of the Union, too, is utterly dishonest.

July 7

6 p.m.: Work on Evergreen State at Pier 18. It was steady hard work sorting cargo from Japan. My partner [was] a partly lame Norwegian by the name of Steve Skarvik; a gentle soul, pleasant to be with. Also in our gang: the Czechoslovak "Reno" who loves words and is consumed with a hunger for the aristocratic way of life. He rolls words off his mouth as if they were candy. When he falls in love with a word he repeats it endlessly. He saw a Negro riding on the edge of a scow and he said to me: "What brinkmanship!" His sympathies are with the Slavs. Any Russian triumph is also his. I can see that he likes me a lot, and it pleases me. In the past I often got his goat by running down Czechoslovakia but we have not touched the subject lately.

July 9

On the Alessandro Volta at Pier 24. One of the pleasantest days I ever had. Both job and people could not be bettered. Cargo—tires mostly, and much sitting down between loads. My partner, Martin Gomez, a Portuguese I have known for a long time but never worked with. Had you asked my opinion of him I would have said that he was a poor worker. Yet he turned out to be one of the most pleasant persons I have met in a long time. A man of character, proud of his family—a son Gilbert, a student of chemistry at U.C.; a daughter Carolina, about 15; and his wife Virginia.

He has just sold his house for $30,000 and is going to build a new one. Has four houses he has built during the past decade which he rents out for about $360 a month. He hires people to build the house but has no contractor; buys the material himself and looks after the job in his spare time; knows how to treat the carpenters, etc., so that he gets the most out of them; pays them $2 more than union scale. You don't have to supervise them—they know their stuff.

Martin himself loves this country, appreciates all his advantages and has apparently the capacity to do more than he is doing.

Clearly a man of his caliber needs no bunch of commissars to tell him what to do and how to manage his life.

It was very hot all day yet I feel unusually well just now, despite the fact that my stomach is not quite right. I have just had a large beer and am listening to a Brahms concerto as I write.

July 10

6 p.m.: Hardest day in a long time, on the Chinese ship Haisin at Pier 41. Steady grind in terrific heat. Was so tired I could not remember my registration number when I went to sign up in the hall. By the same token, I cannot remember a large beer tasting as good as the one I am now drinking. I have to clean up, have something to eat and then go to the union meeting. It'll be awful to sit there and listen to the tiresome speeches and discussions. At the moment I have no use for longshoremen.

11:30 p.m.: The meeting was interesting. Bridges performed superbly. His ability to win and hold the allegiance of any number of workingmen is sky high above that of any other member of the union. He is not a rabble rouser. He reasons lucidly, drives his point home with much logic, and there is not much to distinguish his lucidity and straightforwardness from sheer honesty. All the other would-be leaders can't reach his knees even if they raised themselves on tiptoes. His experience and prestige undoubtedly help, but his main advantage is his natural ability.

July 13

6 p.m.: A day of steady grind at Pier 19. We were practically alone on the dock and it is remarkable how such quiet eases one's day. I feel fairly tired but not strained. My partner, the Slovenian Martin, pleasant and talkative. He said that the greatest difficulty for the Croatians and Slovenians who come to this country is that they have no one to talk to. Back home in the village you were never alone. Men and women were always in groups gossiping, joking,

playing and working. Here you can go for days without talking to a fellow human. He is nearing retirement and he'll probably take a long trip with his wife to the old country.

My Croatian partner said: "In the old country people of my age (he is 63) do not work. They sit, stroke their beards and tell others where to go and what to do. When they go out in the street they are greeted by all. They are important people. Here the old are nothing unless they have lots of money. This country is not a country for the old."

July 14

5:45 p.m.: Finished the job on the Bergalen. It was a hectic day. The bags of coconut meal came out pretty briskly. I sweat buckets. I hate to think what would have happened had I a poor partner. It looks like I am going to put in six days this week. This will justify taking off the whole of next week. I don't know whether it would accomplish much. A couple of good paragraphs on "The Readiness to Work" is all I expect.

There were seven gangs working on the ship today and it again became clear how the hustling of others presses on one's nerves and makes one's work harder.

During the day I thought fleetingly about Berlin [building of the Wall]. My Croatian partner also asked me what I thought of Berlin. I did not know what to say. Berlin must be turned into a bone that will stick in [Soviet leader Nikita] Khrushchev's throat. In Berlin, the Communists are stripped of all camouflage and all double talk: they are jail keepers struggling with all their might to make their prison-lands proof against freedom.

July 15

6:15 p.m.: Hook-on man for Ring's gang at Pier 48A. An easy and pleasant day, yet just now I feel somewhat dizzy. My partner, whose name I don't know, is an exceedingly gentle creature.

Spending a day with him I realized that there are people brittle as fine china who yet spend a long life among roughnecks without getting hurt and without acquiring the tinge of their environment. As I said, the man looked extremely delicate—almost ethereal. He was late for work because he got the order wrong from the hall. I am working with him tomorrow and shall try to find out something about him.

During the day it occurred to me that if it were true that all my life I have had but a single train of thought then it must be the problem of the uniqueness of man.

July 16

8:30 p.m.: 8 ½ hours on the Sagami Marin and Pier 29. We loaded mostly lumber—huge loads off flat cars. My partner was the gentle creature I worked with yesterday. I did not get around to finding more about him than his name: John Reed. The work was not hard but it required jumping and climbing, and the excitement of it made the sweat pour out of me. All during the day, despite the excitement and the continued strain, I had thoughts of Berlin and of the Communist fanatics I come up against now and again on the waterfront.

Yesterday, at Pier 48A, I worked next to the Slavonian [and his partner]. I have known the two hook-on men for many years. They are brothers but quite unlike one another in appearance. One of them has a round face with protruding eyes, somewhat bloodshot, and a quarrelsome expression. The other has angular features, deep set eyes, a quick smile and an air of reticence. It was the rotund fellow that poured out a torrent of Communist rhetoric when we touched upon Yugoslavia. A couple of Yugoslavian ships, newly built, have recently come to San Francisco.

I remembered that things seemed to have improved considerably in Yugoslavia since Tito's break with the Russians. The rotund fellow brushed this aside. Things are good in all Communist countries. Yes, even in Hungary and Poland. The people are really on top, and never before has the worker had it so good. I asked him whether there is any Communist country in which the workingman had living and working conditions comparable with those he and I are enjoying in this country. He sputtered out the accusation that all the money in this country comes from the exploitation of Peru and Guatemala, where workers are paid a few cents a day.

"You just wait and see! Fifty years from now there will not be capitalism anywhere."

Later I talked to his brother. I wanted to know what it was that made his brother so fanatical. He said: "Hand got five fingers, every one different."

Sometime during the day I happened to think of Selden's performance at the meeting with the Ceylonese labor leader. He was telling the man untruths about the union—about corruption and so on. I tried to present the situation as it is. Yet inevitably the dishonest criticisms had to the Ceylonese listener a greater appearance of truth than my truthful defense. To him it seemed that it was I who was exaggerating and that Selden was cutting down the exaggeration to real size.

Hoffer always earned more than he needed for his frugal life. In a 1948 notebook he estimated his annual expenses (including books) at $2,710. In 1956 *Look* magazine reported that "Hoffer reports to work only three or four days a week and takes home between $70 and $80 a week." Strikes he regarded as the equivalent of unpaid vacations, allowing him to concentrate on his writing. He made "crucial advances" on *The True Believer* during the strikes of 1946 and 1948.[18]

In a 1941 letter to Margaret Anderson, Hoffer said something about his writing life before he moved to San Francisco. Somehow, he contrived to sound more like Jack Kerouac (of *On the Road* fame) than Eric Hoffer—writers who could not have been more dissimilar.

My writing is done in railroad yards while waiting for a freight, in the fields while waiting for a truck, and at noon after lunch. Towns are too distracting. Now and then I take a day off to "put myself in order." I go through the notes, pick and discard. The residue is usually a few paragraphs. My mind must always have something to chew on.

The following, from another letter to Anderson written in 1948, sounds more in character. *The True Believer* was mostly written by then but Hoffer was filled with misgivings about it. He could see weaknesses on every page. But he could not tinker with it any longer. Most days he set off for a "five mile hike in the Golden Gate Park," he wrote, and there he found that he could "think according to schedule":

I have done it every day for weeks. Each day I took a problem to the park and returned with a more or less satisfactory solution . . . The book was written in complete intellectual isolation. I have not discussed one idea with any human being, and have not mentioned the book to anyone but you.[19]

Biography as Bibliography

From the time that he settled in San Francisco until the end of his life, Hoffer required little in the way of creature comforts or consumer goods. Early on he had a phonograph, along with some recordings of classical composers—Beethoven's Ninth Symphony among them—but that was a rare concession to modern technology. Even that he later discarded.

"Regarding Eric's one-room apartment," Lili Osborne wrote: "McAllister Street began and continued for many blocks as a second hand sales area. Eric lives in the tough part of it—low rents in old dilapidated houses and areas of prostitution. Gradually Chinese moved in. Their voluble voices made it hard for Eric to think or write. That is when I decided to find him a new home—a traumatic moment for him for many months, but the right one. You will find a large plywood sheet at Hoover. It was propped up to become his table and here he wrote *The True Believer*."[20]

In his four decades in San Francisco he moved only twice, and both times it was noise that drove him away. As Lili said, the change was an ordeal. In fact, the experience of moving might almost have been the source of the title essay of his third (some say his best) book, *The Ordeal of Change*. After seventeen years at McAllister Street, he eventually had to contend with "a madhouse above and a whorehouse beneath."

As to the move, he told Lili: "You have no idea how traumatic it was."

His second apartment, a mile or two away at 1547 Clay Street, was described by James Koerner as a "tiny dilapidated room" on the edge of Chinatown. Jack Bunzel, later the president of San Jose State University, a senior fellow at Hoover, and a friend and admirer of Hoffer, said that it was "a hole in the wall." A visitor from the *Los Angeles Times* described it as a "spare, sunless, almost shabby cubicle, as unrelentingly masculine as the lifelong bachelor who occupies it."[21]

Calvin Tomkins, in town in 1966 to interview Hoffer for *The New Yorker*, went to see him on Clay Street and wrote that "his one room apartment looked barely inhabited":

> "There was one bookcase on one wall, stuffed with a haphazard assortment of volumes—history, philosophy, a few novels, several editions of Montaigne. In the corner was a small table piled with notebooks and a couple of boxes of three-by-five file cards; next to that was a slightly larger work table with a student lamp on it, flanked by a stand holding a big Webster's Unabridged Dictionary. Two straight wooden chairs completed the furnishings. There was no rug, no easy chair, no telephone."[22]

Nonetheless Hoffer took delight in the neatness of his room. He bought flowers to brighten it, and once wrote that when he scrubs the sink, "it smiles back at me." At one point he felt so good that he "went out and bought half a dozen roses for the room."[23] Another time, he "did a thorough housecleaning job (washed the windows even), and bought a dozen golden and blue irises" before copying out an article. A most uncharacteristic bachelor, Hoffer was ruthless about discarding almost everything and was the opposite of a pack rat. Without Lili Osborne's rescue operations, most of his own papers would have been thrown away.

After a dozen years on Clay Street, rowdy children drove him off. This time he moved to the high-rise on Davis Court, where he spent his final years. A visiting reporter, Sheila K. Johnson of the *Los Angeles Times*, said of this apartment: "There are no pictures on the walls, no easy chair, no floor lamps, no television set, no radio, no phonograph. There are in short no distractions." Still no telephone either, she might have added. Hoffer did relent near the end, and one was installed.

It was a Spartan life. As he wrote to an unnamed friend in 1953, it was one that he had deliberately chosen. Working on the docks had its advantages and drawbacks:

> The advantages are: complete independence and a sense of usefulness as a longshoreman, and freedom from pretense and intellectual double talk. There is a saying that no one can think justly unless he is in contact with people who do not think at all. I have this advantage. The drawbacks are lack of intellectual stimulation and also of intellectual demands. I find that my mind responds to questions posed. I have to pose my own problems, and I do so, but it happens at far intervals.

He was above all a thinker and writer, and it is said of writers that they have bibliographies rather than biographies. "Exciting writers and artists do not as a rule lead exciting lives," he wrote. In a

1977 notebook, he wrote: "I am more what I think and write than what I do."

Toward the end of his life, as the guest of Charlie Kittrell, Hoffer gave several speeches in Bartlesville, Oklahoma. In one he said:

> Retirement on the waterfront has been very dangerous. The most dangerous job on the waterfront used to be handling steel—the big steel coming in there. But the longshoremen used to say that retirement is more dangerous than steel."

Hoffer himself received his retirement papers from the longshoremen's union in 1966. He may have already received that news when he accompanied Tomkins to the docks later that year.

A few years before that, in June 1959, Selden Osborne wrote a letter to the editor of *The Dispatcher*, the official longshoremen's publication. He suggested that it was time the union acknowledged Eric Hoffer's existence.

> Dear Sir and Brother:
>
> On the docks in San Francisco there works a man who, next to Harry Bridges, is the most famous longshoreman in the world, and yet a large number of San Francisco longshoremen have never heard of him, and, so far as I know, his name has never been mentioned in the pages of the *Dispatcher*. Almost ten years ago he wrote a book, *The True Believer*, which was acclaimed by intellectuals throughout the United States and England as a work of tremendous importance, and was reviewed by virtually every important newspaper and magazine that carries book reviews, being reviewed in England by Bertrand Russell. In the course of these reviews he was frequently compared with the greatest thinkers in history.
>
> ... [Eric Hoffer's] work is widely known in every college and university in America for the style of his writing as well as for its

content; and in books by other writers in social science one finds frequent reference to Hoffer's ideas and to quotations from him.

Some members who know Hoffer and his writings feel that such achievement by a member of Local 10 is ignored by the *Dispatcher* because the *Dispatcher* follows a policy of giving no recognition to ideas of which it disapproves.

Fraternally,
Selden Osborne
Book 8945, Local 10

In longhand at the bottom of the letter, a Mr. Coleman had written: "Agreed. One of best books I've ever read—it's a classic—The True Believer." And beneath that: "Frazier agrees too."

But across the top of the page, Harry Bridges' opinion was definite and final. There would be no argument. In large lettering, doubly underlined, he scrawled: "No!—HB."[24]

CHAPTER FOUR

Intimate Friendships

*The only person who truly touches my heart is
Eric. He is the only one who can truly get under
my skin. He stirs in me genuine compassion.*

—ERIC HOFFER,
writing about Eric Osborne

After Hoffer moved to his San Francisco rooming house, his life
became more settled but little about it was newsworthy. Most days
he was closeted in his room, grappling with ideas, or working anon-
ymously on the docks. He emerged for meals at local cafes—he did
no cooking at home beyond heating a can of soup—and for repetitive walks.

His regular walk through Golden Gate Park took him from Tenth
Avenue to the Pacific Ocean, a gradual downhill slope of about three
miles. There he would think and compose sentences, retain them in
his head, and rearrange them. He would take the bus back downtown, a distance of about six miles. Maybe he would have dinner
alone at a cafeteria such as Blum's. Then he would walk home.

Having settled into a routine in San Francisco, Hoffer was free
to form the friendships that he had earlier avoided. Selden and Lili
Osborne entered his life in the late 1940s. They became his closest
friends, and Hoffer played an increasingly important role in their
family life. He also became well acquainted with Joe Gladstone, a

long-time member of the Osbornes' circle. Their relationships played out against a background of considerable political disagreements.

Selden Osborne, who became one of Eric Hoffer's few male friends, had a wealthy mother (who later became a Quaker) and a father who worked for the customs or immigration services. Selden's childhood was spent in San Diego County, "on a small ranch, just two miles from the Mexican border," perhaps not far from El Centro in Imperial County.

In 1935 Selden wrote a paper for the Student League for Industrial Democracy, "Why I am a Socialist." The paper provides an in-depth look at Selden when he was a recent graduate of Stanford but unable to find steady employment.

A family tradition traced the Osbornes back "not only to the Mayflower but to Pocahontas herself," he wrote. He was born in 1911, spent his first twelve years on the ranch and then attended high school in the San Diego suburb of La Jolla. The oldest of four children, Selden wrote that he was deeply influenced by a teacher who taught Sunday School at the Presbyterian church he attended. Selden "became very religious" during that time and hoped to become a great political leader who could help create a perfect society. He worked as a laborer in 1928 and had to join a union— which he said he hated doing. He attended Stanford in the fall, was an ardent supporter of Herbert Hoover's candidacy for the presidency, and signed up for ROTC before becoming a pacifist after hearing Sherwood Eddy speak at a YMCA conference. (Eddy was a missionary and national secretary of the YMCA.) He adopted the "religious socialism" of Eddy and Kirby Page, a minister and peace activist.

Selden Osborne graduated from Stanford, lived at home for six months in Mill Valley, and then returned to graduate school in March 1932. He joined a socialist group in Palo Alto and that summer organized a Thomas-for-President Club on campus. That would have been Norman Thomas, who in 1950 traveled to San Francisco to meet Hoffer.

He finished his graduate work that same year, making him eligible to teach, but he couldn't find a teaching job. He put his energies instead into the socialist cause and "working for the revolution." After months of frustration trying to learn how to be a party organizer and holding brief jobs with Stanford and the federal government, he attended the Student League for Industrial Democracy's summer school in 1935. In the essay he wrote for the SLID, he showed true believer tendencies when, rather than be a "Big Shot," he said, "I would much rather be a follower working under the complete direction of someone in whom I had real confidence."

Osborne eventually took a blue-collar job. By June 1945 he had become a "limited longshoreman" in San Francisco (a probationary and easily terminated position), and then a "Class A" longshoreman and full union member on April 22, 1947. Selden married Lillian Fabilli in Fort Smith, Arkansas, in 1944 while he was serving in the military. His military service qualified the Osbornes to live in the Sunnydale Housing Project, built for military families during World War II. It was here that Lili and Eric Hoffer met for the first time.

In 1952 Hoffer wrote to a friend, Sarah Milner, who knew Margaret Anderson. The Osbornes were "in some trouble," Hoffer reported. "They are living in a government housing project and it looks as if they are going to be ejected because Mr. Osborne is a member of a minute socialist clique which is considered subversive."

At the southern edge of San Francisco, the Sunnydale Project survives as a public housing project today. Once considered "a nice place for a family to live," the *San Francisco Chronicle* reported recently, it is now "quite possibly the most dangerous, depressed and decrepit area of the city," littered with bottles and trash. Muni drivers refuse to go there after dark."[1]

Lillian Fabilli, who went by Lili, was the daughter of Italian immigrants who came to the United States, returned briefly to Italy before her birth, but then came back to America to stay. Lili herself was born in Gardiner, New Mexico, in 1916. Soon the family moved to California and she was reared, along with three sisters and a brother, in the small farming town of Delano, in the southern San Joaquin Valley.

After Lili and Selden married, she worked even after their children were born. According to their second child, Stephen Osborne, his mother "was working for the San Francisco school district but lost her job, probably in the early 1950s, when she refused to sign a loyalty oath. Later on she worked for the Unitarian Church, where she organized the nursery school program."

A "Paisano" to Dinner

There is no reliable information as to when Selden and Eric Hoffer first met. It was certainly on the waterfront, and before *The True Believer* was published. Stacy Cole believes that the book was already in manuscript when they met.

One day Selden came home from work and told Lili that he knew an interesting longshoreman who had written a book, soon to be published by a famous New York house. It was something about true believers, and Selden assumed it was about religion.

Lili suggested to Selden that he invite Eric Hoffer home to dinner. When Hoffer phoned, seeking directions to her house, Lili was struck by his voice—his foreign accent. It reminded her of the immigrant accents she had heard all her life. Eric's accent was German while her own background was Italian, yet his voice impressed her all the same.

"The moment I heard his voice coming so strong and with that accent," she recalled, "I just said to myself, 'A *paisano!*'"

Eric's voice took her back to the immigrant world of her upbringing. She assumed that he was an immigrant, too, and in the years to come she continued to suspect that he was.

She doesn't recall details of their conversation that evening. He remembered that she spent a lot of time on the phone because an old radical friend had called. Lili remembered that "it was with wonder that I listened to him talk. It wasn't the usual working-class talk at all."

It was at about this time that Margaret Anderson came out to San Francisco for her first (and perhaps only) encounter with Hoffer. After their initial correspondence she had forwarded some of his material to Eugene Saxton, the editor of Harper & Brothers. Impressed by what he read, Saxton asked Hoffer to write his autobiography. But Hoffer said that he was not interested in personal writing and had no desire to write such a book. Nonetheless, Hoffer stayed in touch with Anderson, and in 1949 sent her the completed manuscript of *The True Believer*.

Selden Osborne was also eager to meet Margaret Anderson because he, too, had a book in mind. It was a part of Hoffer's credo that longshoremen were "lumpy with talent," so he encouraged the idea, as did Lili. Eric always encouraged Selden in his writing and attempts at self-expression, Lili recalled, because he believed that everyone has a God-given talent. "Eric respected the common man," she said. "Selden did not respect the common man."

Lili even bought Selden a special jacket for his meeting with the New York editor. But Anderson seems not to have noticed Selden; nor is he known to have written a book, then or later. Hoffer's faith in the literary abilities of longshoremen generally tended to be on the generous side. It's as though he wanted to play down any suggestion that his own talent was exceptional.

Lili thought that Eric first noticed Selden because he would intervene boldly at union meetings. Selden believed he knew better than Bridges how to run the union. But Bridges and his allies were not impressed by this university-educated longshoreman who had self-consciously joined the working class and now wanted to instruct them on union business. An exasperated Bridges once tried to drive Selden out of the union, Lili recalled.

Nonetheless, Selden impressed Hoffer for his own reasons. He could see that Selden was a "true believer," as he called him more than once, and as such he was worth studying no matter how much they disagreed. Hoffer tried to figure him out:

> The problem of Osborne: His most urgent need is to belong. He must have been a member of some clique from his youth. Was he ever a commie? If so, when and why did he secede? He wanted terribly to play college football. It is perhaps true that the intense desire to be different from others, particularly the people he grew up with, is the result of a frustrated desire to belong.

Later, when Selden ran for union office (and never made much headway), Hoffer was amazed at his ability to deceive himself into thinking that he would gain a following and "lord it over caucuses and meetings." He also noted Selden's "undoubted courage in braving a hostile audience; his moments of lucid intelligence lost in an ocean of opaque self-delusion, self righteousness and sheer intellectual dishonesty. The mixture results in a peculiar instability which is not far removed from insanity."

Selden made friends easily (as Eric did not) and was easy to like. So they became friends, despite the political gulf dividing them. Each saw the futility of trying to bring the other around to his own point of view, so permanent truce was their only modus vivendi.

A month after publication of *The True Believer,* Hoffer applied some of its ideas to Selden Osborne as illustrating the true believer's desire to renounce an unwanted self and embrace a cause greater than himself. Hoffer's April 1951 "Letter to Osborne" is of interest because it instantiates the argument that he made so abstractly in print. (It is not known if he ever sent the letter to Selden.)

"If Marx was not a Marxist why is it imperative for Osborne to be a Marxist? Anyhow it would be worth your while to be an Osbornist for a year and see what comes of it. I understand how terribly difficult it is for you to let go of Marxism even for a day: not because of your attachment to it but rather fear of the void it would leave behind and also the throbbing fear that you have wasted the best part of your life.

One of the main reasons why I wanted to see you accomplish something—see you write something striking and important— was the recognition that such an accomplishment would ease the transition from a confirmed doctrinaire to an independent social psychologist. . . Assume that the transition is temporary—just an experiment.

In plain words: you are going to be just Osborne for one whole year—and whatever you think and write during the year would be as free from Marxist dialectic as from religious casuistry."

A Surrogate Family

Selden's and Lili's first child, Tonia, was born in 1944. The second child, Stephen, was born in 1947, and finally Eric was born in 1955. Hoffer knew them all, especially the boys.

He also came to know about Selden's siblings, particularly his brother, Robert. Selden's two younger sisters were educated at private schools in Switzerland. Robert, on the other hand, "would wander about the world—take up with gypsies or whatever," Lili said. He would arrive in San Francisco unexpectedly and sometimes stayed at her house. Eric Hoffer described one of Robert's visits in February 1959:

> Bob is wholly without defenses, and without a trace of self asser-tion. He is intelligent, intuitive and has an excellent memory. He is not normal. Most of the time he is lost in a haze. He drifts up and down the land, works at odd jobs, hardly talks to anyone, reads a lot (mostly avant-garde crap) and almost starves himself. Here is a case where a genuine belief in God would make a differ-ence. He is obviously drifting to an unmarked grave in a godfor-saken graveyard. In lucid intervals he drifts back to San Francisco but does not stay long.[2]

Hoffer's premonition was accurate. Eventually, Lili recalled, one of Selden's sisters "got information with identification of someone who had died on the streets of San Francisco some years earlier. It was Bob."

Tonia, born in 1944, was not close to Hoffer. In fact she was criti-cal of him as an outsider who had invaded the Osborne household. In 2011, Stephen remembered his sister as "a highly strung, very attractive young woman, and an epileptic. She gravitated toward political causes, like Selden." In the mid-1960s, Tonia moved to New York, where she was employed as a social worker. She died fol-lowing a seizure in 1966.

However, Hoffer had a significant influence on the two boys.

Asked in 2011 what Stephen remembered most about Hoffer, he replied, "Listening. Listening to him pontificate. He is exuber-ant. He is expansive. He is telling stories—stories he has told many times. He has a good sense of humor, a good voice, a positive way of looking at life. I loved him. I would say he was very important in my emotional development."

Stephen also remembered his father's arguments with Hoffer: "They had big political differences, especially over the Vietnam

War. Set-to arguments over the dinner table. Eric was a pretty intolerant person."

As a young adult, Stephen had found Hoffer to be an important influence: "I had joined the Peace Corps and after I left, for some reason I took from him the courage to go back to school. Then I just threw myself in and struggled until I could learn the material. So he was important to me."

Lili and Selden were divorced in 1969. In later years, Lili alternated between speaking admiringly of Selden as an intelligent, articulate man with convictions and criticizing him as a dreamer who lacked practical and political sense. His public quarrel with Harry Bridges over how the union should be run was not a good career move. He didn't know when to pipe down and she criticized him for not using his teaching qualification to earn a living.

"He wanted to change the world, and he wanted to change it *alone*," Lili recalled. "He made a single convert—his mother." Years after his death, reflecting on her former husband's impractical nature, Lili still seemed amazed. "The idea that he chose to express his ideas was by *leaflets*," she said with an emphasis that conveyed her frustration. "He joined many a march for peace." She also believed that he missed his true métier—as a minister. "He would have made a good one," she said. Hoffer also said that Selden should have been a minister, of the Unitarian faith.

Selden remarried eventually and outlived Hoffer by eleven years, dying of mesothelioma in 1994. His ashes and Tonia's are buried alongside each other on the property of family friend Joe Gladstone, who wrote, "Both Tonia's and Selden's ashes are buried in a redwood grove in Pescadero, a place they considered a haven in a heartless world."

Gladstone was an old friend of the Osbornes, having known them in their radical days, and they are featured prominently in his unpublished memoir, *Days of Pain and Pleasure.*

In his memoir, Gladstone described Selden as "a cross between a boy scout and a socialist." He spent thirty years "hassling Harry

Bridges" and his allies in the union. He also became "probably one of the best known 'peaceniks' on the West Coast." At one point, he wrote, Lili refused to sign a loyalty oath, and at that point the FBI took an interest in her.

Hoffer also got to know Gladstone. Sometimes, Hoffer would accompany Lili to Pescadero, a tiny beach community about forty miles south of San Francisco, to visit. Hoffer had a "mysterious autobiography," Gladstone wrote, claiming "to have been born of Alsatian-German parents." Reflecting on Hoffer's account of his early life, and the implausibility of his claim that as a large child he was carried downstairs by a small woman who tumbled and then died, Gladstone said: "I don't believe a word of it."[3]

Joe Gladstone's son Rick occasionally had dinner with his father, Eric, and Selden at Lili's house. He attended the University of California–Berkeley and also saw something of Eric Hoffer there in the 1960s. He recalled that Selden slept in a cot in an upstairs bedroom at Lili's house, with a mimeograph machine beside the bed. He would type out leaflets at night, copy them on his machine, and take them with him down to the docks the next day.

Rick Gladstone expanded on his memories in 2011:

"Any of the Osbornes could come and go to Pescadero. Selden would sometimes take advantage of a break in his work routine, maybe take off three nights in a row on his 'b-gang' schedule and drive one of his jalopies down from the city for a couple of days. Or, after he retired, while on his way to one peace event or another, hitchhike down to the ranch to recharge his batteries, and stay a few days to read and walk in the woods, or contribute a little 'elbow grease' to the myriad chores that were always there to be done. I remember Selden as among the most conscientious of men about making that kind of contribution. He would stay in one of the old dilapidated cabins on the ranch or a spare bedroom in the large rambling farm-house or perhaps in the lodge, if it wasn't being rented out at the time.

"He and my father got on quite well and shared many personal characteristics: keen intellects, social commitment, somewhat emotionally distant. My dad considered Selden an astute political theorist and teacher and a disciplined thinker, and I believe Selden valued my father's erudition and wit (and prodigious memory). They had their fair share of discussions and arguments with each other as well as with Big Eric, who considered both of them to be knuckleheaded Marxists—though Selden had more of an appetite to duke it out with 'Baba' than did my father. Selden often came to the ranch, as he loved the mountains and creek, the forest and fresh air, just as did Eric, the whole Osborne family, and the rest of our far-flung clan."[4]

Young Eric

In a letter to a friend written in June 1955, Hoffer said that "Lili is going to have a baby a few months from now." The baby was born in October. In his book on Hoffer, Calvin Tomkins wrote: "When Lili became pregnant Hoffer made a prediction. 'I say it's going to be a boy, his name is going to be Eric and he will be my grandson. And that's just exactly the way it worked out.'"[5]

His name was Eric—Eric Osborne. A publisher's note in *Working and Thinking on the Waterfront* said he was Hoffer's godson.

Grandson? Godson? Or Hoffer's biological son? Most of the evidence is for the latter.

Soon after Eric Osborne was born, Hoffer drafted this letter to Lili:

"Dear Lili: Most of the dough was saved during the past three months. It was saved for you and the child, and it is yours to do with as you see fit. My feeling is that you ought to cleanse yourself of debt. The child must not come in touch with anything that has not been paid for. It is a matter of honor, decency and even cleanliness. There is nothing we cannot do in a relatively short time if we do not burden and blemish the future with debts."

"Eric was the first baby I ever held in my hands," Hoffer told a reporter. "Sometimes I think that if I didn't have this family I'd have been a dried-up, sour old man. I become more attached to them the longer I know them. I didn't plant, I didn't sow, I just harvested."[6]

Hoffer had a major influence on young Eric. But it wasn't always an easy relationship. He assumed financial responsibility for Eric and kept an eye on him as a teenager. He wrote in one of his notebooks, "He has not learned how to study, never does homework. But it is impressive how he keeps his trouble to himself. No one has an idea what's going on in his mind." Hoffer was "enormously flattered when he introduced me to his counselor as his grandfather." When he went with Lili to see her mother, Giacinta, he noticed that "the old girl actually wants to be alone with her son Albert. The Fabilli women are basically ruthless."

He also stated, "The only person who truly touches my heart is Eric. He is the only one who can truly get under my skin. He stirs in me genuine compassion."

In late 1974, Hoffer drafted the following letter to Eric Osborne, who was then nineteen years old:

> A million thanks for your fine letter. It worried me no end not to know whether you made it to Oregon. I kicked myself after you left for not talking more with you. I am always afraid lest I bore you. People my age repeat themselves endlessly. But I should have taken a chance and shared all my thoughts with you, hoping you would bear with me. It is a momentous event in my life that you claim me as your father. It is a gift of the God and I do not deserve it. I have been nobody's son, nobody's brother, and nobody's

husband. And here all of a sudden I am a father. The thought of it warms my heart. I shall never get used to it, never take it for granted. You cannot imagine the celebration that erupted in my soul when you claimed me as your father. I have become a new man at 72. Think of me often, for I think of you all the time.

Take care of yourself. With much love,

Eric

There was a blow-up in 1977 when Hoffer recorded some of his daily observations about young Eric in the manuscript of *Before the Sabbath*. Eric objected, not so much to what Hoffer had written as to the fact that he had written it at all. Apparently, Hoffer had reassured young Eric that, as a subject, he would be off-limits. The result was that "we are totally estranged," Hoffer wrote. "It is a new experience to love a person who loathes me."

Much of the book was "ripped out" and was reduced to "a collection of thoughts in the form of a diary covering six months." Hoffer told Stacy Cole that the excised material "would have immortalized" the young man. Anyway, new material replaced what was removed. The new thoughts, he wrote, had to flow and he had to guard against monotony. He didn't know whether the revised book was any good. (Excerpted in *Harper's* in 1978, *Before the Sabbath* is among the most readable of his books.)

Hoffer wrote to Eric around this time:

My hunch is that you will think well of me as you grow older. I wish you well. I cannot nurse a grievance. It is legitimate that I should be of service to you. Do not hesitate to call on me. Take care of yourself and do not hate me.

In about 1978 Eric Osborne spent some time in Europe. Needing to earn some money, he went to Alsace-Lorraine to find work.

While there he made an attempt to trace Hoffer's father, but without success. He also found that the soft, Frenchified intonation of the locals was quite unlike Hoffer's harsher Bavarian accent.

In 1979, Eric moved to Alaska, became a fisherman, married, and had a family. He lives in western Alaska to this day.

There are additional references to young Eric in Hoffer's books—in *Working and Thinking on the Waterfront*, in *Before the Sabbath*, and in his later notebooks.

When Selden became aware of the true nature of the relationship between his wife and his friend is unknown. Even as Eric grew closer to Lili, the personal relationship between Eric and Selden seemed to be unaffected. In fact, Selden welcomed the financial support that Eric was able to provide—support that was beyond his own powers. Eric and Selden remained on terms of warm friendship until the day of Hoffer's death. Lili agreed with that assessment.

At the San Francisco reception following his mother's funeral in October 2010, Eric (by now the father of six) was receptive to the idea that Hoffer's account of his early life didn't quite add up. He thought Hoffer's case might be comparable to that of B. Traven, the mysterious German author of *The Treasure of the Sierra Madre*. (B. Traven was a pen name for a German novelist whose actual identity, nationality, and date and place of birth are still unknown. The book, published in Germany in 1927, then in English in 1935, was made into the famous movie of the same name in 1948.)

When he was asked to comment on his statement that he believed Hoffer to be his father, Eric Osborne replied, "I guess I had better leave that unanswered. Both of those guys [Selden and Hoffer] are a part of me and I loved them both." He mentioned that Hoffer had called him his grandson, and he thought that was appropriate because Hoffer was a wise man and he had imparted to young Eric the wisdom that one associates with a grandfather. And in many ways Selden had been a good father to him.[7]

Looking back in 2010, Stephen said he and Tonia were affected as children by their mother's relationship with Hoffer. "I had trouble learning to read when I was very young. I imagine with the emotional difficulties of having a mother who was having a relationship with another person, that that was unsettling to me. I know that it bothered my sister Tonia a lot. So I think there was a lot of confusion as I grew up."[8]

Of the paternity question, Stephen said, "Has there been a DNA test? No. But Eric suspected that Hoffer [which he pronounced Hoafer] was his father. He asked my mother and she said yes."

In the final analysis, Stephen said of Hoffer, "I loved the man. He was a great presence in my life. But his value to the world is in what he wrote."

That Hoffer loved Lili is undeniable. In one notebook, he wrote,

> I must remind myself all the time that I love her and that it will be finis with me if anything happens to her. We are so terribly different from each other and I have never learned to take thought for other people, to be aware of their troubles and agonies.

But that didn't mean he was unaware of the complications their affair had brought to many lives. In what Lili Osborne described as his "last notebook," in the autumn of 1981, Hoffer wrote, in a hand quavering with age:

> The sin of my life has been to invade a neighbor's nest and take his wife. The people I sinned against were not the husband but two of the children, Tonya and Eric. Eric believes he is my son and has renounced both his mother and me. I am on terms of warm friendship with the husband. Tonya is dead, and Eric has run away to Alaska where he lives with an Eskimo girl and fathered

a son, Joshua. My influence on the family has not been all bad, I have been generous with myself and my money and the truth is that Selden did not love Lili and felt my invasion as a liberation. He told me yesterday that my intrusion enriched the children's life and whatever I have saved will be theirs when I am gone. My attachment to Lili after 33 years is undiminished.

In Lili's hand beneath she wrote: "Dear, dear Eric! Always beloved."

CHAPTER FIVE

The True Believer

However different the holy causes people die for,
they perhaps die basically for the same thing.

—ERIC HOFFER

Preface, The True Believer

"Until 1949, there was hardly a person who knew that I existed," Hoffer wrote. "No one watched me or expected anything from me. I was free as the wind. There were no limits, and no repressions."[1] All that changed in 1949, when *The True Believer* was sent to Margaret Anderson. By 1967 the book had sold half a million copies in all editions, and probably outsold all his other books combined.

Any analysis of Hoffer's work must begin with *The True Believer*, the first, most influential, and most difficult of his books. Parts of it exist in earlier drafts in the Hoover Archives and at the San Francisco Public Library; the twenty-three notebooks he donated to that library in 1964 consist mostly of *True Believer* sections written earlier. When he sent the manuscript to Margaret Anderson it had a different title. He drafted the following letter in March 1949:

Dear Margaret:
I just finished the book. It will take several months to rework it. The title is *Thoughts on the Nature of Mass Movements.* I enclose the table of contents and the foreword to give you an idea of what it's all about. The latest waterfront strike was a godsend. I should

have taken a long leave of absence a year ago. But I was afraid—afraid to face the truth ... There must have been a doubt in the back of my mind whether I was capable of finishing this piece of methodical thinking. A leave of absence of several months would have put me to the test. And suppose I got stuck for weeks—as it has happened in the past—what then? Would I lose heart and give up? I was afraid to face the test.

With a strike on things are altogether different. I have to keep up the routine of picketing and the book is still a sideline, though I spend all my time on it. It will have to be so to the end. I must feel that I am first and foremost a workingman and not a thinker and writer. To do otherwise would be to feel a pretentious fraud. Still, I knew all along that to make headway with the book I had to immerse myself in it. An interruption of even two consecutive days on the front is enough to scramble a train of thought and it takes a week of concentrated groping before I regain my grip. What I lack then is confidence that my thinking and writing is not nonsense and that the persistent dedication through the years is not the symptom of some mental aberration.

The book was a "string of thoughts," Hoffer wrote in a later draft, but he was too familiar with them to sense any originality they might have. He was full of misgivings but had already held on for too long. It had taken him almost ten years to get from its biographical shell to its present state. "There must be an end."

He gave Anderson leeway to "drop, cut, switch and change at will." He had unique faith in her judgment. He wanted her to find a typist and could pay $100 or more for the service. Perhaps he should find one himself but in his present mood "I haven't guts enough to speak to a cat." Even if Anderson thought the book unfit for print, he wanted to see it "embalmed and sealed in a perfect manuscript" and out of his life. It is "as much your baby as mine. . . . It sounds presumptuous. Still, it was the thought of you that prevented me from settling down into the fairly pleasant existence of an orthodox longshoreman."

It was Anderson who suggested that the title should be changed to *The True Believer*.[2]

Comparison of earlier drafts with later ones is revealing. At one point, he wrote:

> The important point is that faith is easy. It demands no effort and it presupposes no qualifying achievement. One need not go through preliminary testing in order to qualify for faith. Hence any doctrine which places an emphasis on faith is welcome to those who have no confidence in their own abilities and their capacity for effort and accomplishment.

Later he changed his mind about that and decided that faith was a virtue—"a virtue seen in the acceptance without evidence, in not asking for signs and wonders." He also saw religious tolerance as "a mark of weakness—of little faith."

A few pages after his comment that faith is easy he noted that "there should be a section on the deviousness and trickery of true believers." In an introduction written in early 1949, he recorded one of his earliest conclusions about the psychological basis of the true believer:

> The textbook for the art of starting and promoting a mass movement is to be found in reading the frustrated mind; that the characteristics of the true believer are to be found either latent or in the embryonic state or fully developed in the frustrated mind.

Even in the published book the phrase "true believer" was infrequent. The book is overwhelmingly about mass movements, their appeal, their potential converts, and their propensity for unity. When "The True Believer" was added as the new title, "thoughts on the nature of mass movements" was retained as its subtitle. The text seems to have been little altered to accommodate the changed title.

In short, the book was first submitted as, and largely remains, a set of reflections on mass movements, with comments on true believers thrown in. One of the few to notice this was the anonymous reviewer for the *Times Literary Supplement*, who pointed out that *The True Believer* was ostensibly about the fanatic, or true believer, but in fact

> "is concerned more with crowds than with persons, more with great social tides and currents than with the units that are swept to and fro. The fanatic emerges only as it were incidentally, and then in two very different forms. In one context he is the fugitive from reality who seeks oblivion in the latest craze; in the other the master spirit who directs the whirlwind and controls the storm."[3]

Some of these fanatics act out of the weakness of their personalities, the reviewer added; some out of the strength. But by the end of the book Hoffer had brought "the fanatical leader and the fanatical follower into a single natural species."

What is a Mass Movement?

The phrase "mass movement," common in the 1930s and '40s, has all but disappeared from political discourse today. In the early twentieth century "mass movement" described a popular political movement with an implied element of spontaneity. The goal was the overthrow of an existing regime or system. The Iranian revolution to overthrow the Shah in 1979 was a mass movement, as was the student revolt against the Vietnam War in this country ten years earlier. The modern Islamist movement has elements of a mass movement. But uppermost in Hoffer's mind was Nazism. The book sought to explain "the preposterous manifestations of the Hitler decade."

True believers don't start mass movements, Hoffer wrote. That is achieved by "men of words." But the true believers do energize those movements. Hoffer's understanding of the relationship between true believers and mass movements was Hitler's relationship to the Nazi Party. The German Workers Party—its name was later changed—was founded in 1919. Hitler soon joined it and ousted the founder, Anton Drexler, in 1921. With all the zeal of the true believer, Hitler infused it with fanaticism and Nazism became a mass movement. Hoffer did not make this Hitler relationship explicit in his book but it was his unstated guide.

Hoffer never defines a mass movement. Some are religious, he said, some are social, others nationalistic. In addition to Nazism and Communism, he also characterized Christianity, Gandhi's movement for independence, and "the Puritan, French and American Revolutions" as mass movements.[4] Islam was mentioned, but inconspicuously. At times he seemed to think of mass movements as synonymous with revolutions.

In-house comments on the manuscript by John Fischer, the long-time editor of *Harper's* magazine, saw this lack of definition as a defect: "The more I think about the book the more strongly I feel that what it needs most is a more precise definition of mass movements, to distinguish them clearly from other kinds of group undertakings which often bring about important changes but are not so strongly characterized by the phenomenon of the 'true believer.'"

But Hoffer avoided any such precision. He was looking for generalizations that covered not just particular events but whole movements and ages. Shortly before the book was published, he wrote that "the preoccupation with the book is with theories—right or wrong. I cannot get excited about anything unless I have a theory about it." He was "on the lookout for some observation or experience which, though thin and brittle," might lead him to a general law.

One of his laws was that mass movements share a family likeness, however dissimilar their doctrines. They all tend to breed fanaticism, enthusiasm, and a readiness to die for the cause. They engender fervent hope, hatred and intolerance, and a proclivity for united action. All "demand blind faith, and single-hearted allegiance." They can also release a powerful burst of energy—one that may transform the society in which it erupts.

A second generalization—and here came the true believer—was that these movements "draw their adherents from the same types of humanity, and appeal to the same types of mind." It followed that the adherents of one mass movement might switch to another.[5]

> Though there are obvious differences between the fanatical Christian, the fanatical Mohammedan, the fanatical Communist and the fanatical Nazi, it is yet true that the fanaticism which animates them may be viewed and treated as one . . . He who, like Pascal, finds precise reasons for the effectiveness of Christian doctrine has also found the reasons for the effectiveness of Communist, Nazi and nationalist doctrine. However different the holy causes people die for, they perhaps die basically for the same thing.[6]

The religious character of the Bolshevik and Nazi revolutions was generally recognized, Hoffer wrote. The hammer and sickle and the swastika were in a class with the cross. They all had "articles of faith, saints, martyrs and holy sepulchers."[7] The French Revolution started out as a new religion, but turned into a nationalist movement. A similar transformation occurred after the Bolshevik revolution transformed Russia.

For a movement to prevail, the existing order must first be discredited. And that "is the deliberate work of men of words with a grievance." If they lack a grievance, the prevailing dispensation may persist indefinitely.[8] Sometimes, a regime in power may survive by co-opting the intellectuals. The partnership between the Roman rulers and the Greek men of words allowed the Roman Empire to last for as long as it did.[9]

On the other hand the British in India were of a type altogether lacking in the aptitude for getting along with intellectuals. So Gandhi won. Similarly, a bishopric conferred on Luther at the right moment might have cooled his ardor for a Reformation.[10]

As Hoffer saw it, then, men of words laid the groundwork for mass movements by creating receptivity to a new faith. This could be done only by men who were first and foremost talkers or writers, recognized as such by all. If that ground had not been prepared, the masses wouldn't listen. True believers could move in and take charge only after the prevailing order had been discredited and had lost the allegiance of the masses.[11]

Mass movements are not equally good or bad, Hoffer wrote. "The tomato and the nightshade are of the same family, the Solanaceae," and have many traits in common. But one is nutritious and the other poisonous.[12] In adding this he was probably responding to another caution from Fischer, who wrote that some in-house readers ". . . got the impression that Hoffer is implying that all mass movements are equally good or bad, that the ideas on which they are based are always predominantly irrational, and that from the standpoint of value judgments there is not much distinction between, say, the Nazi movement, Christianity, and the Gandhi movement in India."

Publication and Reception

The book's acceptance by Harper & Brothers was not plain sailing. Publication was supported by Fischer but opposed by Evan Thomas, a senior Harper editor. He criticized the manuscript on these grounds: "I was so impressed by the author's gift of expression and apparent insight that I was sure I was going to vote for acceptance. However, after finishing the book and turning it over in my mind, I feel quite the opposite. This is basically an extremely cynical book . . . . I wish to deny the author's plausible cynicism with everything in me." Fischer, on the other hand, thought it an important piece of original thinking and very much hoped "we can work out a contract to publish it." They did.

The Harper contract to publish the book was sent to Hoffer in June 1950. Harper scheduled the book for publication and, not surprisingly, wanted some independent report about this mysterious author who was unreachable by phone, worked on the docks, had never gone to school, and yet wrote so well.

Norman Thomas, having recently completed the last of several presidential runs as the candidate of the Socialist Party, went to see Hoffer in San Francisco in 1950. He found the longshoreman to be "big, bald, thickset, strong, tie-less, a bit awkward but in manner active and eager."[13] Norman Thomas could not possibly have heard of Hoffer at that point, and it is highly likely that he went to San Francisco at the request of his son Evan Thomas. (The publishing house evolved into Harper & Row and eventually into HarperCollins. Evan Thomas was the father of the journalist and author, also named Evan, who now teaches journalism at Princeton.)

It must have seemed improbable to New York editors that an unknown longshoreman who had never gone to school could have written a treatise as abstract and polished as *The True Believer*. They wanted independent confirmation from Norman Thomas that the author really was who he said he was. That surely was the undeclared purpose of his visit with Hoffer.

After publication, some reviewers, including the *New York Times*'s Orville Prescott, also called the work cynical—"as cynical about human motives as Machiavelli."[14] The libertarian author Murray Rothbard, writing for *Faith and Freedom* under the pen name Jonathan Randolph, was also highly critical. "Hoffer may be anti-Communist," he wrote, "but only because he sneers at all moral and political principles."[15]

The reviewers' consensus was nonetheless highly favorable. The historian Arthur Schlesinger Jr. called the book "brilliant and original." The philosopher Bertrand Russell wrote that it seemed "as sound intellectually as it is timely politically." *The New Yorker*'s Richard Rovere called it "a work of almost pure cerebration and intuition." Crane Brinton in the *New York Herald Tribune* called Hoffer "a born essayist-philosopher." In the *New York Post*, Dorothy Schiff struck a more independent note, calling the book "very controversial and contemptuous."

In addition to calling the book cynical, Prescott said it was "one of the most provocative books of modern times," glittering with "icy wit." Hoffer himself wrote that he had approached the subject as a technician, not as a moralist. His goal was not to pass judgment but to find out how and why things happen: "The true believer is everywhere, we have to cope with him, and it is well that we should know all we can concerning his nature."

It was Hoffer's neutrality about his subject—reminiscent of his report on the migrant camp in El Centro—that led reviewers to call his book icy. Some applauded Hoffer's scientific spirit. The *New York Post*'s Murray Kempton called the book "a model of detachment about the kind of person who has generally lent himself to anything but detached treatment."[16] Others expected an authentic member of the working class who had surfaced in the world of publishing to be more politically engaged.

But that wasn't Hoffer. Social science was still his model. He wanted to observe and describe, not praise or condemn. He was dispassionate about the "Hitler decade" and he approached Stalinism in the same spirit. *The True Believer*, his only footnoted book, included 187 references covering ten pages.

Hoffer later became openly political, attacking Stalin, Communism, and leftist intellectuals en masse. He had "a savage heart," he reflected, and "could have been a true believer myself."[17] America and Israel were to become his great causes. But the neutrality of *The True Believer* contributed to its critical success.

The Charge of Cynicism

The "frustrated mind" gave rise to the true believer, Hoffer wrote. Frustration was sufficient to generate his peculiar characteristics. The true believer wants to escape from an unwanted self and looks for a sudden and spectacular change in the conditions of life. He rejects the spoiled present and lives for a hope-filled future.[18] He has a "passion for self renunciation."[19] He may even sacrifice his life for the cause. In an aphorism sometimes cited as a one-line synopsis of *The True Believer*, Hoffer wrote: "Faith in a holy cause is to a considerable extent a substitute for the lost faith in ourselves."[20]

"What ails the frustrated?" Hoffer asked. "It is the consciousness of an irremediably blemished self." The true believer wants to escape that self—and that leads to united action and self-sacrifice.[21] He quoted poet and historian Peter Viereck as saying that most Nazi leaders initially had artistic or literary ambitions but were unable to realize them:

> Hitler tried painting and architecture; Goebbels, drama, the novel and poetry; Rosenberg, architecture and philosophy; von Schirach, poetry; Funk, music; Streicher, painting. "Almost all were failures, not only by the usual vulgar criterion of success but by their own artistic criteria." Their artistic and literary ambitions "were originally far deeper than political ambitions: and were integral parts of their personalities."[22]

Personal frustration convinces true believers that they cannot find "a worthwhile purpose in self advancement."[23] Self-interest is itself tainted. Anything "undertaken under the auspices of the self seems to them foredoomed."[24] In a 1941 notebook, Hoffer noted that the Italian socialist activist Angelica Balabanoff had written in *My Life as a Rebel* (1938): "Life lived on behalf of a great cause is robbed of its personal futility." Hoffer incorporated that more or less directly into *The True Believer*.

The word "frustrated" was not meant as a clinical term, Hoffer emphasized. Nonetheless, the book owed something to the interest in psychoanalytic thought that was widespread at the time. In 1947 Hoffer filled three pages of a notebook with quotations from Erich Fromm's *Escape from Freedom*. Born in Germany and Hoffer's exact contemporary, Fromm was a student of psychoanalysis who came to America in 1934. He was not mentioned in *The True Believer*, but Hoffer echoed Fromm when he wrote:

"Unless a man has the talents to make something of himself, free-dom is an irksome burden. Of what avail is freedom to choose if the self be ineffectual? We join a mass movement to escape indi-vidual responsibility."[25]

Hoffer might find Freud's *Civilization and its Discontents* "both stimulating and useful," Fischer added in his memo. Freud was not mentioned in the book, and Hoffer later expressed contempt for him, saying he had not read his books. (His indexed quotations include twelve cards on Freud, a few from *Civilization and Its Discontents* and *The Future of An Illusion*. But some of these came from authors who quoted Freud, so it's possible or even likely that Hoffer never had read those books.)

Fischer also pointed out that the book would be more readable "if the author would make greater use of examples and illustrations." Readers of *The True Believer* do indeed encounter a sea of abstrac-tions—fanaticism, enthusiasm, substitution, conversion, frustra-tion, unification—and many will have scanned its pages, often in vain, looking for the tall masts and capital letters of a proper name.

Criticism of the Book

By claiming that people become true believers because they lose faith in themselves, Hoffer had indeed opened himself to the charge of cynicism. Evan Thomas's father, Norman Thomas, ran on the Socialist Party ticket in several presidential elections. Did he embrace socialism because he had lost faith in himself? We cannot rule out the possibility that socialist ideas really appealed to him, whatever his self-assessment. The same could be said of those drawn to any other "holy cause."

But in claiming that those drawn to such movements had found a substitute for the self, Hoffer was judging the individual rather than the reasons that he gave. It was an *ad hominem* argument. Such arguments are not necessarily wrong on that account. An individual may indeed recognize his own inadequacy and so enlist in a cause larger than himself. Normally, however, we take at face value the reasons that people give for supporting causes. Hoffer assumes that a diagnosis is what is really called for and confronts such devotees with a clinical explanation for their position. In finding something that may never have crossed the mind of the person being analyzed, Hoffer was also appealing to the Freudian idea of repression—the idea that people find ways to avoid unpalatable thoughts about themselves.

Hoffer himself eventually found the self to be a slender reed. Viewers of Eric Sevareid's interview of Hoffer in 1967 can see how vehement he became in support of both Israel and the United States. The tone of his remarks illustrated better than words his own "Passionate State of Mind"—the title of the CBS program.

Only a handful of true believers were identified in the book. In addition to Hitler and Stalin, Luther and Gandhi were mentioned, but we have to hunt for them. St. Paul and Jesus by implication were also pegged as true believers.

A wholly critical review of the book was written by Bernard Theall, a Benedictine monk who later became an editor of the Catholic Encyclopedia. He wondered why a Christian had to be categorized as a fanatic and whether putting Christianity on a par with Communism was appropriate. He took issue with Hoffer's claim that "charlatanism of some degree is indispensable to effective leadership," and with the following:

> Jesus Himself might not have preached a new Gospel had the dominant Pharisees taken Him into the fold, called Him Rabbi, and listened to Him with deference.[26]

Hoffer's generally unflattering treatment of Christianity may account for the book's favorable reception by such reviewers as Bertrand

Russell. As a historical assessment, nonetheless, Hoffer's treatment was questionable on several fronts. Longevity was just one. Nazism lasted for twelve years, Communism's span was measured in decades, while Christianity has endured for two thousand years and shows no sign of disappearing.

Further, Christianity does not fit the claim that true believers immerse themselves in mass movements to avoid "individual responsibility." Christianity does hold the individual responsible, both in this world and the next. Hoffer later recognized this. He noted in 1955 that "to those who believe in God and a hereafter, there is no escape from the scheme of things."

Hoffer never embraced the Christian creed (or any other) but he later conveyed a much more respectful tone, even an admiring one. He noted in 1976 the "misfortune that the age-old Catholic Church chose to initiate unprecedented reforms at a time when so many countries were about to be racked and disoriented by drastic change."[27] He stopped representing Christianity as a mass movement; and he said in 1981 that if he met the pope, he would advise him to "go slow" before changing anything.

He never criticized Judaism, and later composed what was close to a prayer in praise of Jehovah. A reference to Jewish extremists, "the fanatics of the Irgun and the Stern group," found in an earlier draft of *The True Believer,* was omitted from the final book.

The Place of Communism

If Nazism was uppermost on Hoffer's mind when he wrote the book, Communism was a close second. Apart from Hitler, the leaders most frequently mentioned were Lenin and Stalin. But was the Bolshevik Revolution a mass phenomenon? The Stalinists did use some techniques that Hoffer imputes to mass movements. Show trials and confessions evoked "in the faithful the mood and frame of mind of a repentant criminal," Hoffer wrote.[28] But asked whether Communism itself was a mass movement, Richard Pipes, a professor of

Russian history at Harvard, responded: "The Russian Revolution had two stages: the February one was in some ways a mass phenomenon, especially in its opening days in St. Petersburg; the October one was a coup d'etat, plotted at night by a small group of conspirators. The masses had no inkling of it."[29]

Pipes has great admiration for Hoffer and assigned *The True Believer* to his Harvard class. "Mass movements do occasionally occur," he added, "but my feeling is that most such movements are organized and directed by minorities simply because the 'masses,' especially in agrarian societies, have to get back to work to milk the cows and mow the hay. They don't make revolutions: they make a living."

Communism resembled a religion but it was the faith of disaffected Western intellectuals, not of the masses. After the immediate revolutionary fervor cooled it was sustained, in Russia and everywhere else, by coercion and terror. Communism never did bring about a release of human energies—or if so, only for a short time.

Over the next decade Hoffer spent much of his own energy trying to write a sequel to *The True Believer*. He hoped to specify the conditions needed to unleash the human energies that the postcolonial countries of Africa and Asia wanted to harness. He eventually abandoned the attempt. By the late 1950s he came close to Professor Pipes's point of view, doubting that "the masses" had much to do with anything.

With the single exception of the United States, Hoffer wrote, "it would be difficult to point to a single historical development in which the masses were a prime mover and chief protagonist." In neither the underdeveloped world nor the advanced countries "are the masses restless, militant and vainglorious."

In his 1967 interview, Sevareid asked Hoffer about mass movements. He replied:

People ask me: How about mass movements in this country? And I tell them that mass movements haven't got a chance in this country for the simple reason that mass movements are not started by the masses. Mass movements are started by intellectuals.[30]

The explosive component in the contemporary scene, Hoffer wrote, was not "the clamor of the masses but the self righteous claims of a multitude of graduates from schools and universities." An "army of scribes" was working to achieve a society "in which planning, regulation and supervision are paramount, and the prerogative of the educated."[31]

In another notebook he said that mass movements were not the seedbeds of released human energies but a manifestation of egotism and destruction. Why so? Because "we all carry around a little Hitler and a Stalin in our heads."

A mass movement is the vomit of the 'I'—the innermost self externalized. What dungeons, what pits of bedlam and what savage jungles are hidden within us! Civilization is possible only when the pestilential cesspools of the 'I' are sealed airtight. Once they spring a leak we have concentration camps, and also modern painting, modern music, modern poetry.

Islam's True Believers

Until recently, *The True Believer* resembled a piece of theoretical machinery that lacked an application more recent than "the Hitler decade." Hoffer assumed that he was living in a godless age, and the discussion of mass movements and true believers seemed more relevant to an earlier time. There were a few mentions of Islam in the book, but in the mid-twentieth century that faith was hibernating, at least in terms of its impact on the West. Godlessness seemed to be equally widespread in the East and the West. But a remarkable feature of *The True Believer* is that the Islamist revival, unforeseen when the book was written, confirmed Hoffer's ideas in detail.

Ultimately, it was the rebirth of Israel that produced the wake-up call. By 1959, Hoffer saw that the "dormant past of the Old Testament has come to life, and the stirrings in the Arab world echo the happenings of 600–1300 AD [the period of Arab conquests] . . . The devil is loose in such times and all over the map buried cesspools are pried open and poison the air."

With the September 11, 2001, terrorist attacks on New York and Washington, *The True Believer* was rushed back into print. Jihadists seemed to be following Hoffer's fifty-year-old script. Young men were joining the Islamist cause with little in the way of coercion, volunteering for death in return for promised rewards in a transformed existence.

Mass movements deprecate the present, Hoffer wrote in *The True Believer*, "by depicting it as a mean preliminary to a glorious future." The hope released by the visualization of such a future "is a most potent source of daring and self-forgetting."[32] Dying or killing "seem easy when they are part of a ritual, ceremonial, dramatic performance or game."[33] The leader of such a movement has to promote a devil—ideally a foreigner—and he "has to evoke in his followers the illusion that they are participating in a grandiose spectacle."[34]

The conditions that generate true believers, in Hoffer's analysis, are conspicuous in the Arab world. The Islamist revival has shown that the book doesn't just belong to a particular time or place.

In its May 22, 1983, obituary on Hoffer, the *Washington Post* said that *The True Believer* is "difficult to summarize [but] easy to admire." That was true on both counts. A succession of insights rather than a train of reasoning, the book was a loose structure into which Hoffer poured many original ideas. His later work more openly took this fragmented, aphoristic form. His generalizations were at times extreme, and an academic would have hesitated to propose them. But he liked to say that to get almost any idea across, one must "exaggerate much."

It was "a rather rambling piece of work," the *Times Literary Supplement* reviewer noted, "but it has the cardinal virtue of open mindedness." The concept of a mass movement was problematical, but Hoffer's analysis of the true believer was in some ways inspired. He continued to reflect on the type for the rest of his life:

> The fact that all dreams have so far turned into nightmares has not sobered the addicts of commitment. Only when private affairs become engrossing and pregnant with possibilities is there any likelihood of true believers finding fulfillment in an individual existence.

In contemplating the mystery of Eric Hoffer, Lili Osborne would ask herself how a self-educated laborer came to write so abstract a work. His early manuscripts had shown that he was a polished writer before he (apparently) had much experience of writing anything. His comments to Margaret Anderson give one or two clues. Looking back over his earlier notebooks, he was surprised to find how hard it had been for him to reach insights "which now seem to me trite." The key was that "the inspiration that counts is the one that comes from uninterrupted application." Sitting around waiting for lightning to strike got one nowhere.

His rewritten drafts of *The True Believer* showed how much he owed to perseverance. His self-assurance and stylistic mastery were remarkable coming from someone who had not yet published anything. But if his success with *The True Believer* were to be attributed to any single quality, it would be his capacity to concentrate and persevere. His ability to exercise these talents also explained his self-confidence.

Still, the mystery never quite goes away.

Hoffer's "Book Tour"

When *The True Believer* was published, Hoffer gave one or two press interviews in San Francisco, and a few articles appeared in the local papers. Completely unknown outside his circle of workers on the waterfront, he became a prominent author overnight. The contrast between his debut as a literary stevedore—a publicity photograph showed him in his familiar working-class rig—and his learned abstractions and footnoted references was without precedent in American letters. It was also irresistible to the press.

But Hoffer hid from reporters. About a month after the book's publication he took time off from the waterfront and traveled incognito. He went on the very opposite of a book tour, as though nostalgic for his migrant-worker anonymity. He traveled from San Francisco to Modesto in California's Central Valley, taking a bedroll with him. At least some of the time he seems to have slept out-of-doors. He wrote in a notebook:

> You have to be a stranger and a lowly one—for I pack a bedroll— to get a full taste of their kindliness. I had the feeling all during the past four weeks that, where no one knows me, everyone is my brother.

In *Truth Imagined*, Hoffer transformed this anonymity into a make-believe account of Modesto. He found this agricultural town to be "a huge park of trees and lawns" and he wandered through its streets trying to discover the secret of its lawns—without success.[35]

What Hoffer was looking for was not the secret of Modesto's lawns but a retreat where "no one knows me." He could be as shy personally as he was self-confident intellectually, and his hobo escape removed him from the literary spotlight. Fame was a new experience for him, and at this stage he actively avoided it. Later on he enjoyed the attention, but even then only briefly.

In one of his last notebook entries, written in September 1981, he recalled his isolation when *The True Believer* came out.

"When my first book was published, there was no one near me, an acquaintance let alone a friend, to congratulate me. I have never savored triumph, never won a race."

A Footnote: The Book Ike Liked

One of the better-known facts about *The True Believer* is that President Eisenhower admired the book. He urged cabinet members to read it, and Charles E. Wilson, his secretary of defense, kept a stack in his office and handed them out to visitors. Ike's admiration for the book was widely reported. *Look* magazine published "Ike's Favorite Author" in 1956. A couple of months earlier the *New York Times* had given a full account.[36]

The story was first published in 1952 and then again in 1953 by Marguerite Higgins, a foreign correspondent for the *New York Herald Tribune*. Eisenhower had given her his own copy of the book in August 1951, while he was still in uniform in France. He had scribbled his thoughts in the margins and, Higgins wrote, "there are pages of the book on which there is almost as much written by Eisenhower as by the book's original author."[37]

In 1952 Eric Hoffer wrote a note to the unidentified man who had first put *The True Believer* in Eisenhower's hands. In the note Hoffer wrote that the "best ending for Miss Higgins's piece would be a photograph of a page from *The True Believer* with the General's notes on the margins, identified as 'An American president reading and annotating a book written by an American workingman.'"

But Ike's comments on the book were never divulged, and years later *The New Yorker* reported that Hoffer "was not particularly flattered" by Ike's attention. "It proved to me something I always knew, which is that this is the kind of book that any child can read."[38] But the book was really not an easy read, and of course the president had done Hoffer a great favor.

Years later, after an overdose of the "Terrible '60s," Hoffer looked back on Eisenhower's America as a golden age.

In his first newspaper interview, Hoffer allowed a local reporter from the *San Francisco Examiner* to visit him at home. Dick Pearce wrote, "The author is 48, big and genial. He occupies a single room on the second floor rear at 1438 McAllister Street. There, on a crude bench against a blank wall, he wrote *The True Believer* in longhand after his days' stints on the waterfront.[39]

Before posing for a photograph, Hoffer "insisted on putting on his work coat and white cap with its union button." Some of the men on the waterfront "wouldn't believe it was me if I didn't have the cap on," he said. In the picture published with the article, Hoffer looked triumphant, with a copy of his new book in his hands.

At the end of his life, toward the end of *Truth Imagined*, Hoffer wrote:

> The only moment of unalloyed happiness I ever had was when I received a wire from Harper telling me that they would publish *The True Believer*. I felt like a darling of fate, an immortal raised above the common run of humanity. There were no doubts about my worthiness and no fear about the future.

In the *Examiner* photograph, Hoffer's expression as he holds his just-published book conveys this moment of an achievement realized. The photo caption reads,

> NEW AUTHOR—Eric Hoffer, a San Francisco longshoreman, holds a copy of the book he has written which will be published March 14. "The True Believer" is a study of mass movements such as Communism and religion, declared by publishers "one of the boldest ventures in original thinking."

CHAPTER SIX

Hoffer as a Public Figure

*... being in the White House with Johnson was to me a
tremendous thing. I slept there one night and I walked
and I said, 'We are here, we are here! We are here!'*

—ERIC HOFFER

to Eric Sevareid

The sixties became notorious for attitudes that Hoffer grew to detest.
He also became well known—a figure on the national stage. He was
interviewed on public television, then he triumphed on CBS. He
was invited to the White House by one president and urged others
to run for that office. He became a senior research professor at the
University of California–Berkeley, an institution which became a
leading source of the unrest that he despised. He published books
and was profiled by *The New Yorker*. He started a newspaper column,
but after it was successfully syndicated abruptly discontinued it. He
was appointed to the National Commission on the Causes and Prevention of Violence, and plunged it into controversy. Newspaper
editors sought his words of wisdom on the moon landing. In short,
he became a public figure.

It began unexpectedly, with his concerns about automation.
Although he later concluded his fears were unfounded, they dis-
lodged him from his entrenched routine.

Something strange happened to me early in 1964. After a lifetime of hardly ever sticking my nose outside the San Francisco

waterfront, I found myself running around, shooting my mouth off, telling people of an impending crisis, a turning point as fateful as any since the origin of society, and warning them that woe betides a society that reaches a turning point and does not turn. For the first time in my life I became possessed by something.

I am not by nature one of the doom around the corner boys. But this automation thing has hit me between the eyes and I haven't recovered yet.[1]

He worried that if workers' skills were no longer needed they might become "a dangerously volatile element in a totally new kind of American society." America itself might be undermined—no longer shaped by "the masses" but by the intellectuals. Hoffer increasingly saw them emerging as villains in the continuing American drama.[2]

He lectured at schools, churches, and Rotary clubs and turned out to be a spellbinding speaker. His earlier ventures in public speaking had already shown that he had this gift. Now he again found that he could hold audiences in the palm of his hand. "I could have done anything with them," he said. "I hated that feeling—I could see how Hitler was able to move the masses with his words—but I was possessed by this idea."

That he could sway even a hostile audience he showed at the height of the antiwar protests. Speaking to a packed house at the Stanford student union, he said something provocative about the Vietnam War. The details of the exchange are long forgotten. But an infuriated student stood up shouting: how could Hoffer possibly know what he just said? Hoffer held out his arms, palms up, pleading no contest: "I was guessing!" The students burst out laughing and were immediately on his side.[3]

His thoughts on automation went back and forth. His second opinion stirred him to daydreams of social reconstruction. He imagined brand-new jobs and allocated them as he saw fit. Hoffer was sometimes disposed to engage in such utopian reveries, and this was one of those moments.

We know of the suffering and dislocation to be expected in the wake of total automation. It is interesting, however, that the culmination of the industrial revolution might give us back all that we lost in the rush of industrialization—not only the leisure but also the handicrafts, and many other things which the high price of handwork has kept beyond the reach of the majority of people.

With so many superfluous hands might we not eat hand-baked bread, fresh-churned butter, drinks and dishes which require time and care? If the automated factories can operate without our help we shall be forced—not by hunger or need but by the need to acquire and exercise skills—to use our hands in a hundred ways and we shall learn and conserve all the skills of non-industrialized societies past and present.

The culmination of the industrial revolution should enable the mass of people to recapture the rhythm, the fullness and the variety of pre-industrial times.

As we now know, automated factories never could "operate without our help." So neither vision—whether of jobless masses or restored pre-industrial handicrafts—was realized. The future turned out to be more like the past than he imagined. But his fears served to push Hoffer in a new direction.

Berkeley Professor

At some point in the 1950s Hoffer became acquainted with Norman Jacobson, a member of the Political Science Department at UC-Berkeley. They corresponded. In a 1955 note, Hoffer sounded almost deferential: "It is altogether new to me, Norman, to have someone like you with whom to exchange ideas; to be stimulated and to stimulate in return."

By 1959 they were on cordial terms. Jacobson was holding a series of seminars on "mass democracy and the creative individual" and Hoffer agreed to preside over one of them. He would talk about how he "first stumbled into thinking and writing." He was interested in "the creative potentialities of common people," he told Jacobson, and "should have enough ideas to play with for an hour or so."[4]

By 1963 Hoffer was sixty-five years old and his involuntary retirement from the waterfront loomed as a possibility—the union still had not clarified its decision. Hoffer had no desire to retire. "Largely at the instigation of Selden Osborne and Norman Jacobson," Calvin Tomkins wrote, Hoffer became a senior research political scientist in Jacobson's department, with an office on the top floor of Barrows Hall on the Berkeley campus. Interested students could find Hoffer there every Wednesday afternoon from 2:00 until 5:00 p.m.

Selden Osborne apparently contacted his old college roommate Clark Kerr, the university president, letting him know that Hoffer was available if the university had anything to offer. By October 1963 Jacobson told Hoffer that he had heard from Kerr, and "I break my long silence to let you know where things stand at the present time." He continued, "Kerr and I agree that you ought not to be attached to any single department. Accordingly, the title Professor of Social Theory has been tentatively assigned, hopefully with full support of three departments: Political Science, Sociology and Economics. Kerr has given me permission to go ahead with the plan. In fact the authorization came to me only this morning. I will speak to my Chairman this week, if possible, and set the vast machinery in operation!"[5]

In January 1964 Jacobson wrote again (without a phone, Hoffer could not easily be reached any other way) with the news that he would go on the payroll in March. A further letter from Jacobson, dated March 21, 1964, alluded to a speech Hoffer had recently given in Utah.

> I trust that all went well among descendants of the Lost Tribes, that you enjoyed your stay at Brigham Young, and that the voyage itself was pleasant. I am eager for details.

We would love to have you at our Seder, on Saturday, March 28, around 5 p.m. There is no reason why *our* Tribe should not get together either! Please call during the week, and let us know whether you can come.

Eugene Burdick wrote a note to Hoffer in March 1964 saying he was delighted that "you are going to be with us on the Berkeley campus . . . You are probably the most popular and widely discussed new appointment in the last decade."

A few years later, Hoffer and Jacobson fell out. Jack Bunzel, who became a senior fellow at the Hoover Institution and knew both men well, said that politics was the cause.

Jacobson, renowned for his course on American political theory, had been Bunzel's thesis adviser. Bunzel meanwhile had befriended Hoffer and went on long walks with him in San Francisco. When he taught political science at Stanford in the early 1960s, Bunzel invited Hoffer to speak to his graduate seminar. Appearing in his usual workingman's rig, Hoffer kept the Stanford students enthralled for four hours with his passionate views on almost any subject. Bunzel became chairman of the Political Science Department at San Francisco State College when that campus was embroiled in the longest and one of the most violent conflicts in the history of American higher education. Meanwhile Jacobson moved to the left, eventually identifying with the more radical camp of Sheldon Wolin, who was then teaching in the Political Science Department at UC–Berkeley. At the same time, Hoffer was moving to the right.

Public Figure

In the spring of 1963 Hoffer's book *The Ordeal of Change* was published, collecting some of his best essays and ending a literary drought. Twelve years had passed since *The True Believer*. Meanwhile his public appearances had attracted the attention of James Day, who had helped found KQED, a public television station in

San Francisco. It became part of the National Educational Television network, the predecessor of the Public Broadcasting Service, PBS. Day helped pioneer the interview format later popularized by Dick Cavett, Charlie Rose, and others.

Day later told Tom Lorentzen, an admirer and friend of Hoffer's, that he had somehow heard that Hoffer was a "longshoreman who wrote poetry," an intriguing combination.[6] In 1963 Day filmed six half-hour conversations with Hoffer. They were a great success, and Hoffer returned for six more interviews the following year. Day found that Hoffer needed little prodding. A single answer to one of his questions might take up a full ten minutes.

By now Hoffer's life story was fixed. The KQED version became, in effect, the canonical account. In later interviews—by Tomkins, James Koerner, Eric Sevareid, and others—Hoffer stuck to the same script, sometimes almost word for word. He told the same anecdotes with no new details. The inconsistencies in his earlier accounts were gone. It was as though by 1963 he had settled on the story of his life and he no longer deviated from it.

CBS producers saw the KQED programs and also regarded Hoffer as a promising subject for their network. Harry Reasoner would interview Hoffer for a half-hour program. Later it became an hour, and Sevareid replaced Reasoner. CBS filmed Hoffer walking in Golden Gate Park, but mostly sitting in the corner of a hotel room, an awkward-looking space, talking volubly. His strong German accent must have made things difficult for some viewers. Often he spoke rapidly, ranging in volume from a whisper to a shout. He spoke with great passion, responding almost instantly, smoking cigarettes and frequently mopping himself with a handkerchief.

Hoffer boomed out praise of America and the workers, and denounced the intellectuals who, he said, were by then on their familiar fault-finding mission against the country. A bemused Sevareid, also smoking, mostly just listened and seemed to relish Hoffer's contrarian views. The audience, he knew, was hearing something unusual.

On December 7, 1967, Sevareid wrote to Hoffer: "The Hoffer hour is about to be carried over the BBC in England. I had my heart set on this from the beginning, because your vision of this country is almost alien to the British."

Hoffer didn't see the program, but "they tell me I delivered a sermon in defense of America."[7] America was "the only mass civilization there ever was," he had said. The masses "eloped with history to America and we have been living in common law marriage with it."[8]

Sevareid emphasized Hoffer's working-class credentials—something that "makes him a phenomenon." Several such reminders were inserted into the program, and no doubt they helped immunize CBS against Hoffer's critical comments about the black leadership—"phonies, all of them." (He exempted civil rights activist Roy Wilkins.)[9] The black leadership had "no faith in the Negro masses, no concern for them," Hoffer said. The riots of the mid-1960s had been used "by a relatively prosperous Negro middle class to attain its ends," namely political power.[10]

But what attracted the most comment was Hoffer's praise of President Lyndon B. Johnson, whose popularity was suffering as the Vietnam War dragged on.

> Hoffer: I'm not going to tell Johnson what to do because I have faith in Johnson. Johnson will do the right thing. I've lived with Johnsons all my life, see. I know them. He'll do the right thing and he'll figure out . . . Let me go all the way, he'll be the foremost president of the twentieth century.
>
> Sevareid: You're saying that Johnson will be the foremost president of the twentieth century.
>
> Hoffer: Absolutely. I'm convinced.
>
> Sevareid: He's got to get out of Vietnam one way or another, doesn't he?
>
> Hoffer: We will find a solution to the Vietnam problem. You know, we fumbled. We've never fought a war like that before. We have to learn how to fight, see.[11]

Hoffer was promptly invited to the White House and photographed tête à tête with LBJ in the Rose Garden. A *Newsweek* columnist called it "an intimate 50-minute chat."[12] Hoffer later told Sevareid:

> ... being in the White House with Johnson was to me a tremendous thing. I slept there one night and I walked and I said, 'We are here, we are here! We are here!' Now we ain't going to be here with Nixon, although I think Nixon will make a good president. But Johnson to me is something very special.[13]

Aired in June 1967, the program was so well received that it was rebroadcast two months later. Sevareid wrote that "the program broke just about all records for telephone and mail response from the people." CBS then returned to San Francisco for a second interview in November 1968. Sevareid said later, without exaggeration, that after these conversations were broadcast nationwide, Hoffer became "a kind of popular celebrity." ... "When the first TV hour with him ended, late at night, the telephone switchboards in every CBS station across the country lit up. The next day, I was told, his little books sold out in virtually every bookstore that had them."[14]

It was thanks mainly to the Sevareid interviews that Hoffer was so easily recognized by strangers in San Francisco.

Violence Commission

After Sen. Robert F. Kennedy was assassinated in June 1968, President Johnson appointed a National Commission on the Causes and Prevention of Violence. Johnson wanted Hoffer to be a commissioner, and he accepted. It was mainly a political exercise dressed up as sociological research, as such commissions tend to be. But hearings were public and Hoffer soon realized that political tact was not his strong suit. So he wrote a letter of resignation: "I have to tell my president that I am not worthy of the trust he has placed in me.

I am not fit to serve on the Commission on the Causes of Violence. It is my savage heart."

But President Johnson did not accept his resignation.

Hoffer's letter was drafted the day after a public hearing that made news. The *New York Times* headlined its story on the episode: "White and Negro Clash at Hearing; Hoffer Disputes Argument of Militant Sociologist."[15]

The militant sociologist was Herman Blake, an assistant professor at the University of California–Santa Cruz. With another sociologist named Jerome H. Skolnick, director of a task force on the commission, Blake had interviewed Huey P. Newton, then awaiting trial in the Alameda County Courthouse for the murder of a white policeman. (The "minister of defense" of the Black Panther Party, Newton was convicted of voluntary manslaughter in that trial.)

Newton, considered a legitimate voice of black protest, had consented to be tape-recorded in jail, but only on the condition that the tape not be transcribed. It could simply be played for the benefit of the commissioners, Hoffer among them.

Assembled in a Senate hearing room, commission members were "having trouble following Newton's rambling sentences and ghetto language," the *Times* reported. Blake, the go-between who was testifying on behalf of the absent Newton, realized that his message to the nation was not getting across as hoped, so he cut off the lengthy tape and told in his own words "the frustrations of ghetto life."

"These people in the black community are angry," he began. The Panthers gave blacks "a rhetoric and an ideology that explain their situation." Commissioners could not know the frustration of the "impoverished Negro," as the *Times* reported. "The anger and rage is something that cannot be put into words."

When it was Hoffer's turn he said to Blake: "Your rhetoric went down fine with these people [the other commissioners]; it didn't go down fine with me. It wouldn't go down fine with the longshoremen." He went on: "Rage is something that doesn't come from frustration. Rage is cheap, rage is a luxury and you can't afford it."

Mr. Hoffer: I say that you have to build a community and you are not.

Mr. Blake: We can't build a community with white people like you around telling us we can't be what we are.

Mr. Hoffer: You are not going to build it by rage. You are going to build it by working together.

Mr. Blake: You are defining it.

Mr. Hoffer: They haven't raised one blade of grass. They haven't raised one brick.

Mr. Blake: We been throwing them, baby, because you been out there stopping them from laying bricks and raising grass.

UPI reported that Hoffer "clenched his fists in obvious anger and shouted: 'All my life I was poor. When I was picking cotton Negroes were eating and living better than I was.'

"The bearded Blake, wearing an African tribal shirt and dark glasses, began yelling back and finally got up, turned on his heel and walked away from the witness table."[16]

Blake was invited back by another commissioner, federal Judge A. Leon Higginbotham, who wanted to note "on the record, how totally in error Mr. Hoffer is on the most elementary data." He cited as evidence unemployment figures of 30 or 40 percent in Watts, in Southern California. Judge Higginbotham added:

I think that Mr. Hoffer's statements are indicative of the great racist pathology in our country and that his views are those which represent the mass of people in this country.

When Hoffer "exploded with indignation, shaking his fist," according to Stacy Cole, television cameras caught it and that night Daniel Schorr of CBS News referred to the "racist Eric Hoffer." Then he "had to sit through the humiliation of being chastised by Judge Higginbotham."

How often do we think, too late, of the reply we wish we had made? Few get the chance to make that rejoinder on network television.

But Hoffer did. When Sevareid interviewed Hoffer for a second time, in November 1968, Higginbotham's comment came up.

> Mr. Sevareid: A great many of the New Left and the Negro militants have been awful hard on you, Mr. Hoffer. They say you're old hat, or that you're a racist, or that you don't really understand what's going on today. Does this upset you much?

> Mr. Hoffer: No, no, no. You saw that scene in the commission there, big Higginbotham calling me a racist. Now as a matter of fact I am less afraid of being called a racist than Higginbotham is afraid of being called an Uncle Tom.

Hoffer added that he had "a higher opinion of the Negro masses than Higginbotham."

Skolnick, who had interviewed Newton in jail, produced a task force report for the Commission called *The Politics of Protest*. The journalist I.F. Stone called it "brilliant and indispensable." But in a March 1969 notebook entry, Hoffer said something different:

> "Skolnick's report would be ideally fitting if it were written for a commission appointed for the justification and encouragement of violence. For all I know such a commission is in existence. Perhaps Skolnick's task force was such a commission."

In a 1970 article for the magazine *Transaction: Social Science and Modern Society*, a journal published by Irving Louis Horowitz of Rutgers University, Skolnick wrote that staff members on the earlier Kerner Commission on Civil Disorders, formed in 1967, had produced a draft document with exactly that in mind. Called "The Harvest of American Racism," it excused the riots of the day as the first step in a developing revolution. Blacks will feel that "it is legitimate and necessary to use violence against the social order," the draft alleged. A "truly revolutionary spirit has begun to take hold."

Higher-ups on the Kerner Commission were appalled, however, and many of the social scientists responsible for the "Harvest" document were "released." It was not published.[17]

As to the Violence Commission, Skolnick said that Hoffer, "the president's favorite philosopher," presented "the backlash voice of the American workingman." That was no doubt true, and Lyndon Johnson surely had it in mind when he appointed Hoffer to the commission and then refused to accept his resignation.

Skolnick noted that in the minute or so of hearings shown on national television, Hoffer was seen "shouting at a bearded black man in a dashiki," so "it is doubtful that much enlightenment was achieved."

Hoffer also criticized affirmative action and those who supported it:

> The well meaning people who want us to do everything for the Negro and do not expect him to do much for himself are convinced that the Negro is inferior. They are part of the conspiracy of least expectation which has sapped the Negro's confidence in himself.

Stacy Cole said he thought that Hoffer suffered a loss of status as a result of his experience on the commission. Perhaps a change of status was closer to the truth. Hoffer became more popular with the masses. But intellectuals began to see him in a new light. It had not been immediately obvious from his most recent book, *The Temper of Our Time* (1967), but Hoffer was by then becoming close to a reactionary political figure. By 1968 it was plain for all to see.

Hoffer wrote about violence in a 1970 notebook:

> Thought and feeling can beget violence only when they are first transmuted into violent words. It is impossible to deal with the causes of violence unless violent words are taken about as seriously

as violent acts. It is doubtful whether a society can have order and stability if insults and obscenities which outrage personal and community sensibilities go unchallenged and unpunished.

This raised debatable (and much debated) First Amendment questions. But on a related issue Hoffer's position was unassailable. If it were true that poverty is the root cause of violence, he said, then the 1930s should have been an extremely violent decade. But it wasn't, as Hoffer knew at first hand.

There was less juvenile delinquency, less racial conflict and bitterness, less crime in general during the hungry years of the Depression than in these affluent times.

Free Speech at Berkeley

To reach Berkeley for his sessions as conversationalist-at-large, Hoffer traveled by bus across the Bay Bridge from San Francisco. His arrival at the campus coincided exactly with the Free Speech movement, involving protests against the Vietnam War in particular, student riots, and impassioned speeches by Mario Savio and others.

Early in Hoffer's career at Berkeley, he observed:

It is much easier to be a rebel than a hard-working student. This is particularly true of students with meager talent but it also holds true of the more richly endowed. It is also much easier to be a hero or a martyr than to strive day in day out mastering knowledge and acquiring new skills.

Later, he reckoned that many students' lives were wasted because of the rebellious mood prevailing on campus. "The sudden license and the sky-is-the-limit experimentation blemished thousands of minds," he wrote in 1972.

In 1965 he made a written note of something he planned to tell the students:

> Let me tell you what you look like in the eyes of an old man. You are right now nature's fifth column and you are doing nature's work when you want to wreck Sproul Hall, set Los Angeles on fire, or roam in packs or gangs to vent your rage on whatever attracts your fancy. Negro Assemblyman Willie Brown, though a phony, was putting his finger on the truth when he recognized a close kinship between the Free Speech Movement here and the orgy of burning and looting in Watts.

(Willie Brown, a San Francisco Democrat, went on to become speaker of the Assembly for fifteen years and then a two-term mayor of San Francisco.)

In 1967, the New Left magazine *Ramparts* published an article about Hoffer, written by Peter Collier, who moved to the right himself in later years and wrote books with David Horowitz.[18] He described Hoffer's office commanding "a prime view of the now famous plaza and steps over which more than 700 true-believing students once walked to occupy Sproul Hall." As for Hoffer himself,

> "The upper part of his body is still thick and powerful but beginning to bow at the shoulders. Hoffer dresses in the cap and heavy coat he must have worn on the waterfront. He ushers all those waiting for him—usually seven or eight, the number remaining constant for the afternoon despite arrivals and departures—into his office, chatting loudly in his Alsatian accent.
>
> "When he talks to a student, he demands a first name and a short biography. Later he may use this data to gently play one of them off against another for rhetorical leverage; but mostly he conducts a monologue—crooning and swaying, squinting his eyes shut as he reminisces. 'The President is an overwhelming

person face to face,' he says. 'I told him all about the Johnsons. I've known nothing but Johnsons all my life. On the docks, in the fields. They are very unassuming people.'"

Hoffer had met the president earlier that year. He also told the class how he had won over the students at Stanford. He had defended "everything they don't like—Vietnam, law and order, everything. And at the end of my speech they all came up and were hugging me and kissing me. It was wonderful."

When a Berkeley student sought Hoffer's opinion of the New Left, Collier reported, Hoffer pointed to Sproul Plaza outside. One more ad hoc demonstration had just been held there, with students rallying for their "final assault" on the Oakland Army Induction Center. Hoffer dismissed them as clowns. The New Left belonged to "the nineteenth century."

When the student replied that the Oakland police were "breaking the heads of doctors, clergymen, journalists and protesters with an indiscriminate ferocity unusual even for them," Hoffer exploded:

> What about that little bitch at the rally here yesterday noon, the one who came up and began hitting the boy who dared say some-thing about the Oakland police being human too? What kind of fanaticism is that? Why is it that the past is condemned to repeat itself? This New Left, this bunch of clowns down there, they would all of them have been the isolationists I saw objecting to this country entering the last war. They are the same ones I saw on this campus in 1939 pleading and whining for non-intervention.

It was one of the few times that Hoffer encountered a journalist who was not wholly sympathetic. Collier saw, correctly, that Hoffer's fre-quent method of argument was to view "the desire for revolutionary change in terms of the motives and purity of heart of those who promote it." But his monologue was given with humor, and he had a winning manner. He used his charisma "as incisively as he does epigrams from Montaigne and Pascal in his books." Despite its basic aggression, his performance was immensely interesting.

Stacy Cole

"Hoffer was quick to discourage disciples," Tomkins noted. "His usual method, when a student too obviously sought his approval, was to tell him to go and write down his ideas clearly and explicitly, and preferably on one page."[19]

Stacy Cole was Hoffer's only real disciple—he does not object to the word. He taught American history at Washington High School in Fremont and then at Ohlone College. He started attending Hoffer's Berkeley seminar in 1968; when it ended in 1972, he continued visiting him in San Francisco almost every week. He kept that up until Hoffer's death.

Hoffer had spoken at a high school in South San Francisco, so Cole sent him a letter asking if he could do the same at Washington High. Hoffer wrote back and suggested bringing his class to Berkeley. Cole's class drove up in cars. Hoffer "enjoyed having these 17-year-olds, boys and girls," Cole recalled. "They were extremely interested in him and his ideas." After that, Cole returned on his own. From early April of 1968 until the end of May of 1972, he may have missed only four or five weeks. He recalled the seminar:

> "Usually seven or eight people showed up. It was a drop-in situa-
> tion. Some came early and would leave, some came later. After
> 1969 I would come at about 2:30 and stay till 5. Sometimes public
> service people would come in seminar groups. The offices were
> arranged around an anteroom, so 15 or 20 people could be out
> there sitting on the floor. Hoffer would bring his chair over and
> sit in the doorway. Three or four students from Stanford came on
> a regular basis.

Later, the FBI heard that Ted Kaczynski, the Unabomber, an assistant professor at Berkeley at that time, might have visited the class; at one point, agents combed through Hoffer's papers at Hoover. "Anyone could drop in to Hoffer's class," Cole said. "But they never established that Ted Kaczynski was there. Lili asked me if I remembered him. I didn't."

Hoffer had no set lecture at Berkeley, Cole recalled. "He might introduce a topic, or someone else might. He could go thirty or forty minutes on a given topic. He loved questions, loved for people to challenge him, loved the interplay of ideas. He would bring a handful of note-cards and would read quotations. They might be from the ancients, or contemporary. I found them not only illuminating and instructive but a guide to my own reading. Now I've got thousands of cards of my own."[20]

Stacy Cole particularly remembers a visitor in 1971 who sat next to the desk while Hoffer, his chair pushed back, was smoking and listening. The man's conversation covered literature, art, philosophy, poetry, and history; Cole reckoned he "was in the presence of a man with a first-class mind who had had the advantage of a first-class education."

Eric introduced him during a break. He was Milton Himmelfarb, an associate editor of *Commentary*, brother of the historian Gertrude Himmelfarb and brother-in-law of Irving Kristol, the well-known conservative writer.

Evidently he had come to pay a tribute to Hoffer. For an hour and a half he was the center of the discussion. Hoffer was enjoying it, not saying much, sometimes feeding him a line or two. Then the topic turned to something close to Hoffer's heart—the role of the Jews in history, particularly "their story of the creation." Himmelfarb described the creator as one "who creates something out of chaos, then creates human beings with minds capable of comprehending it, then resting on the seventh day and giving them dominion over it, rather than making them subject to it," Cole recalled. "He puts human beings in charge of it. In other words, they can be creators, too."

Hoffer then joined in. Man considered as separate from creation was something unique to Judaism, he said. Himmelfarb listened for a while and then said: "Mr. Hoffer, there is a psalm in which the

Jews praise creation and in effect pay tribute to it." He picked up his briefcase and pulled out a well-thumbed copy of the Bible. He began to read out loud the psalm he had in mind. Hoffer then astonished everyone in the room.

Himmelfarb was about three verses into it, Cole recalled, when Hoffer began quoting the psalm in the original Hebrew. "Verse by verse, he quoted the entire psalm." Himmelfarb stopped reading and his eyes grew wider. "When Hoffer was through he quietly said, 'Mr. Hoffer, you amaze me.'"

What impressed Cole—in addition to Hoffer's knowledge of Hebrew—was the spontaneity of his intervention. He could not have known what was coming. Cole thought it "the greatest piece of one-upmanship" he had ever seen. Several years later he was with Eric at Lili's house one Sunday night and he mentioned it. Hoffer roared with laughter. He said it was "the only verse in the whole Bible that I knew in Hebrew from beginning to the end, and he happened to pick that one."

How came Hoffer to know Hebrew? He said that when he was "on the bum and working in the fields" in the Imperial Valley he walked outside one morning when the fields were covered with hoarfrost, white and glistening like diamonds. He was struck by the beauty of it and remembered having read this psalm in translation. "And I said to myself: you have to learn Hebrew, you have to learn the psalm in the original, because the translation cannot have done it justice."

So he taught himself Hebrew, "and his pronunciation was wonderful." Cole heard Hoffer "more than a few times say something in Hebrew. He had such a great ear."

Hoffer told another interviewer that he had learned Hebrew while on skid row in Los Angeles. "I think I mastered it. I can speak it, but I cannot make out the text," he said.[21]

Hoffer learned in June 1972 that the university had not renewed his contract. His position there had lasted for eight years. "Finally I am a free man, truly retired," he wrote. "I shall not really miss the job. I might feel nudged now to start writing."

Wednesday I found out by a short phone call to the chairman's office that my "academic career" has come to an end. I shall not miss much the three hours each Wednesday and I shall not miss the $8500 a year. I have a base income of $15,000 a year. I also have 150,000 dollars in the bank. Even if I were to live to be ninety I would still be safe and secure. There is, it is true, an unpleasant feeling when we are diminished in some degree even if we are denied what we do not really need or even want. But such a feeling does not last where there is no hardship.

His time at UC–Berkeley was "my first taste of getting paid for doing nothing," Hoffer said. As to the campus disorders, the underlying problem was that "the power structure of the university was manned by toothless lions," and the students knew it. Clark Kerr "knew how to build a great university but did not know how to defend it. He had not an inkling of the vulnerability of institutions."[22]

Newspaper Columnist

Hoffer's career as a newspaper columnist was short-lived, but a great success. His talents were well-suited to the task, and the column, syndicated by The Ledger Syndicate, promptly took off and was carried by over a hundred newspapers. He wrote in a 1973 notebook:

Sometime in 1968 I was tricked by a one-legged tragic looking Irishman by the name of [John] Higgins into signing a contract as a once a week columnist. It was a two-year contract. He told me I won't have to write them—that he would extract the columns from my published books. It seemed easy and the man looked so tragic. The moment I saw samples of his extractions I realized that I would have to do the columns myself. They caught on. My share (50%) came to more than $500 a week. At the end of two years I quit and Mr. Higgins put on all sorts of tragic act. I promised him then that eventually I would write fifty columns and make them as good as I know how.

A few days later he added a few reflections on the great potential of the newspaper column—his own was published under the rubric "Reflections." It was a "powerful and delightful literary genre."

> To say something meaningful and with several punches and good sentences all in 500 words may seem difficult and discouraging to a person who has not too many ideas or does not know precisely what he wants to say. But to someone who delights in the play of ideas yet is impatient of expansive discourse the column is an ideal vehicle. Its counterpart in painting is the sketch with a minimum of lines. The column becomes art par excellence when what is not said echoes in the mind of the reader. What you need for writing columns is the seed of ideas.

Hoffer began the column in February 1968 and kept it up for two years. His last column, "The Effects of the Negro Revolution," was syndicated on March 15, 1970. The columns sometimes had a topical lead, sometimes not, but always benefited from his gift for concision. He knew that his strength lay in the short form, and the newspaper format required it.

He memorialized this appeal to brevity by funding the Lili Fabilli and Eric Hoffer Essay Prize at UC–Berkeley. It is awarded each year for the best essays of 500 words or less on a topic chosen by the Committee on Prizes. In July 1970 Hoffer donated $10,000, and now a total of $3,000 is divided among the winners at the judges' discretion. In 1977 he wrote to a Mrs. Blumberg:

> Wordiness is a sickness of American writing. Too many words dilute and blur ideas. An average American book is twice as long as a British book on the same subject . . . There is not an idea that cannot be expressed in 200 words. But the writer must know precisely what he wants to say. If you have nothing to say and want badly to say it, then all the words in all the dictionaries will not suffice.

His best column on Israel (appendix 3) is only 400 words.

When he "bustled into the *[San Francisco] Examiner* editorial offices" one day in February 1970 and announced that he was discontinuing the column, he said it was "not my type of writing."[23] Nonetheless, his newspaper column was highly effective. Particularly influential were three columns on Israel, widely distributed by Jewish groups. They were probably the source of Milton Himmelfarb's interest.

At least one of these columns was read by Pauline Phillips, the author of the "Dear Abby" column, who had been friends with Hoffer for some time. She wrote to him in January 1970: "Dear Eric: Your recent piece on Israel was magnificent. You know I share your views, but then it's a matter of my being loyal to MY people. But Eric . . . You?"

At Hoffer's recommendation, the UC–Berkeley political science Professor Aaron Wildavsky tried out as Hoffer's successor, but he didn't work out. The column was discontinued.

Poor John Higgins was disappointed that there would be no more columns, especially given the offhand way Hoffer had let him know. Neither he nor the syndicate had advance warning of Hoffer's visit to the *Examiner's* office. Hoffer also said at the time that "the columns weren't good enough to put into a book," having told Higgins that he could publish them as a book. Higgins wrote to Hoffer saying that he had made both the author and the syndicate look bad. Hoffer tried to make it up to Higgins, promising to write fifty more columns, specially dedicating them to Higgins, whom he always liked. He could then reprint them as a book.

Soon, Hoffer was writing that "all the 50 new columns" should be about "the new lessons that we have learned since the First World War, particularly in this country, during the 1960s." The recent turmoil "should contain enough revelations about the human condition to fill a small book." His ambition seemed to be over-reaching once more, yet two months later he said that he had finished column thirty-nine, "A use of History." The moment he finished writing something, he added, he was not confident that he "could do it again." He still had "eleven columns to write."

Higgins never did receive his fifty columns, but in 1976 Hoffer published a small book, *In Our Time*, containing thirty-two short pieces. Many of those thirty-nine columns are among them.

On his visit to the *Examiner's* office in 1970, Hoffer announced his retirement not just from column-writing but also from public life. His career at Berkeley would continue for another two years, but he described himself as "very tired, very spent . . . not much inside." So there would be ". . . no more columns, no more television, no more lectures, no more teaching. I don't need it and I don't want it. I'm going to crawl back into my hole where I started. I don't want to be a public person, or anybody's spokesman. I am not the type for it and I dislike it."

The *Examiner's* executive editor, Thomas Eastham, noted that Hoffer had not led the life of most public personages. "Though flooded with offers, he has consistently refused appearances."

"Any man can ride a train," Hoffer added. "Only a wise man knows when to get off." Besides, he said, he was getting to be an old man. "I don't want to die barking."[24]

CHAPTER SEVEN

The Literary Life

*Remember, patience is your only asset. You must hang
on, month after month and year after year until the
thing takes shape. Familiarity—long familiarity—is the
only way of penetrating and mastering the subject.*

—ERIC HOFFER

notebook

After he appeared on national television in the 1960s, Eric Hoffer
was often recognized on the streets and sometimes approached by
strangers. Later, in the 1970s, he wrote that people in San Francisco
had been asking when his next book was coming out.

"It reminded me how frightened I was during the stagnant 1950s
when longshoremen asked me about my next book," he said.

"Stagnant 1950s" did not refer to the nation as a whole. By the
1970s Hoffer saw the 1950s as a "paradise of lost innocence." But the
fifties really had been a difficult time for his own writing. The books
he struggled to write had not worked out. After his great success
with *The True Believer*, it was a setback.

And yet an overview of Hoffer's entire literary output reveals
him as a prolific writer. In the 1950s, he published two books: *The
True Believer* (1951) and *The Passionate State of Mind* (1955). He
published three books during the sixties, *The Ordeal of Change*
(1963), *The Temper of Our Time* (1967), and *Working and Thinking
on the Waterfront* (1969).

During the 1970s, when he was also in his seventies, he produced four more: *First Things, Last Things* (1971), *Reflections on the Human Condition* (1973), *In Our Time* (1976), and *Before the Sabbath* (1979). Before his death in 1983, two more books appeared under his name: *Between the Devil and the Dragon* (1982) and *Truth Imagined* (1983).

It was the books that he wanted to write but didn't that frustrated him.

In 1950, six months before *The True Believer* was published, he was making confident notes on its sequel. Sometimes he referred to it as "vol. 2." The earlier book had dealt with the nature of mass movements. In a notebook, he wrote, "The present volume sees mass movements as one of the devices for the release of man's energies."

He worked on this project for seven years, but he never could pull it together. He retitled it several times. "The Release of Man's Energies" became "Stagnation and Renascence," then "Explosive Change." Notebooks refer to the book on Fanaticism, sometimes on Enthusiasm. He told Calvin Tomkins that he had spent as much time on it as he had on *The True Believer*.[1] He also struggled with a book on "Intellectuals" for much of the 1950s, but that promising project didn't work out either.

His political views changed, heading in a more conservative direction. *The True Believer* had not been seen as a conservative book, and the early notebooks showed little such tendency. He favored the revolutionary overthrow of incompetent governments, for example, even if that meant a "frightful waste in lives and wealth." We also find him saying that an educated and articulate minority was "essential to maintaining the vigor of a group." Later he referred to educated minorities as intellectuals, and they became his *bêtes noires*.

He wrote magazine articles, some of which were collected in a highly regarded book, *The Ordeal of Change*.[2] In the mid-1950s he also published his first book since *The True Believer*—a collection of aphorisms called *The Passionate State of Mind*.[3] Here his ideas were compressed into a few lines, and sometimes he said he preferred this form to any other. He wrote to an otherwise unidentified correspondent in 1956:

> Dear Josine:
>
> A strange weariness has been weighing on me for over a year. The events in the Middle East and in Hungary revived me for a while but the old dullness soon returned.
>
> The waterfront has been unusually busy for over a year and I have been working more than I should—in part to justify my inertness. How are you both? I want very much to hear of all that concerns you.
>
> As to *The Passionate State of Mind*, it is yours to do with as you please. As you know, our literature is not overly rich in aphorisms, and so a compact little volume of aphorisms should have a rightful place. I need not tell you that neither of the two books is selling well and *The Passionate State* even less so. The American reader has no time for this kind of concentrated writing. Yet strangely, the wisecrack, which is an American product, is a near relative to the aphorism and I hear now and then sparkling specimens of them.
>
> Some should have been thrown out and new aphorisms added. But there is no use worrying about it.

In 1972, when he was working on a later collection of his work (published as *Between the Devil and the Dragon* in 1982[4]), he planned to include a set of his aphorisms. He wrote in a notebook:

> A good aphorism is a seed—often a barbed seed—that sticks in the mind of the reader and there germinates. An aphorism even when very brief has in it the embryo of a large train of thought. The reader feels a jar the moment the aphorism has hooked into his mind. Some aphorisms as they hit a mind stab and also titillate. The reader knows that something hit him.

But, like a meal of chocolates, a book of aphorisms is a rich diet; it's too much for most readers. *The Passionate State of Mind* enjoyed only a limited success. Murray Kempton of the *New York Post* wrote that Hoffer's books are short "because they are without preliminaries and documents and most of all without the facts which are so often the substitute for conclusions. Mr. Hoffer writes short books which cry out for long reviews."[5]

In the 1950s Hoffer learned the important lesson that the book-length treatise was not his forte. He excelled at shorter pieces, whether aphoristic or article-length. Once he became reconciled to that discovery, he found his authentic voice. His style was also well suited to the newspaper column. So the decade was far from wasted. But the experience was an uncomfortable one, because he was inclined to blame his difficulties on physical decline. He wrote in 1957:

> It is comforting to discover in days of decline that others before us have petered out; some more or less abruptly. It is on the way down that we need others. It is then that we fear to be alone.

In early 1963 he wrote in a notebook:

> What do you do when you are over 60 and a worry the size of a mountain weighs on your mind? Well, you can do many things. You can go on working, eating, sleeping as usual and with every breath, every move, feel the weight pressing you down.

As his successes to come would show, he had far from petered out. But something had gone awry. In his notebooks, in which he often addressed himself in the second person, his steps can be retraced.

The Release of Man's Energies

Hoffer began his numbered notebooks in November 1949, when the revised *True Believer* was sent to the publishers. Within months he was taking notes on its sequel, with outlines and chapter headings in constant flux. The underlying issue was this: if you look at societies throughout history, most of them, most of the time, do little more than produce a minimal subsistence. Occasionally, however, there is a great release of energy. What causes it? What makes a community active or stagnant? Stagnation is the rule for centuries. Fervent action is the exception.

"The energies of man," he wrote. "What a subject!" The following notebook entry, written in November 1950, was intended as an introduction to the new book:

> The most striking example of the release of man's energies is the awakening and modernization of stagnant, backward societies. This phenomenon of national renascence is one of the most peculiar characteristics of the present era and one of its chief sources of unrest and strife. Though the phenomenon of national renascence has occurred now and then in the distant past (the modernization of Europe since the Reformation, the awakening of Arabia at the time of Mohammed), its frequency and diffusion have increased enormously since the French Revolution, and it is one chief characteristic of our era.
>
> As pointed out in a previous book, the renascence of a stagnant society is in almost every case the work of a mass movement [or] the religious, revolutionary or nationalist enthusiasms generated by a mass movement. The present volume deals with the nature, role and varieties of mass enthusiasm and its relation to other types of enthusiasm.

"It's an awful lot," he wrote a few months later. "Still, this is your subject: The Release of Man's Energies."

He girded himself for the struggle ahead: "Remember, patience is your only asset," he told himself. "You must hang on, month after month and year after year until the thing takes shape. Familiarity—long familiarity—is the only way of penetrating and mastering the subject."

Communists had seized power in Peking in October 1949, so Mao's revolution was on the front pages. Hoffer assumed that this momentous event had involved one of those explosive releases of energy. He had also persuaded himself, as the above quotation from his notebook shows, that revolutionary events drew their energies from mass movements. That, after all, had been a key argument of *The True Believer.*

He was therefore committed early on to two propositions that led him astray. The first was that Communist revolutions are mass movements; the second was that Communist regimes are highly productive (because they release energies). He was unwilling to abandon these ideas for several more years.

In other countries, Czechoslovakia for example, the market system had worked well enough in the pre-war period. But because Communism had prevailed since, individualism had been shown to be unworkable (for Czechs). In Russia, the problem was that "sloth, anarchy and pathological suspiciousness are deeply engrained, and are likely to assert themselves whenever the individual is left to his own devices."

Asian countries had their own problems. So they, too, needed Communism to shake things up. Hoffer had written in *The True Believer* that one of China's great misfortunes was that its mass movements (that of revolutionary leader Sun Yat-sen, for example) had deteriorated too soon, before a new Stalin could keep a genuine mass movement going long enough for drastic reforms to take root.[6] That was written shortly before Mao seized power.

In Russia, meanwhile, Communism was proving to be "a vitalizing, modernizing and integrating force." Stalin's secret weapon, Hoffer believed, was his ability to inspire fanaticism in all masses of people. But if Stalin was to hold Russia on the path to modernization, he would have to use the following method:

[He] must keep his 200 million Russians drunk with this potent elixir; must keep out the fresh air of doubt and tolerance blowing from the outside world; must keep his Russians thoroughly united and needs hate, strife and danger threatening from without as unifying agents.

Hoffer continued to hold these ideas for about two years. In an article published by the *New York Herald Tribune* in late 1951 (and never reprinted) he argued that what we had seen in Asia was not Communist manipulation and propaganda so much as the awakening and renovation of stagnant, backward societies.

> The modernization of a backward society can succeed only when undertaken in an atmosphere of wild hope, blind faith, spectacular defiance, and in what Milton called "a sea of defiance and hoarse disputes."[7]

Hoffer didn't welcome the idea, but as he saw it Stalinism was "a most effective instrument for the conversion of millions of backward Russian peasants into modern industrial workers." It could even be achieved by "fanaticism, ruthlessness, charlatanism and pestilential double talk." The "soul plasticity requisite for the rapid and wholehearted adoption of a new way of life is a by-product of fanaticism."[8]

For a while he justified the Iron Curtain, recently erected. Why must Stalin segregate the Russians from Western civilization? Later he realized that it was simply to prevent Russians from escaping. But in 1951 Hoffer's answer was that by creating a separate, segregated Russian civilization, Stalin was "laying firm foundations for his structure of collective submissiveness and the complete submergence of the individual."

At the time of the anti-Soviet revolt in East Germany in 1953, Hoffer recognized the Communist evil. He noticed, too, that the West held Communism in awe.[9] But he was also impressed by what Communism had apparently achieved. Stalin had shown unbounded contempt for human beings, but he could justify it by pointing to "the breathtaking results of sheer coercion." Cruelty worked, in other words. "Idealism, courage, tremendous achievements both cultural and material, faith and loyalty unto death can be achieved by relentless, persistent coercion."

High officials of the Truman and Eisenhower administrations held similar views. They accepted Soviet claims of economic achievement, journalists repeated them, and the Soviet nuclear tests seemed to confirm them. The launch of Sputnik in 1957 further persuaded most of the world that the Soviets had moved ahead of the United States—in production, if not in freedom.

That industrial production had in fact collapsed following the Bolshevik Revolution and had made only a faltering recovery was not appreciated for decades. Led by U.S. government agencies that took Soviet statistics at face value, policy analysts and economic textbooks continued making the same mistake right up to 1989.

Longshoremen on the waterfront also influenced Hoffer. Some were Communists, and he noticed that this boosted their pride.

> I know their attachment to Communism is motivated less by the excellence of Communist teaching than for the beneficent effect the Communist faith has on their lives. It gives them a sense of self importance and ingrains in them a habit of self discipline. In short, the wholehearted attachment to the Communist faith makes it possible for them to live sober lives full of hope and interest. It makes it possible for them to save money, acquire property and in addition feel that they are superior to their fellow men and that they are somehow connected with the winning side.

He read Max Weber's *The Protestant Ethic and the Spirit of Capitalism*, R.H. Tawney's *Religion and the Rise of Capitalism*, Henri Bergson's *The Two Sources of Morality and Religion*, and many other books. Still more "dynamic factors" were added to those needed to unleash human energies. By August 1952 he was proposing nothing less than a "general theory of action." His daunting list, compiled in August 1952, shows that the book was getting out of hand:

> Your job is to evaluate a whole series of conditions and emotions as dynamic factors. Hate, of course, and love, hope, fear, discontent, malice, greed, envy, pride (and humiliations), faith, persuasion, compulsion, necessity, individualism, boredom, group existence, isolation, migration, change in general, music, drugs (alcohol), mass spectacles, symbols, ideas, visions, imagination, a sense of weakness or strength. A probing of all these factors should offer clues for the formulation of a general theory of action. All this is, of course, but the backdrop for the problem of stagnation.

He saw man's energies as normally blocked, but the pent-up forces could be sprung open if the right human factors were combined. Perhaps it was like a chemical reaction, or fermentation. He talked of enzymes. But the Open Sesame formula continued to elude him. He turned to psychology. The most fruitful investigation, he decided, lay in the way "such factors operate in man's soul." How do they "shape our thoughts, feelings, dreams, tastes; by what chain of reactions do they reach and influence literature, art, music, manners, fashions and so on?" If we knew, we would be able to manipulate life. Then revolutions and violent upheavals would no longer be necessary.

The Awakening of Asia

Further clues appear in "The Awakening of Asia," an essay he published in *The Reporter* in 1954. By now he had toned down his acceptance of Communist achievement. Max Ascoli, an anti-Communist immigrant from Italy, may well have played a role. Hoffer's reference to Asia, with its many and diverse countries, overrode all specifics about China, India, and Japan, not to mention the recently divided Korea. As always, he was aiming for the widest generalization.

How did the present revolutionary turmoil in Asia arise? In newsreels, Hoffer took note of the upturned faces shouting and marching. Do they demand bread and clothing? The good things in life? "No! The clamor that is rising all over the Orient is a clamor for pride."

Before the Europeans arrived, the individual in Asia "was integrated into a more or less compact group—a patriarchal family, a clan or a tribe." Such an individual never felt alone or isolated. But Western influences had cracked apart the traditional way of life, draining communal structures of their prestige. And once isolated, individuals became explosive, a breeding ground for the convulsions that had shaken these societies to their foundations.

Europe in the fifteenth century had "witnessed a similar release of the individual from the corporate pattern of an all-embracing Church." With the Reformation, the Church lost its hold on the minds and souls of the people. This in turn produced "an outburst of vitality that has since been characteristic of the Occident." Now something similar was happening in the Orient. It was a vast and fruitful subject, but Hoffer still had not worked out the energy-releasing combination.

He was still looking for the key as late as 1957. An ever-expanding range of activities came under his purview, not just business and industry but "exploration, migration, gold rushes, crusades [and] war." He had taken on an enormous subject, he realized. Its appeal was that it covered "*all* the items you are interested in."

In 1957 he drew up a final list of the factors which release man's energies, and came up with abstractions that included hope, despair, example, pride, and humiliation. He would also have to look at "religion, nationalism and socialism as factors in the release of energy." But one form of released energy could also be channeled into another, so he should also work out the connections between them all.

Having surveyed his task he wrote, in an understandably weary hand: "You have a lifetime to work on it."

Freedom and Economics

Not until the very end did Hoffer find that *freedom* was the key ingredient. In "The Readiness to Work," written in 1959, he concluded that "it is individual freedom which generates the readiness to work." But this was a "startling conclusion," and to get there he had taken enormous and time-consuming detours.

By February 1959, diary entries show, he was "beginning to think that the activation of the masses—their readiness to work and strive—is a function of individual freedom." In March, he returned to the readiness to work and was "itching to write a chapter on the subject," with particular reference to the United States.

> To me it is a miracle that 200 million people who are largely the descendants of rejects and dropouts from Europe should have created in this country the most important material power on the planet.

Significantly, he also saw that the intellectuals *cannot* "induce in the masses a readiness to work."[10]

"The Readiness to Work" was finally published in *The Ordeal of Change*. Given the years of note-taking that he was now repudiating in all but name, it is one of his most significant essays. The main problem confronting Communist regimes was "how to make people work—how to induce them to plow, sow, harvest, build, manufacture." Yet to us in the West these activities were entirely natural and matter-of-fact.

He had come a long way from believing that the Communists had created an atmosphere of "wild hope, blind faith, spectacular defiance" to get people to work. In *The True Believer*, he had accepted the "prolonged dynamism of the Communist movement" as a reality.[11] Now he was abandoning such ideas. "Communism has not changed people," he bluntly noted.

An enduring problem was that Hoffer was not interested in economics and paid little attention to political institutions. He either took private property and the rule of law for granted, or thought them unimportant.

"Far more important than the structure of a governmental system is the make-up of the men who operate it," he wrote in 1952. He disparaged economic incentives and as late as 1970 denied that they "invariably release a steady flow of energy." He thought there was "probably need for an illusion, a myth, or a certain folklore if people are to exert themselves to the utmost." He lumped together the Sudan and modern Britain in denying that high wages can induce a willingness to work. (By 1970, there were indeed serious problems in Britain, but they were mainly caused by militant trade unions.)

Hoffer paid little attention to such thinkers as Milton Friedman or Friedrich Hayek, and at times viewed economic explanations as beside the point. "How naïve it is to see in economic self-interest the motive of all our actions and attitudes," he wrote soon after *The True Believer* was published. "The Marxists who poke their fingers into every human manifestation [do so] with the sole intent of finding the obscene kernel of economic motivation."

His essay, "The Madhouse of Change," first published in 1968 in *Playboy*, summarized some of these views. The countries that had won independence in Africa and Asia after the war had attempted to modernize themselves. But they had mainly succeeded in turning "every country into a madhouse." Was this really necessary? he now wondered. After all, modernization "is not an occult process." It requires everyday activities like the building of roads and factories.

He had spent two decades groping for an answer. In fact, almost everything he had written during that period had dealt with some aspect of this problem.[12] It is remarkable that he stayed with it for as long as he did. He surely recognized that he had expended much valuable time on a search to which his gifts were not really suited. Hence the worry, "a worry the size of a mountain," weighing on his mind.

He persisted, surely, because his underlying argument—mass movements had animated societies by releasing pent-up energies—came from *The True Believer*.[13] Abandon this search, then, and his argument about the role of mass movements might collapse. He had referred to his new book as "vol. 2." His prolonged difficulty with that unwritten book was rooted in "vol. 1," on which his reputation was largely based. Later on, Hoffer was inclined to ignore and even to disparage mass movements.

There was another factor. The obvious answer to the question, "What drives people to work every day?" is that most have a family to support. Hoffer never seemed to give much weight to something so mundane. And perhaps that was because it didn't apply in his case. He had no wife and no debts, and his rent was as low as rents in San Francisco ever get. His expenses were minimal and his frugality ingrained. Pen, paper, and books from the public library were for him the key ingredients of contentment.

When book royalties and article fees started to come in—the *Saturday Evening Post* paid him $2,500 in 1961 for an article on human nature—he could probably have afforded to stop working as a longshoreman. He certainly needed his salary through the 1940s, at a time when he had no other income. After *The True Believer*, however, he probably could have survived without his longshoreman's pay. But he not only enjoyed his work on the docks, he derived considerable non-monetary benefits from it.

Image certainly played a role. His literary reputation was helped by the public knowledge that he was a working longshoreman. With his distinctive Filson jacket and his workingman's cap, he dressed the part and he continued to do so after he retired. Hoffer was a master of style, and his style was not just literary.

He wrote in 1952:

This food and shelter theory concerning man's effort is without insight. Our most persistent and spectacular efforts are concerned not with the preservation of what we are, but with the building up of an imaginary conception of ourselves in the opinion of others. The desire for praise is more imperative than the desire for food and shelter.

It is appropriate for a philosopher to say that, and one admires the clarity with which he says it. One sees also its unfashionable kernel of truth. But a man with a family and a mortgage might have had neither the time to think it through nor the confidence to write it down.

Slowing Down

The 1960s were a whirlwind decade for Hoffer—as they were for the country as a whole. By the early seventies he was beginning to slow down. But he remained productive, publishing four books. They were admittedly short, consisting of pieces that were also short (thirty-two of them in the case of *In Our Time*; 183 aphorisms in his ninety-seven-page *Reflections on the Human Condition*; nine essays in his 132-page *First Things, Last Things*). To an editor at Harper & Row who complained that his books should be longer he replied that they included original ideas in every essay—wasn't that enough? Hoffer's own editors were sometimes included in his campaign against prolixity.

His notebooks became more concrete and less given over to abstractions (such as "change," and man's energies). Influenced by his newspaper column and his Berkeley encounters, he focused more on current events. The notebooks also became more personal, telling an inside story about his fears for America and about his own health and mortality. "I know that I am going to die soon," he confided. "Yet I go about my daily tasks as if my life will never end. The mind shies away from certainties."

He told himself that he had earned the right to take it easy, but sitting up late reading a novel made him feel guilty. "Strange that when wasting my time doing nothing I have no feeling of guilt; but reading a novel is dissipation . . . I never know how to ration myself when reading a novel."

He was full of foreboding about America, but had no solutions. He still loathed the intellectuals and thought that racial integration wouldn't work. Still, it was unseemly to "go to the grave scolding the new generation." Work brought him short-lived contentment. But it became harder and harder to discipline himself to sit at his desk; he quickly ran out of words. Whatever he had to say he wanted to say "in few words and then stop." He recommended brevity for others. "We always use more words than are necessary when we try to say more than we know."

Writing well was a never-ending task. A related theme was often found in his notebooks: "What tires us most is work left undone." He kept insisting that he was not a writer, but to continue functioning he had to keep on writing:

> And I can write only when I have the confidence in my capacity to think and write. I can derive the confidence from an achievement. What is an achievement? You write something and somebody else says it is good, publishes it and pays you for it. My own judgment cannot be decisive, since I can easily fool myself.

By 1970, he reported, the 1950s had receded to an almost "archeological distance." "Read a book written about America in the late 1950s and it seems totally out of date. No one would now dream of saying that we are the hope of the world." The 1950s seemed like "a paradise of lost innocence"; America was surely in decline. He also saw reasons for believing that "Russia's day of judgment will come sometime in the 1990s." (The Soviet Union was always "Russia" in Hoffer's lexicon.) "And when the day comes everyone will wonder that few people foresaw the inevitability of the end."

Great dissatisfaction can nonetheless prevail in free societies. His reflection on this captured some of his best ideas:

He who feels that he is growing will feel free even in prison. A Tolstoy engaged in writing *War and Peace*, a Beethoven in the throes of composing the Ninth Symphony or the Missa Solemnis would feel free in a prison cell. Dostoyevsky said that one needs to believe in God when imprisoned. But the feeling of growth is more effective. Those who do not grow and do not do useful work do not know what to do with their freedom and are likely to feel miserable in a free society. The lust for power grows best in the souls of men who lack the endowment or the temperament to employ and realize talents.

Hoffer thrived in the marketplace, but like an eighteenth-century artist who never knew when he might need a patron, he also had an instinct to flatter those in power. Joseph Alioto, the mayor of San Francisco, was "a statesman philosopher." In a letter to Warren Burger, Hoffer praised something the chief justice had written as "the most lucid piece of writing I have laid eyes on in what seems a lifetime." He joined a Citizens for Humphrey Committee and met with the soon-to-be presidential candidate. Hubert Humphrey wrote, "It warmed my heart to see you looking so well." Lady Bird Johnson wrote, too, saying she was "thrilled you will be coming for the dedication of the [LBJ] Library."

He wrote to Richard Nixon several times. His notebooks showed that his immediate political judgment could be unreliable. Nixon's "place in history is secure," he wrote at the time of his second inaugural address. His "steadfastness and superb courage" are so conspicuous that even his enemies are "paying tribute." The Nixon haters "are almost unfailingly wrong in their forecasts."

He wrote to Nixon: "We pray to whatever Gods that be that you prevail over our enemies here and abroad. We also pray that you do not let Israel down." When Nixon was close to resigning Hoffer wrote:

There will be no peace in this land for decades. The journalists have had a taste of history-making and have become man-eating tigers. Life will become a succession of crises ... What will political life be like when history is made by journalists?

He was not just old but old-fashioned, he decided. He was "too crabbed and prejudiced" to write about the present, but he didn't want to write about anything else. "Surely the only problem worth tackling just now is: What has happened to this country during the past decade?" His pessimism came and receded in waves. "Things are crumbling everywhere," he wrote. But he was also aware of his disdain for what most journalists and publicists say. He found himself "full of reveries of murder. Anyone I dislike I want to kill and be done with. I catch myself machine-gunning masses of punks and their champions."

Books: His Own and Others

He allowed James Koerner to tape an interview for his forthcoming book on Hoffer, but he warned Koerner:

> Let me try to be as truthful as I can. I have not read Tomkins' book and I shall not read your book. Do not hesitate to wipe the floor with me. It is your book and you only have to please yourself. My feeling is that you are the least malicious person I have met in adult life. It is not good for me to see myself in the eyes of others. The taping was done to please you. I do like to shoot my mouth off and I do it once a week in Berkeley. Lili sends her love.

Hoffer's America was published in 1973.[14] Lili did read it, and she disliked it. Stacy Cole thought that Koerner had "captured Eric's temperament and his conversational style perfectly." It was, after all, a transcript of conversations that he had taped. But, Cole added:

> It caused a break with Lili, and to a lesser extent, with Eric. She was offended by the book and even Eric thought it should have

been edited so that he did not come off as savagely blunt and outspoken. I had mixed feelings about it, but thought that it effectively captured Eric as he was in his unguarded moments.

Hoffer worked on an anthology for Harper & Row, "Quotable Hoffer," which promised to be a "hefty book." Something very similar, *Between the Devil and the Dragon: The Best Essays and Aphorisms of Eric Hoffer*, was published in 1982, shortly before Hoffer's death.

By 1972 he had completed *Reflections on the Human Condition*. It was originally titled "Unfinished Man," but when another book with that title was announced the title was changed. Hoffer's new book consisted of reflections, mostly paragraph-length. This one explained Hoffer's original choice of title. It is one of Hoffer's greatest insights:

> Nature attains perfection, but man never does. There is a perfect ant, a perfect bee, but man is perpetually unfinished. He is both an unfinished animal and an unfinished man. It is this incurable unfinishedness which sets man apart from other living things. For in attempting to finish himself, man becomes a creator. Moreover, the incurable unfinishedness keeps man perpetually immature, perpetually capable of learning and growing.[15]

When Hoffer heard from Cass Canfield, an executive at Harper & Row, that the editors were enthusiastic about the new book it cheered him up to no end. But he couldn't "savor the originality of the text because of my long familiarity with it." And there was this: He was "getting weary of patching together ideas I have worked out long ago." It would be better to have something wholly new to work on. He also noted:

> I'll have to compose several more poems on death etc. if I am to include a collection of poems in Quotable. I have three fairly

good ones. There ought to be a dozen. My present mood is right for this sort of poems.

He looked back at the aphorisms he had composed for *The Passionate State of Mind* in the 1950s, but mostly they seemed flat. It was getting more difficult to write, but perhaps over the years his judgment had sharpened. Earlier, his language had been too labored. So there was a silver lining:

> It is actually comforting to discover that *The Passionate State of Mind* is not impressive. I wonder whether, with all the inevitable decline, there has been a line of development running through the seven books I have composed. I have become more savage but perhaps also more clearheaded.

"How rare it is that anything I read touches my heart," he marveled. Re-reading parts of *The Idiot* was exhilarating. But he hungered "for a piece of writing that is original, objective and lucid." Two contemporary writers did impress him. An article by George Gilder in *Commentary*, "In defense of Monogamy," was "one of the very best pieces of writing." Malcolm Muggeridge on the British social thinkers Sidney and Beatrice Webb was "as good writing as I know."

Hoffer was "beginning to realize how miraculous [is] the ability to stir minds to thought." The praise for his new book made him feel good for a moment. But the glow was speedily dissipated. His own creative flow had practically ceased. He found himself dipping into his *Ordeal of Change*—essays written in the 1950s—and realizing that he could no longer write like that. Still, a word of approval from someone whose judgment he valued had the power "to reconcile me with myself for a while." Elizabeth Lawrence's letter to him about his new book gave him deep satisfaction.

At Harper & Brothers she had handled *The True Believer* as its first editor in 1950. A quarter-century and many authors later, she told Hoffer that "by strange routes you have become one of the true professionals in the writing business, and it is a pleasure to work with you."

Hoffer found that he barely understood books by academics:

My mind is not attuned to vagueness, to artificial complexity, and to abstruseness. I can learn only from the lucid. I could never learn from [American economist Thorstein] Veblen, hard as I tried, whereas Tocqueville's profundity never gives me the least trouble. I want things spelled out, not hinted at, implied or evoked. And I don't mind repetitiveness.

The hour was late, but there were still some books to read.

Before I die I ought to read one book each of Rousseau, Marx and Freud. I doubt whether I would have the persistence. Still, I should have a mouthful of each. Without having read them I loathe all three. Yet they all wrote extremely well.

There are so many important books I have not read. I never, until today, laid eyes on *Das Kapital* and the *Interpretation of Dreams*. I have the two books on my table. Will they stir my weary mind? I shall only dip into them. It's beyond me to study two thick volumes. So far I have been getting along fairly well without them. I scorn Marx without having read him. He never did a day's work in his life and knew as much about the proletariat as I know about chorus girls. As to Freud: He lived all his life in the city of Vienna, a fairly compact city. Within Vienna there was the compact Jewish community, and within that community the compact Freud family. Freud was encased by a triple layer of compactness and wanted desperately to break out.

Freud was popular with the intellectuals because he catered to their instinct for self-dramatization. The one who is analyzed sees himself as "dealing with the intricate affairs of a state rather than with the paltry doings of a striving mortal."

In 1977 he had a deflating thought about writers and their modern influence:

> Will writers and artists be ever as important as they were during the Renaissance and the 1700s? You cannot see Presidents, prime ministers and heads of business corporations vying for the favor of an Erasmus, Voltaire and Diderot. Will ever men of power treat writers and artists as friends? The total elimination of superstitions and the belief in magic may have robbed writers and artists of some magical power they had over men's souls.

As a symptom of aging, he noted what many in retirement have reported: he felt hurried though no one was pursuing him. "Of course, I am not doing the one thing I ought to do and hence have no time for anything else." But he constantly felt pressed. "Hardly ever in my life have I been pressed for time. My sort of stuff is chewed on for months and written down in minutes."

> It is clear that I no longer talk with myself—no longer report to myself. I don't feel like noting the savage thought, the daily incidents—not even the books I read, the pictures I see and the people I meet. Why? Obviously I have come to the edge of life. Also my self esteem is very low. I am not worth bothering with.

> Logic and experience suggests that I won't live to see the end of the seventies, and this should make me light hearted. But it is clear to me that even to my last breath I shall not feel at ease unless I do what I must do.

Working on an essay about the old, he knew that "to function well the old need praise, deference, special treatment—even when they have not done anything to deserve it. Old age is not a rumor." The "disease of age is upon me." "We grow and died in quanta—in jumps. Now and then I can tell the day or even the hour at which a jump occurs." He quoted Tennyson as saying in his old age: "I am the greatest master of English who ever lived—and I have nothing to say." Reading a book on Ibsen, Hoffer became depressed.

> The helplessness of old age. I ought to have some capsules of cyanide. But I have the gun. I will not die a lingering death. I must also see about the trust fund.

Occasionally his morbid thoughts were lightened by a dash of humor:

> They say that on his deathbed Voltaire, asked to renounce the devil, said: "This is no time to be making new enemies."

Old age taught him "to take joy in the existence of beautiful and desirable things without wanting to possess or even savor them. I have not enjoyed the mere sight of beautiful women in the past as I do now."

A Measure of Contentment

He found contentment by lowering his sights. He didn't have "anything more to say, nor any problem to grip my mind." Still, it was good to be alive.

> The only temptation is novels and I manage to resist it. I read more than enough of newspapers and periodical literature to keep up with what's going on in the world. No money worries of any sort. I eat my food (two meals a day) with gusto. One drink a day helps. One page of manuscript a day is something I ought to be able to keep up.

Nov. 30, 1975: I have not spoken half a dozen sentences in two days. Yet I have no impulse to speak to people. Being alone is with me a normal condition. I have not taken a drink nor eaten an elaborate meal. In other words I didn't try to escape from being alone; I don't feel lonely. Still, I feel exhilarated when drinking, eating and talking with people.

He did not hunger for companionship. "Indeed, when I meet people and have to talk I tire easily and feel relieved when I am by myself again." Taking care of himself throughout his adult life had allowed him to have "a peaceful existence and [he] never hankered for anything better." He considered that to go on publishing "would be to write myself out of whatever favorable reputation I have as a writer." He recognized that his judgments were getting to be less balanced and true.

The best thing would be to stop worrying about his "inability to go on writing much. Is there no retirement from creating? Are those who have savored creative work condemned to eternal servitude? Does not the inner slave master grow weary too?"

Existence was bearable, "even if it is made up of common everyday activities, eating, talking with friends, reading no matter what, scribbling a paragraph." There was no need for uncommon deeds, lofty goals or noble dedication.

This talk of living a life of quiet desperation is the blown-up twaddle of juveniles and if it hits the mark it does so with empty people. I have no daemon in me; never had. There is a murderous savagery against people I have never met; a potential malice which is not realized because of a lack of social intercourse.

Disraeli felt that "nothing could compensate his obscure youth, not even a glorious old age." But Hoffer saw things differently. He wrote in 1977:

Practically all artists and writers are aware of their destiny and see themselves as actors in a fateful drama. With me, nothing is momentous: obscure youth, glorious old age, fateful coincidences—nothing really matters. I have written a few good sentences. I have kept free of delusions. I know I am going to die soon.

He reckoned that it should be possible to keep on writing "without any immediate prospect of publishing. But what one writes must be entertaining." Meanwhile, the people he loved "will remember me during their lifetime after I am gone. This is enough."

CHAPTER EIGHT

America and the Intellectuals

The intellectual will feel at home where an exclusive elite is in charge of affairs, and it matters not whether it be an elite of aristocrats, soldiers, merchants or intellectuals. He would prefer an elite that is culturally literate, but he will put up with one that is not. What he cannot endure is a society dominated by common people. There is nothing he loathes more than government of and by the people.

—ERIC HOFFER

quoted by Calvin Tomkins

Hoffer's hostile attitude toward what he called intellectuals is complicated, even contradictory. On the one hand, he admired well-educated, articulate people, corresponded with them, and wrote down hundreds of quotations from their books. On the other, he despised those he identified as "men of words" and expressed contempt for them and their followers.

In the usual sense of the word, Hoffer himself was an intellectual. He read books and wrote them. But he had no desire to teach others, he said, and this made him "a non-intellectual." For the intellectual is someone who "considers it his God-given right to tell others what to do."

What the intellectual craves in his innermost being is to turn the whole globe into a classroom and the world's population into a class of docile pupils hanging onto the words of the chosen teacher.

"Even in a union meeting of more or less unlearned longshoremen, I never have the feeling that I know best, that I could tell them what to do," Hoffer pleaded. He had faith in the competence of ordinary Americans to solve their own problems.

When it came to union business, certainly, Hoffer had no desire to instruct. Setting up the union's rules was of no interest to him— let Harry Bridges worry about such matters. Hoffer had no desire to challenge a system that let him stay home on days when he didn't feel like working and left him free to pursue his own thoughts when he did. Even as he steadied loads and hauled pallets on the waterfront, he liked to say, his mind could remain engaged by the article or book that he was writing in his head.

As for teaching: Hoffer was hired to show up in a Berkeley classroom once a week and tell students what was on his mind. In one sense, he was certainly an intellectual despite his denials. He demonstrated it in various ways, above all by his penchant for expressing ideas at the broadest level of generality—sometimes to the detriment of his writing.

He also showed his affinity with intellectuals by corresponding with them, including the sociologist Robert Nisbet; Harvard professor Daniel Bell; Nobel Prize laureate William Shockley; Democratic Senator Daniel Patrick Moynihan; and the educator and senator-to-be, S. I. Hayakawa. Another correspondent was the community organizer Saul Alinsky.

What he had in common with most of these writers, however, was not their intellectualism so much as their favorable disposition toward the United States at a time when an adversarial stance was on the rise. So "intellectual" in Hoffer's vocabulary should be qualified. It was intellectuals hostile to the structures of influence and power in the United States whom he detested.

One target was Herbert Marcuse, a Marxist political theorist who taught at Brandeis University. America suffered from "repressive tolerance," Marcuse believed, and many leftist radicals of the day (such as Abbie Hoffman and Angela Davis) admired him. Hoffer called Marcuse "a shabby would-be aristocrat."[1]

Two others were playwright Arthur Miller, who set out to denounce the Soviet invasion of Czechoslovakia but somehow ended up "denouncing America," and Jean Paul Sartre, who had demonstrated that intellectuals enjoy the privilege of being "scandalously asinine without harming their reputation."[2]

Hoffer made the same point about the political theorist Hannah Arendt, whom he met at Berkeley. They went on walks together and corresponded amicably. But in a late notebook he said that she "has been consistently wrong in her explanations and predictions, without incurring lasting damage either to her self confidence or to her reputation." He compared her unfavorably to her "unlearned mother," who "discovered America the first week she arrived." The learned Hannah, on the other hand, was "scribbling about the country's imperfections till the day she died."

He criticized British author Rebecca West's *The Meaning of Treason*[3] as "a hazy, poetical, metaphysical treatment of the fanatic; the language is cryptic because the idea is not clear." He was also highly critical of Noam Chomsky.

Among Hoffer's unwritten books, the most promising addressed intellectuals, those "men of words." He planned it, outlined it, mulled over it for decades, but in the end he didn't write it. "There is not going to be a book on the intellectual," he wrote. "This is certain." And yet, the role of the intellectual was closer to his heart than some of his earlier preoccupations, such as the release of man's energies or the problems of the underdeveloped world.

Hoffer at one point defined an intellectual "as one who saw himself as born to teach, lead and command"; later as "a literate person who feels himself a member of . . . an intellectual elite."[4] He began to develop these ideas even as he was writing *The True Believer*. Mass movements are generated by non-creative men of words, he believed. He outlined a book on intellectuals less than a year after

The True Believer came out and he never ceased reflecting on the type. Long after he decided that there would be no book, observations about alienated or adversarial intellectuals continued to flow from his pen.

He viewed them as a dangerous species. They scorn profit and worship power; they aim to make history, not money. Their abiding dissatisfaction is with "things as they are." They want to rule by coercion and yet retain our admiration. They see in the common criminal "a fellow militant in the effort to destroy the existing system." Societies where the common people are relatively prosperous displease them because intellectuals know that their leadership will be rejected in the absence of a widespread grievance. The cockiness and independence of common folk offend their aristocratic outlook. The free-market system renders their leadership superfluous. Their quest for influence and status is always uppermost.

> A free society is as much a threat to the intellectual's sense of worth as an automated economy is a threat to the worker's sense of worth. Any social order, however just and noble, which can function well with a minimum of leadership, will be anathema to the intellectual.

These ideas stayed with Hoffer until the end of his days. In America he saw Henry Adams, the grandson and great-grandson of presidents, as the prototype:

> Henry Adams simply loathed man—the vulgar creature. In the whole of the universe there were at most a thousand people worthy of life (about a dozen in the U.S.). Surely this is a case where simple envy and the treacherous craving for power have molded the whole intellectual life of an apparently gifted intellectual.

Intellectuals preach democracy, but insincerely. They support it only to oust disliked regimes. In practice, democracy might oblige them to submit to the low taste of the majority. They clamor for equality

but they neither want it nor believe in it. Egalitarian rhetoric nonetheless works to conceal their class-consciousness.

> The intellectual knows with every fiber of his being that all men
> are not equal, and there are few things he cares for less than a
> classless society. No matter how boundless and genuine the intel-
> lectual's altruism, he regards the common man as a means.

> Their temperament is aristocratic.

> My hunch is that for the typical intellectual it is a dull empty world
> where there are no longer genuine kings and real aristocrats and
> real castles and palaces. The intellectual's cast of mind is basically
> aristocratic and no matter how much he railed against kings and
> nobles they were the only people he really admired. This is true
> even when the intellectual is Karl Marx.

They disdain the masses, even as they enlist mass support for their
abiding cause: generating a sense of prevailing injustice. A year
before *The True Believer* was published, Hoffer argued that the intellectual "goes to the masses in search of a grievance." He is "in the
position of the shyster who looks around for a curse against someone he hates."

The intellectual regards the masses much as a colonial official views the natives. Hoffer thought it plausible that the British
Empire, by exporting many of its intellectuals, had played a counter-
revolutionary role at home. Employment and status abroad for a
large portion of the educated class may have "served as a preventive
of revolution."

He reckoned that there had been "a continuous revolt by the intellectual for the past 200 years," and it was "now coming to a head."
Hoffer continued:

> But the intellectual who expounded and wrote about this revolt
> invariably failed to give it its true name. He wrote about the revolt

of the middle class, the revolt of the masses, the revolt of the oppressed and exploited. He always saw himself as fighting other people's wars and bleeding for their sake.

By 1967, he was writing that "mass movements are the creation not of the masses, but of the intellectuals."[5]

All intellectuals are homesick for the Middle Ages, Hoffer wrote. It was "the El Dorado of the clerks"—a time when "the masses knew their place and did not trespass from their low estate." Intellectuals enjoyed their first taste of blood when they started the French Revolution. Writers and revolutionaries had a new sense of their power. "They knew that the world was vulnerable to the potency of thought and that they were the new makers of history."

But the nineteenth century had been a big disappointment. The workers had shown unwelcome signs of wanting to join rather than rebel against the bourgeoisie. The members of the intelligentsia, pushing too openly for revolution, had overplayed their hand and were discredited in the failed European revolutions of 1848. They didn't return to the stage of history until the Russian Revolution.

Unless they are consulted and flattered, Hoffer argued, intellectuals constitute a destabilizing force in society. When a prevailing order is discredited or overthrown, it is often "the deliberate work of men of words with a grievance."[6] Even a vigorous and meritorious regime is likely to be swept away if it fails to win the allegiance of the articulate minority. When we hear of widespread disaffection within a society it is really the intellectuals who are disaffected. On the other hand, where that minority lacks a grievance, the prevailing order—however incompetent or corrupt—is likely to remain in power.

The modern faith in education as the solution to society's ills had only made matters worse. Shortly before *The True Believer* was published, Hoffer noted that if it is true that "... the most rabid fanatic comes from among the non-creative men of words, then it is obvious that a spread of education and a reverence for creativeness is likely to multiply the number of those thwarted in their attempt to create."

Possibly, then, "the diffusion of literacy in the Western world . . . has created a reservoir of fanatics of the most virulent kind."

Educational efforts in Asia had kindled more resentments and grievances than solutions, he thought. "Many of the revolutionary leaders in India, China and Indonesia received their training in conservative Western institutions."

The Hunt for Status

The intellectual craves a status "above the common run of humanity," and as long as that status is acquired and held securely—as long as "he does not have to prove each day his right to a special position"—he is likely to be free of fanaticism. Astute leaders can often neutralize trouble-making intellectuals by the use of diplomacy and tactical grants of power.

Appealing to the concept of repression, Hoffer wrote that "nary an intellectual is aware of the true nature of his passions, fears, dedications and pet hatreds." He may see himself as the champion of the downtrodden, but "the grievance which animates him is, with very few exceptions, private and personal."[7]

What saddens the reformer is not sympathy with those in distress but his own "private ail." But such insights were not available to the intellectual, who "can never have a lucid conception of what it is that eats him and embitters him against the status quo."

He sees himself as born to teach, lead, and command:

> Where he is held in high honor and clothed in distinction, he will put up with a considerable amount of injustice to others and himself and will champion the prevailing dispensation. Where he is left out in the cold and is not taken seriously, let alone honored, he will deprecate, decry and defame every aspect of the existing

order. He will see his chief role as that of a critic and equate criticism with truth and moral courage.

Those who instruct others crave power and status, Hoffer argued. For centuries they lived off crumbs, often eking out a living. As teachers, they were treated as poor relations by boards of trustees. Their status remained low. But once their superior status is acknowledged, men of words will usually find "all kinds of lofty reasons for siding with the strong against the weak."

Hoffer pondered the role of universities and what he perceived as their less-than-impressive results in the realm of artistic creativity. Universities, he wrote,

> are organizations dominated wholly by intellectuals; yet, outside pure science, they have not been an optimal milieu for the unfolding of creative talents. In neither art, music, literature, technology and social theory and planning have the universities figured as originators and as seed-beds of new talents and energies.

He also believed that the intellectual "is not at his creative best in a wholly free society, where he is left to his own devices and allowed to say and do anything he pleases."

> To be left alone is to be ignored and the intellectual would rather be persecuted than ignored. Yet the creative intellectual needs a certain mode of freedom—the freedom to challenge and decry. An inefficient despotism that galls but does not crush gives the intellectual just grievances and leeway to protest.

Writers and artists who could not find fulfillment in creative achievement and who spurned the practical world were likely to form a "brotherhood of resentment [and] self dramatization."

A Book Outlined

Hoffer began to outline a book on the intellectuals in 1952. The first chapter would deal with literacy and its spread in the Western world ("it was the men of action: statesmen, businessmen and military men who spearheaded the spread of literacy. The Intellectuals were against it . . .") Chapter two, "the Literati," would encompass Egypt, the Phoenicians, China, the Jews, Greeks, Romans, Charlemagne, the Middle Ages, and the Renaissance. Chapter three would address "the anatomy of Intellectualism."

> It would be interesting to sketch the contempt of the intellectual for the masses through the ages. Quotations from the Egyptians, the Talmud and some Hindu writing. A beautiful thing might be made of "the Intellectuals," their origins and their proclivities and the various roles they play.

Only the critical success of *The True Believer* gave him the confidence to take on such a task. Experts could be expected to challenge him at every turn, but he was undaunted and he remained so three years later.

"The book to be written is 'The Man of Words,'" he wrote in 1955. It should concern itself with nothing less than "the nature of the intellectual through the ages and the role he played in cultural, social and political development"; a series of articles would later be expanded into chapters. The book would deal with "the genesis, proclivities, attitudes and reactions of the intellectual."

"This is definitely your subject," he reminded himself.

> You have the intellectual as a literate person, the intellectual as a courtier and time server, the intellectual as ecclesiastic, as a prophet, as a bureaucrat, as a philosopher, as a scientist, as a statesman, as a revolutionary, as an oppressor, as a Messiah and

so on. Then the relations between the intellectual and the aristocracy, the bourgeoisie and the masses.

By then he had written a substantial article, "The Intellectual and the Masses," reprinted in *The Ordeal of Change*. "The intellectual as a champion of the masses is a relatively recent phenomenon," he began. Today they must seek wide support for their ideas but in earlier centuries they preferred to monopolize literacy rather than disseminate it. But that monopoly had become ever more difficult to sustain, thanks to the printing press.

The first chapter of the new version of Hoffer's book would make that case; the second chapter would address "the peculiar attitudes of the ancient Hebrews" and the idea of a chosen people—something that he regarded as also peculiar to the intellectual. His ambition seemed unlimited. He would explore the invention of the alphabet, the spread of literacy, and beyond that:

> ... the role of the Hebrew Prophets; the mandarins, the Brahmins, the Phoenicians, the Greeks. [There would be] something too about the scribes and then finally the clerics. The information should be lucid and precise and all the instances should illustrate the tendency toward monopolization of the art of writing and its connection with the bureaucracy.

A year later, he proposed that his book would be about "the man of words in history, beginning with the invention of writing about 3000 B.C." He had no end of ideas on the subject.

A Book Offer

Beacon Press in Boston offered Hoffer a $3,000 advance to write a "small book" on intellectuals, reminding him that he had briefly outlined it in an article for the magazine *The New Leader*. Titled "A Future for Intellectuals," it was reprinted as "Deeds and Words" in

The Ordeal of Change. Here, Hoffer said that in the Western world intellectuals had lost power compared to their glory days in ancient Egypt, imperial China, or medieval Europe. Now, embedded in the market order, they were considered no better than poor relations and had to pick up the crumbs. But they had come into their own in the Communist world. Even when they were free to travel beyond the Iron Curtain, Soviet bloc intellectuals rarely took advantage of the opportunity to escape.

> However much they abominate the crudity and cruelty of a Stalinist regime they realize it is a regime run and dominated by the intellectual. A Communist regime is a government of an elite by an elite for an elite.

In modern times, Hoffer wrote, Communist regimes called upon intellectuals to shoulder the most difficult tasks and exercise unlimited authority. In planned economies, after all, planning took precedence over action and intellectuals were the planners.

> Lenin predicted that when the intellectual had done his work the masses will manage to get along without intellectuals. What happened? The intellectuals have made common cause with the communist exploiters; and the masses must manage by themselves.

The overall influence of Communism was due less to its new doctrines than to the entry of intellectuals into the economic, political, and military fields, Hoffer thought. "During the past 50 years intellectuals, particularly schoolmasters, have taken possession of half the world, turned it into a vast schoolroom and reduced whole populations to the status of children and juveniles," he wrote in a 1961 notebook.

Sometimes, to be sure, intellectuals in Russia were imprisoned or worse, but that was a small price to pay. They wanted to be taken seriously and "treated as a decisive force in shaping history." They "would rather be persecuted than ignored"—the latter being their fate in the United States of the 1950s.

In 1957 Hoffer read in *People's World* (published by the Communist Party U.S.A. and available on the waterfront) that a writer called Michael Gold "exults that the poet Ginsberg is harried by the cops." Such a "compliment hasn't been paid to an American poet since Walt Whitman was fired from his job," Gold wrote. Nixon's enemies' list provoked a similar reaction among the intelligentsia fifteen years later.

Later, with reports from the Gulag, enlightened opinion began to take the problems of Communism more seriously. In fact, intellectuals soon felt "disgruntled and disaffected both in capitalist and Communist countries."

> Our intellectuals writhe with loathing at the sound, sight and smell of an America that leaves them alone to say, write and act as they please. At the same time, the events in Czechoslovakia and the Solzhenitsyn affair have revealed the predicament of the intellectuals in Communist society. It is true that the Russian Osip Mandelstam, hounded and starved by Stalin, still sarcastically gloried in the fact that his persecutors had a boundless, almost superstitious respect for poetry. "Why do you complain?" he teased his wife. "Poetry is respected in this country—people are killed for it." But he did not enjoy his martyrdom.

A short book on the subject was exactly what suited Hoffer's temperament. But he turned down the Beacon Press offer because he disliked the "yoke of promise." Instead, he made his task still more encyclopedic and therefore less manageable. On the history of scribes, those copiers of manuscripts before the invention of printing, for example, he aimed to establish:

> "The mentality of the scribe: his penchant for status, his fear of manual labor, his tendency towards exclusiveness even to the

extent of making of writing and of the very language a mystery open only to the initiated. You have to trace the origins of each of these traits and indicate its presence not only in Egypt, China, Greece and the Middle Ages, but even today."

He saw that the intelligentsia enjoy a key advantage compared to earlier social classes: it is always open to new membership.

One of the reasons that an elite of intellectuals is singularly endur- ing is that it is open. In a society ruled by intellectuals the school and the hurdles of examinations are a clearly marked road to exclusiveness and privilege. No such clearly marked and routin- ized road to privilege is present in societies dominated by elites of birth or of money.

He said something in 1957 about his proposed book in a letter to an unidentified correspondent named Josine:

It'll be difficult for me to say anything about the intellectual with- out seeming crude. My ideas on the subject are simple. It is the role of the intellectual to create—in literature, art, science and whatnot. It is his job to think, theorize, criticize, dream, inspire, warn and so on. It is not his job to act, command and lead. When philosophers become kings it fares ill with the common people, and with the philosophers.

In the end Hoffer was overwhelmed. His hunches and guesses would be enough for a chapter but not for a book. He had decided by then that it could not be a scholarly history, and he believed his own insights were not enough. "Obviously, the intellectual would have to be part of a larger subject."

By the 1960s, however, Hoffer really did have his larger subject, and it dovetailed perfectly with his concerns about intellectuals.

He had already seen that the homelessness of the intellectual was evident across all Western societies, but it was nowhere more pronounced than in our own common-man civilization. America had been running its economy, its machinery of government, and most of its cultural needs without the aid of the typical intellectual. "Nowhere has the intellectual so little say in the management of affairs." It was natural, therefore, that the intellectuals outside the United States "should see in the spread of Americanization a threat not only to their influence but to their very existence."[8]

Intellectuals had long managed to thrive in societies dominated by aristocrats or merchants, "but not in societies bearing the imprint of the tastes and values of the masses." What galled intellectuals everywhere was not so much the dominance of business. The problem was that America had become home to "a genuine mass civilization—the only one that ever existed."

The "Americanization of the world is an almost unprecedented phenomenon," he wrote a few years later. As a rule, such penetration of outside influence into a society "depends upon the receptivity of the educated or the well to do." Yet something new was happening.

> The worldwide diffusion of American attitudes, tastes and habits is taking place in the teeth of the shrill protests of the intellectuals and the hostility of the better people. The only analogy which comes to mind is the easy spread of Christianity with the difference that the Americanization is not promoted by dedicated apostles and missionaries, but like some powerful chemical reagent penetrating of its own accord.

Here, then, was his larger subject. America in the post-war period was leading the world in a new and unexpected direction. It was creating a "genuine mass civilization." And in so doing it was undermining the position and status of intellectuals everywhere. Henceforth, Hoffer would champion America at every opportunity.

America His Cause

As early as 1953, Hoffer composed an American manifesto, a "revolutionary doctrine that America could propagate." It was "unlike any other doctrine ever preached." Hoffer evidently had been thinking about these matters for years.

> It is the doctrine of individual revolt against any form of tutelage and direction, against bureaucratic meddling; against do's and don'ts propounded from above. The individual on his own, who has shaken off his masters who rode, goaded and guided him from immemorial time—kings, priests, prophets, aristocrats, intellectuals, managers and bureaucrats. The common man inarticulate, unrefined, uncultured, undoctrinaire—the common man whom God filled the Earth with.
>
> This is our pride and our doctrine—the common man on his own who mastered and won this vast continent; who dared more and accomplished more than any king or any chosen one ever dared or accomplished; who needs no King or Hitler or Stalin to build his roads, his dams, his factories, his schools, his playfields, parks and pleasure houses. Here, for the first time in history the common man knew the taste of real freedom and not the counterfeit and illusory freedom of other countries. It is a difficult doctrine to preach, and perhaps the most subversive.

Intellectuals at home began to take aim at America and before long were sounding as antagonistic as those abroad. Hoffer worried that if they were to assume power in the United States, as he believed they had done in the Communist world and, more recently, in the developing countries of Asia and Africa, it would not bode well for the world.

> The militant intellectual is profoundly convinced of the dullness, narrowness, selfishness, vulgarity and dishonesty of the common

man. Never before in America had so many among the educated had so low an opinion of the lowbrows, and never before had their elitist conceit been flaunted so openly.

An increasing number of gifted people in the United States were working overtime "and with passionate absorption to find reasons to dislike their country." "Whence comes this passion?" he wondered. He could not understand "the pleasure some people derive from hating this country and praying for its ruin."

> Earlier in the 19th century there was a Russian who wrote "how sweet it is to hate one's country." I have not had the love of America inculcated in me from childhood. Yet it seems that most of my adult life I have worried more about the country than about myself.

The military draft and then what he called "the Vietnam debacle" played important roles, of course, especially on campuses. To make matters worse, America's adversaries were crowing.

> The professors and their hangers-on are preparing their funeral orations. America is to be buried. It is becoming crystal clear that America has never been a good country for the 'educated'; for people who want to live important lives but lack the talent ... America has also not been exceptionally good for the rich. Right now it is only the common people who grieve about America; who want to keep it unchanged.

Reagan's blue-collar Democrats would bear him out, but that was still a decade off. In 1970 Hoffer reflected how far removed the common people's reaction was from the vision of the future that progressives held in the 1930s.

> As recently as 30 years ago it was generally assumed that the disintegration of the middle class would be followed by the rise

of the masses. Hardly anyone has seen that the nemesis of the middle classes would be the alienated intellectual, members of the middle class, rather than the masses. And how many have foreseen that the middle class during its prolonged decline would absorb most of the workingmen who made up the core of the masses and that the fall of the middle class would also be the fall of the masses.

The Sixties at Berkeley

From his vantage point on campus, Hoffer was not just well placed to observe the sixties close up, but—overlooking Sproul Plaza—was practically in the eye of the storm. In fact, he was far too close to take the detached view that was his preferred vantage point on any topic.

"Sitting in my cubicle high up in Barrows Hall every Wednesday afternoon," he wrote one day, "I feel a foreign world, wholly non-American, flowing and ebbing below me—a crummy, shoddy world." He wondered: What would America have been like if only college graduates had been allowed to enter the country? It didn't bear thinking about.

At times he thirsted for vengeance:

> Let us immediately do unto them what they say they will eventually do unto us. They want to be listened to and taken seriously—let's do it. They preach violence against us; let's practice violence against them. Let their words condemn them.

Once, limping along with a pinched sciatic nerve and one more peace demonstration blocking his path, his fury boiled over.

> May 11, 1972 10:30 a.m. I am aware of a reluctance to write down the things that happen and the musings that float through the mind. It is a moment of crisis in Vietnam (Nixon's mining of Vietnam waters) and inside the U.S. (the riots in Berkeley and

elsewhere, the abdication of police and city governments). It is a moment of crisis for me (with the continuous deterioration of the right side of the body). My savagery is becoming pathological. Every time I open my mouth I advocate killing and actually mean it. My reveries [are] about throwing hand grenades and bombs at the rioters—of shooting and hanging.

11:45 p.m. I was caught in the midst of the anti-war demonstration about 2 p.m. They blocked the street and I had to get off the bus and drag my lame leg. The police acted tamely. Instead of urging the buses to ram their way through the few punks who blocked the street, the police stopped the traffic. The bystanders, many of them boiling with rage against the demonstrators, did not lift a finger. I told one punk who tried to give me a leaflet to stick it up his ass . . . The police and the courts are a joke. There is no law. The majority is paralyzed. The extra walking brought a tearing pain so that by the time Lili came to get me I could barely walk. I was in an ugly mood, consumed with rage.

Notebook entries more or less bracketing his time at Berkeley showed him in a more dispassionate mood.

"Idealistic movements gather force only when they are anti-American," he wrote in 1965. It was becoming clearer every day "that the intellectual's militancy can be aroused only by antagonism to America." By 1972, he argued that his own "preoccupation with America didn't start until the 1960s when America came under attack by the intellectuals."

He had by then become what is now called a neoconservative, although occasionally he viewed these events from a more traditional perspective. In 1969, for example, we find him in unusual if short-lived alliance with his adversaries:

The obvious truth of course is that America is becoming un-American. It is un-American for America to become a world power, to have a large mass army, to have bases all over the globe, to tax its people to the utmost, to exalt men of words above men of action. The recent youth movement is un-American. When the American government engages in un-American practices its people begin to react and act in an un-American way.

A Single Theme

America and the intellectuals became the two poles of a single and absorbing theme. The more the attacks on America mounted, the more his advocacy of the country increased. Hoffer had the book that many publishers would have welcomed. The enduring obstacle to its completion was his commitment to unearthing the origin or genesis of intellectuals and their role through the ages. Such an effort would have intimidated the most ambitious of scholars. Probably the book could only have been written as a polemic, presenting the intellectual as a class broadly antagonistic to the United States.

He wrote a few essays along these lines. In *The Temper of Our Time* (1967) he restated a few favorite themes: that the intellectuals' temperament is aristocratic; that they would rather be persecuted than ignored; that America's "mass civilization" was their true target.

In a later book, *In Our Time* (1976), he argued that in Weimar Germany the blind hatred of the adversary intellectual had played into Hitler's hands. One repentant Weimar intellectual, Kurt Tucholsky, had fled to Sweden, and only in exile realized "the enormity of what he and his like had done to undermine Germany's first democratic society."[9] When the intellectuals had done their work in the 1930s, "Weimar Germany could not defend itself against the wreckers—the Communists and the Nazis."

In the United States, meanwhile, alienated intellectuals lacked an "organized revolutionary force," and this deprived them of the apocalyptic denouement that they desired. But the confidence of America's defenders had nonetheless been weakened. The country had lost its nerve. He regarded the "salons of Manhattan and Washington" as imposing their unwritten edicts on almost everyone. Nowhere was there "such a measureless loathing of their country by educated people as in America." They want America to be "not a melting pot but a seething cauldron."

It was no longer his world, and it was unseemly that he go to the grave scolding the new generation, he decided. But "the middle and lower class who do most of the work and pay most of the taxes are without a voice."

> The intellectuals are wailing that they are without honors in America. But has not America been without honors among the intellectuals?

He could still be optimistic:

> When America pulls through and revives its national pride there will be a flexing of muscles that will jar the new world from the North Pole to the South.

"This is a mighty oak of a nation," he wrote in 1976 at the time of the bicentennial, when earlier passions had cooled. It needs "the earth for its roots and heaven for its branches."

Hoffer had placed the problem of the alienated intellectual in an impressively broad canvas. Above all, he saw that the new American civilization had reduced the intelligentsia to a minor role.

In his last press interview, in February 1981, Hoffer discussed the problem in a historical context.[10] Franklin D. Roosevelt had now become his key villain. He told a freelance writer, Gene Griessman, that "we are the only real mass civilization that has ever existed":

> EH: We have all the virtues and defects of the mass. America is a nation that has run on morals, almost independent of its leaders

or Congress. For a long time America almost didn't need a government. People from all over the world came here, worked hard and made America work. [The government] almost ran itself until Roosevelt. The best way to measure the vigor of a society is by its ability to run well without outstanding leaders.

GG: You said "until Roosevelt."

EH: Today America is becoming just like Europe. I was born with this century. I've seen a fundamental change occur in America. America isn't the same nation it was even 20 years ago. The Roosevelt administration brought about the change. You can divide American history into B.R. and A.R.—before Roosevelt and after Roosevelt.

GG: What do you mean?

EH: Roosevelt didn't understand what America is all about. He appointed judges who changed the Constitution, and he was surrounded by intellectuals and other nincompoops.

GG: What did Roosevelt change?

EH: Before Roosevelt, if a man failed he blamed himself. After Roosevelt, a man who fails blames the government, society or somebody else. The idea of work is gone. Today we are just like Britain. Had Hoover been re-elected, America would have continued to be unique.

CHAPTER NINE

God, Jehovah, and the Jews

*The most awful thing that could happen would
be to discover that God really exists.*

—ERIC HOFFER, *1954*

Eric Hoffer said that he subscribed to no faith or creed and that God was a human invention. Yet, he devoted a significant amount of time and effort to questions about God and religion. Predominantly, his interest was in the fate of the Jews.

Lili Osborne's son Eric as a youth marveled at the contradiction that Hoffer said he was an atheist but was always talking about God. He also remarked that he "wouldn't be surprised if Hoffer had Jewish blood."

Eric Osborne recalled one humorous incident: "Once Eric Hoffer was talking and a rabbi was in the audience; or maybe Hoffer was talking to a bunch of rabbis, and he was telling them that there is no God. One rabbi said, 'Mr. Hoffer, there is no God and you are His prophet.'"[1]

Was Hoffer Jewish? Details of his early life are so meager that no definite conclusion can be reached. Nonetheless, some details of his life raise the possibility that he was a non-practicing Jew. Lili recalled that when Hoffer completed the manuscript of *The True Believer* he took it to Rabbi Saul White of Congregation Beth Sholom in San

Francisco and asked him to say if there was anything (in Lili's word) "non-kosher" in it. She said that Hoffer "received a response that he should proceed."[2]

Hoffer said that he grew up in a flat with a hundred or more books. In Hoffer's account, his father brought them with him from Europe—unusual baggage for an immigrant artisan in the 1890s. Another possibility is that Hoffer indeed did grow up in a house with books and bookcases, as he said, but that this early home was in Europe, not the Bronx.

Hoffer was often invited to speak at Jewish events and there was nothing he enjoyed more than a discussion with a group of rabbis. A relative of Norman Jacobson's gave Hoffer two yarmulkas. Among his effects at his death was a prayer shawl, probably given to him by one of the groups that invited him to speak. But in the late 1950s he wrote that "never in all my life have I prayed."[3]

Selden Osborne's old friend from Pescadero, Joe Gladstone, himself a Jew and "one hundred percent atheist," said he did not think that Hoffer was Jewish but certainly was "Judeophile."

Supporting this description are Hoffer's knowledge of Hebrew, his conspicuous omission of Judaism from his list of religions that inspire fanaticism, his pre-publication submission of *The True Believer* to a rabbi, his frequent references to Jehovah, and his growing and overriding concern about the fate of Israel.

Asked if he believed in God, Hoffer would say that he subscribed to no faith or creed. Yet he continued to ponder the nature of God. It was speculation without faith—more philosophy than religion—but it was never far from his mind. In his notebooks he often wrote as though God was a reality whether he believed in Him or not. And he did (sometimes) capitalize the pronoun.

"He never spoke about being a believer or a non-believer," said Lili Osborne. "But God was a part of his life. The Old Testament was always real to him." He enjoyed the company of Lili's mother, Giacinta Fabilli, a devout Catholic who lived into her nineties. "They used to sit and discuss Old Testament characters such as Solomon and David as though they both knew them," Lili recalled.

Eric Osborne said, "Giacinta and Eric Hoffer were close, and he really listened to her. She was a tribal Italian gal from the Apennines. She would pray for somebody nonstop, and it was the old faith, the kind you don't see in Christianity any more. He valued her prayers. It wasn't spoken, but it was there."

Once Giacinta wrote Hoffer a letter (in Italian) after watching him on television. We "appreciate all that you say," she wrote. But "the best is lacking to make you more appreciated." She continued, "Do you know what is lacking? Faith in God is missing—that God who created you, and redeemed you with his precious blood . . . You are in debt to him, and you should acknowledge, praise and thank Him. It is a great mistake that an intelligent person with a charitable heart like you should lose yourself."[4]

"Faith" was missing, certainly, but God—whom Hoffer increasingly referred to as Jehovah—was somehow a reality. Saying that Hoffer was an atheist puts the case too strongly. "The atheist is a religious person," Hoffer himself wrote in *The True Believer*. "He believes in atheism as though it were a new religion."[5] Hoffer more closely resembled a non-believing theologian whose speculations about God were based on reason and inspiration, not revelation. He seemed to regard such speculation as a basic task of philosophy.

He rarely mentioned Jesus and did not accept his divinity. "The presentation of Jesus as a son of God was a device to blur the reality of Jesus the son of a Jew," he wrote. He liked to contrast the Old Testament prophets (elitists) with Jesus' disciples (working-class people), but that was a rare point in the Christians' favor.

In *The True Believer* he more or less wrote off Christianity as just another mass movement. The question of its truth or falsity didn't arise. The true believer attracted to Christianity might as easily have been drawn to something else, Communism for example.

The fanaticism animating these movements "may be viewed and treated as one."[6] At that stage he seemed to dismiss all religion as the delusion of true believers. But as the years passed he became more interested in religion, and more supportive of it.

Judaism was omitted from unflattering comparisons. His notebooks show that the Jews were never far from his thoughts, especially with the rebirth of Israel a current event as *The True Believer* was written. As the years passed he became more and more concerned about Israel's fate.

In 1974, Hoffer attended the Nuptial Mass of Lili's son Stephen Osborne to Beatrice Jonama. At Lili's request, Hoffer sat next to Lili's older sister, Mary Fabilli, who worked for years at the Oakland Museum. She was briefly married to William Everson, a poet of the Beat Generation who was known as Brother Antoninus while a member of the Dominican Order. In later years her Catholicism became more focused on the Latin Mass and the traditional doctrines that she had absorbed from her mother. Her relationship with Hoffer was difficult, as her unconcealed goal was to convert him to Roman Catholicism.

Mary and Eric "would disagree about God in a way that could not be resolved," Lili recalled.

Mary recalled that she would sometimes object to Eric's ideas about God, "but he would crush me and get angry with me for disagreeing with him. It was impossible to argue with him." She thought he was "anti-Christian to a certain extent." He had "no understanding of Christ and I thought that was very sad." However, Eric "loved the Old Testament," and he loved discussing it with her mother. "But he thought it was written by man, not by God. He thought it was a great book, but human."

At Stephen's wedding, Lili wanted Mary to explain the Mass to Hoffer. But Mary knew by then that liturgical details would not interest him. They sat next to one another, and throughout the service Hoffer "kept up a running commentary on irrelevant things."

Then he said something that made Mary laugh. "If I ever came to believe in God I would commit suicide," Hoffer said.[7]

She marveled at this illogical remark from one normally so logical. "As though committing suicide would get him away from God's attention," she said.

Hoffer clearly saw the contradiction. In a notebook he had questioned whether belief in God was wishful thinking, as Freud and others claimed. Do we really welcome the idea of an omniscient deity minutely scrutinizing our lives? As a possibility, Hoffer considered it to be more discomforting than hopeful.

"The most awful thing that could happen would be to discover that God really exists," he wrote. An omniscient God would know our secrets. Therefore, "to those who believe in God and a hereafter there is no escape from the scheme of things. They are eternally trapped." Suicide offered no escape. He thought that more overpowering than any discovery in outer space "would be the discovery that there really is a God." Hoffer sometimes went with Lili to have dinner with Giacinta and her son Albert, who for a while was a brother at the Trappist Gethsemani Abbey in Kentucky. Later he returned to California to live with his mother (at her request). Describing the scene at the house one evening, Hoffer said that "the mother, brother and sister Mary seemed to me like tourists packed up for a journey to a fabulous beyond. Life on this earth is a preliminary—like waiting in a railroad station."

Jehovah and the Jews

Hoffer said his interest in the Jews began when he read the Old Testament in the 1920s. "Reading the Old Testament for the First Time" is among his early manuscripts in the Hoover Archives; a close paraphrase was published in *Truth Imagined*.[8] Hoffer's father had been a "small town atheist," he said, and until the 1920s Hoffer had not read one sentence of the text of the Old Testament. When he did, he was unprepared for its grandeur and its freshness.

Just as the scientific mind gives equal attention to the movements of the stars and the efforts of a worm, he wrote, so here "a primitive mind" sets out to find the whys and wherefores of the skies: love and death, the enmity between the man and the snake, the need to work.

> So absorbed were they in the reality of this world that ancient Jews gave no thought to a hereafter; no blessing exceeded life on this earth. The greatest reward was to have one's life prolonged. Not one word about a future life. "As the cloud is consumed and vanishes away, so he that goes down to the grave shall come up no more." (Job 7:9) "Man lies down and rises not till the heavens be no more, they shall not awake, nor be raised out of their sleep." (Job 14:12)[9]

The faith of the ancient Jews in an abstract God was joined with "a vivid expectation of a millennium," Hoffer wrote. "The Jews, perhaps alone among all ancient peoples, had faith in the future and expected it to surpass present and past."

Hoffer sketched out many of his ideas in an unpublished article called "Jehovah and the Occident." In it, he wrote that a case could be made that "the Jews were the first Occidentals." He said they invented the division between kings and prophets, between the Pharisees and the secular power. This created a tension that "stretched Occidental souls." With the destruction of the Second Temple and the birth of Christianity, Hebraic influence then moved west, and penetrated Europe directly.

The Jews were also the first to proclaim a clear-cut separation between Man and Nature. In other civilizations they were united. "The whole structure of magic was founded on the assumption of an identity between human nature and nature." It was "Jehovah's injunction to subdue the Earth" that had sustained the American pioneers in their attempts to tame a savage continent.

"The one and only God created both nature and Man, yet made man in his own image and appointed him his viceroy on Earth,"

Hoffer wrote. Nature thereby lost its divine attributes. "To us in the West nature is not the image of God but his handiwork." And "our cocky attitude toward nature has its roots in the downgrading of nature by the ancient Hebrews."

In this article, Hoffer attributed key developments in Western culture—science among them—to the Jewish spirit. His views on this and related issues to some extent echoed arguments made by his contemporary, the German-born Jewish philosopher Leo Strauss. Like Strauss, Hoffer believed that politics in America was threatening to recreate the avant-garde experimentation and assault on traditional values that had prevailed in the Weimar Republic after 1919. Demoralized by hyperinflation and cultural iconoclasm, some Germans saw Hitler as the antidote.

Although Hoffer submitted "Jehovah and the Occident" to an editor as late as 1980, it was never published. Possibly it was considered too similar to an earlier article, "Jehovah and the Machine Age," published in *The Ordeal of Change*.[10] In the later, unpublished version his argument was "Judaized." He wrote in a 1967 notebook that the Judaic religion had eliminated nature as a source of mysterious powers:

> My conviction is that this elimination of the awe of nature was
> a precondition for the rise of the Occident's science and religion
> and the resulting unprecedented mastering of nature. This simple
> statement is not found in [German psychiatrist Karl] Jaspers'
> books and in any of the books dealing with the ongoing of the
> West's technology and science.

The Death of God

Hoffer early on discussed the decline of religious faith in the West and wondered what lessons could be drawn from it. Faith in the future had also waned and nations had set themselves up as substitute idols. As to the Nietzschean claim about the death of God, he wrote in an early notebook (1950) that "God died sometime in the 19th century," and that it should be possible to fix the date:

> It is since then that people in the Christian world have become terribly serious about their politics, their ideologies and their bank accounts. I doubt whether the Pope himself really believes in God. What I am driving at is that Godly religion is no longer a formidable force. If Catholicism exerts influence, it does so as a political and economic organization. The only living religions at present are nationalism and Communism, and only the latter, because of its universality, can substitute an integrating force for Christianity.

In a simultaneous letter (written a few months before *The True Believer* was published) he argued:

> Like other nations, we lack a universal faith. Were Catholicism a living faith, it could do the job. It could convert Japan, and generate in the Japanese the feeling that they are part of Christian humanity. However, no Godly religion is any longer a formidable force. God died sometime in the 19th century . . .

He was influenced by Max Weber's *The Protestant Ethic and the Spirit of Capitalism*, but that was more in the context of his ideas about "the release of man's energies." The Reformation had brought about such a release. Protestant societies had been energized and individualism then became a substitute for God. He kept returning to the idea:

> A century or so ago, when a Jew lost faith in Jehovah he became more or less a gentile. When the gentile lost his faith in God he could not become anything. His only way out was to substitute himself for God. Thus loss of faith can become a potent factor in the release of individual energies when the alternative of becoming "something else" is restricted.

Where faith flows into the official canals of a church it cannot penetrate into practical affairs. It is only the faith that flows through a myriad of rivulets of individual lives that can energize everyday affairs. The Reformation made every individual a priest and every family a church. The personal God with whom one can commune is undoubtedly a potent factor in the release of individual energies. And yet you have societies with a personal God, yet stagnant in the economic and political fields.

It was a weakening of the Christian faith which marked the birth of our present civilization . . . It is this rejection and usurpation of a once ardently worshipped God which has had fateful effects on society and the individual in the modern Occident.

In the 1950s a correspondent asked Hoffer what he thought about God. His reply conveyed an agnosticism that was genuine and an indifference that by then was fading:

I do not know the least thing about God—whether he is good or bad or whether he exists, etc. He never worried me one way or the other. Nor is it in my nature to advocate aught. My curiosity is concerned with connections. Why did not the Chinese and the Hindus and of course the Greeks develop a machine age? . . . How did the modern Occident originate? I am no scholar and no authority. I speculate as I please. It is good to play with ideas.

By now he was writing more frequently about God, and "in rare moments," he wrote later, he had "an inkling of what it meant to have a real belief in God."

There is probably not one person in the whole world at present who really has such a belief. Two hundred years ago there were many, both great and small—and what an enormous role did such a belief play in human affairs.

He conveyed a sense of disquiet at the decline of faith, not because it was something that might benefit him personally but because society needed it. He was critical of the changes instituted by the Second Vatican Council during the 1960s, which he thought were more likely to weaken the Catholic Church than to benefit it. He also became more doubtful about some of the familiar atheistic claims:

> Sometimes you think how much of a better world it would be if Judaism, Christianity and Islam with their driving vehemence had never happened. Then you think of all the misery and boundless cruelty practiced in lands that never heard of Jehovah, his son and his messenger.

In one respect he became anti-Nietzschean. Nietzsche considered Christianity to be a slave religion, because it praised weakness as a virtue. Nietzsche blamed St. Paul and touted the Übermensch, or superman, as a superior faith. But Hoffer saw "the survival of the weak" as a great feature of the Western world, and for this we had Judaism to thank. "It is by the grace of the Jews that the weak survive," he wrote, "for it is by the grace of the Jews that we made the tremendous discovery of faith."

> We hardly see things as they really are when we view man as a mere animal. In the human species, unlike the pattern which seems to prevail in the rest of life, the weak not only manage to survive but develop capacities and talents which enable them to triumph over the strong. There is a sober realism in St. Paul's stilted words that "God hath chosen the weak things of the world to confound the things that are mighty."

By 1971 Hoffer believed that the decline of faith in the Western world had come with a high price. It might bring about the very slavery that Nietzsche thought Christianity had welcomed:

They are terrible times when people have an intense feeling that they have only one life to live, that once you are dead you are dead forever, and that the living dog hath it better than the dead lion. Such an age may eventually end in slavery.

Some Thoughts on God

Hoffer's thoughts about God were dispensed at random, but he never tired of the subject. In the early 1950s he wondered how "the religious impulse" had originated, and decided that it involved an "escape from the lonesomeness, the burdens and the transitoriness of an individual existence." In fact, anything that separates us "from ourself is of a religious nature. And how strange indeed is this dissatisfaction with the self and the devices used to escape it."

"Man needed God so desperately because he felt so terribly alone," he wrote. "It is fearfully simple":

> The incomplete individual cannot stand on his own, cannot make sense by himself. He is a part and not a self-sufficient whole. He can make sense, have a purpose and seem useful when he becomes part of a functioning whole.

Man was lonely, but maybe God was lonely, too. Possibly, "God created man out of loneliness—he created man in his own image to have his equals to argue with, punish and reward. He created them in his image to be creators." He also liked the idea that "God created man to be reverenced and prayed to by them." God wanted us to depend on Him:

> It is highly questionable whether God approved the invention of agriculture, which reduced man's dependence on providence. God sent thistles and thorns, pests and droughts to make the farmer's lot less secure and the necessities to pray and supplicate

more imperative. He did all he could to give the quality of a curse to the blessing of domestication.

Hoffer closely followed developments in the Soviet Union. Shortly before the death of Stalin he saw a parallel between "our conception of an Almighty who is the seat and source of all power" and the Soviet dictator. Perhaps in truth we visualize "an implacable enemy rather than a friendly protector."

> Men loved God the way the Russians loved Stalin. Only by convincing ourselves that we really and truly love an all-powerful and all-seeing enemy can we be sure of never betraying ourselves even by a word or gesture.[11]

> Those who managed to live under Stalin should find it easy to live in a world dominated by an omnipresent, all-seeing God. The return to God of some ex-Stalinists is not at all anomalous.

Is God really all-powerful? Hoffer wondered about that, too. "If absolute power corrupts, then God must be absolutely corrupted." What is certain is that when man tries to be all powerful he becomes not just corrupted but an anti-God. To be like God is to have absolute power, but in human hands absolute power is an instrument of dehumanization.

> You savor absolute power not by moving mountains or telling rivers whither to flow but by commanding people and making them do your will—by turning human beings into unresisting, pliable matter. In the hands of a God absolute power is creative; it turns clay into man. But absolute power turns a man into an anti-God—it turns a man into clay.

> God automated the whole of creation but did not succeed in fully automating man—his runaway experiment in creation. It

is significant therefore that the Hitlers and Stalins should strive above all to automate man and thereby prove their superior godhood. But to automate man, whether by iron discipline, blind faith or sheer coercion, is to reintegrate man with matter—to turn him into clay, and thus reverse God's act of creation.

In 1959 he wrote a lengthy article on "The Unnaturalness of Human Nature." It was published by the *Saturday Evening Post* and reprinted in *The Ordeal of Change*.

The chief point of "The Unnaturalness of Human Nature" is that it sees the dominant role of the weak in human development not as perversion of our natural instincts and vital impulses but as the starting point of man's uniqueness and his deviation from the rest of creation. What others have seen as degeneration is seen here as the generation of a new order of life.

Hoffer's ideas about the uniqueness of man and the great error of trying to assimilate man into nature—a key dogma of modernity—was perhaps his most original venture into philosophy.

God and Man

By 1958 he considered that the idea of a God grew out of man's "vague but poignant awareness that he is an outsider on this planet and in this universe; that he is unlike any other part of creation. You needed a God to create a man. All other forms of life could just happen—but not man."

Man was the great mystery to Hoffer—the one and only mystery. We are "the great unknown to ourselves." He steadfastly refused to join the parade of thinkers who aimed to demote mankind to the status of a talkative ape. The unique qualities of man encouraged Hoffer to think about his creator. God had "automated the universe" and then "created Man in a playful moment." Man in turn saw God as the master creator. In building his own machines, Man was imitating God.

> Man's impulse to build a machine has its roots in his striving to imitate God—to breathe thought and will into inanimate matter and create a living thing. What God felt when he created life, man wanted to feel when he created the machine. But up to this moment he could not do it. He could not create the perfect machine. He made only a half machine and to make this half machine he had to incorporate living man into it so that for over a hundred years of the machine age men were turned into gears and levers and wheels as a "stopgap of inventiveness."

The imitation of God also bordered on rivalry—a "skirmish against God." It had started at the time of the Renaissance. Then labor-saving machinery, technology, and medicine "reversed God's curse that with the sweat of his face Adam shall eat bread and that Eve shall bring forth her children in pain." With its increased mastery and its miraculous achievements the West began to feel it was catching up with God.

In this there was also defiance—a "revolt against God." In searching for meaning we "spy on God, we try to find his secret plans." We hope to "crack his strong box wherein are locked his mysterious powers." It is "but a farther step in the revolt against God which began some four centuries ago."

Hoffer was strongly opposed to the modern tendency to see science and religion as antagonists. On the contrary, religious ideas about the Creator had inspired the early scientists. They tried to work out how God had created the world and science emerged from this study.

His article "God and the Machine Age" (1954, reprinted as "Jehovah and the Machine Age" in *The Ordeal of Change*) made the point that early scientists such as Galileo and Kepler "really and truly believed in a God who had planned and designed the whole of creation—a God who was a master mathematician and technician." Those present at the birth of modern science "felt in touch with God in every discovery they made." Their search for the laws of nature was partly a religious quest. Nature was God's text, and mathematical notations were His alphabet.[12]

Influential opinion-makers today have reversed this ancient worldview. Nature now approaches the status of a deity, while man has been downgraded to the status of an animal. We forthrightly condemn the idea that anyone should subdue the Earth. The God discerned by the ancient Hebrews is now anathema to the West. With the coming of Darwin in particular, science sought to obliterate the distinction between nature and human nature—a profound revolution in thought.

> When God died in the middle of the 19th century there was immediately set in motion a process which tended to reverse the separation of human nature from nature. Darwinism, nationalism and dictatorial regimentation aimed at reducing human nature to nature. When man is conceived as a superior monkey or as an atom of a compact corporate body or as a regimented, manipulable and predictable automaton he loses that uniqueness—that apartness from the rest of nature, whether inanimate or animate.

At times Hoffer bordered on embracing the supernatural.

> If man is an eternal stranger on this planet then he is truly a mysterious being—the one and only mystery. Some contagion from outermost space reached this planet and injected an ovum and this was the beginning of man. Perhaps the fascination outer space has for us and the early preoccupation with stars, heaven and God is a sort of homing impulse which draws man back to where he came from. Man has been an outsider from the very beginning and from earliest time he had to pretend and masquerade that he was of this earth.

Do we really believe in the "minute dovetailing" of the machinery of nature that life entails, achieved without the intervention of mind? Hoffer had his doubts:

> The mindlessness of nature frightens us, particularly when we see the minute dovetailing and mathematical precision of its structure . . . That chance should accomplish over immensely long periods what only the subtlest intellect could devise frightens us. And it is this fright which drives us to see the hand of an all-knowing God in the workings of nature. We cannot stomach chance, and at bottom we really do not believe in it. We more readily believe in God.

To the direct inquiry in 1980, "What do you think of evolution?" Hoffer similarly replied: "It's easier to believe in God."

> The elimination of God, his substitution by chance, makes the world utterly fantastic. Why should nature obey mathematical laws? And greater than all mysteries is thinking man stranded on a tiny planet in the infinity of space puzzling at his own fate.

The Reformation had seen the "downgrading of God," and that was followed by the nineteenth century's "death of God." Now the twentieth century was witnessing the downgrading of man. The demotion of God had led to the rise of the autonomous individual. How would the demotion of man end? The rise of Islam as a political movement threatening the West happened after Hoffer's death, but in a 1980 article he noted the significant fact that "no Islamic country has so far been modernized."[13] The great gulf separating the Muslims' conception of an all-powerful Allah and the law-bound Jehovah of the Jews may have been the crucial difference.

His speculations were not remotely systematic and he never arrived at any conclusion. In late notebooks he appeared to apply these thoughts more personally. "You must make it easy for God to help you," he once wrote. In a later notebook: "All that we receive from others is a gift from heaven. We do not deserve anything nor does the world owe us anything."

Perhaps most impressive was his idea that it is our duty to complete God's work. He never quoted the Parable of the Talents. But he produced his own eloquent version in a late notebook:

> When I speak to an audience of common people I tell them that if they believe in God they know that God loves them because He made so many of them. He is also a just God. It would therefore be blasphemous to believe that a living, just God has showered all his gifts on a chosen few and left our minds and souls empty and shrunken. It cannot be so. We are actually richer than we think. God has implanted in us the seeds of all greatness and it behooves us to see to it that the seeds germinate, grow and come to flower. We must see learning and growing as a sort of worship. For God has implanted capacities and talents in us, and it is our sacred duty to finish God's work.

Devotion to Israel

Hoffer became ever more interested in Israel, apprehensive or joyful depending on the headlines. He subscribed to the *Jerusalem Post's* weekly edition. But at the time of the Yom Kippur War in 1973, he said he could not bring himself to read the newspapers. One day he was in a restaurant when the papers were changed on the stand outside. The new headline seemed to report an Arab victory. He thought it read "Arabs Score Victory." On the way out he saw that it was "Agnew Quits, Guilty."

He said it would require all his capacity to "weather the terrible days ahead." He could not live in a world with an Israel destroyed or even defeated. His concern about the fate of Israel eventually became a near obsession and it came to dominate all his religious reflections, especially after the Six Day War in 1967. He became quietly upset by "renegade Jews" in the United States who "defile and defame both their own race and the country in which they live." They are "repeating in America what they had done in Weimar Germany" when some had used their influence in the press to criticize or satirize German society. They have not learned a lesson, and now "they have a hand in endangering the existence of Israel."

He believed Israel revealed that history is not a mere process, but an unfolding drama. Sometimes he thought of providence and the mysterious working of history.

> For me and for millions like me, the meaning of history and the meaning of life depend on Israel's survival. It will be a meaningless empty world if anything should happen to Israel.

> July 14, 1972, 11:20 a.m. Never have death and resurrection been enacted so breathtakingly on the stage of history as Hitler's Holocaust followed by the birth of Israel.

To those steeped in Christian eschatology, he wrote, "the return of Jews to Palestine could be seen as the penultimate step to the end of the world."

"The fate of the Jews is a greater mystery to people who do not believe in God than to those who do."

"Jehovah Is My God"

The closest he came to a statement of personal faith was written in the form of a poem in 1966:

> *I don't have to believe in him*
> *I live with him.*
> *Jehovah, man's most sublime invention*
> *Is my God.*

He is with me in all my thoughts,
And I treat him as a God and not an errand boy;
To fetch what I need,
Or nurse me or defend me or comfort me.
No! He and I discourse about the wonder that is man,
That I am in him and He in me.

CHAPTER TEN

The Longshoreman Philosopher

*The insights and thoughts that survive and
endure are those that can be put into everyday
words. They are like the enduring seed—compact,
plain looking and made for endurance.*

—ERIC HOFFER

Hoffer was one of the few people in American history known to the general public as a philosopher. Yet he once said that he "never could figure out what the great philosophical problems are about." The statements that he came across seemed to him "at best a storm in a tea cup."

In a "hierarchy of self evaluation," written in 1949, he thought of himself first as a human being, second as an American, third as a workingman, fourth as a longshoreman, fifth as a thinker, sixth as a writer. Philosopher didn't make the cut, although "thinker" covered the territory.

Despite his disclaimers, he really was a philosopher in the old sense. A philosopher was expected to display insight and show wisdom. In public, Hoffer could be vehement and passionate, a far cry from the phlegmatic imperturbability that we might expect from a philosopher. But privately he was "philosophical" in the sense of being resigned to life's trials and uncertainties. Hoffer particularly admired the French writers and philosophers of the seventeenth and eighteenth centuries, and did so more for their clarity and insights than for their conclusions. Voltaire he rarely mentioned; La Rochefoucauld, in his maxims, delighted Hoffer with his brevity and wit, sometimes bordering on cynicism ("We are always strong enough to bear the misfortunes of others").

Philosophers today are usually associated with university philosophy departments, and philosophy there has been diminished. Bertrand Russell gave an explanation for this in *The Problems of Philosophy*. He allowed that philosophy had not enjoyed "any very great measure of success in its attempts to provide definite answers to its questions." In other fields, such as mathematics and science, researchers could recount their discoveries and triumphs at great length. Philosophers, on the other hand, had little to boast about. Why was this?

Russell concluded, "As soon as definite knowledge concerning any subject becomes possible this subject ceases to be called philosophy and becomes a separate science. The whole study of the heavens, which now belongs to astronomy, was once included in philosophy; Newton's great work was called 'The Mathematical Principles of Natural Philosophy.' Similarly, the study of the human mind, which was a part of philosophy, has now become separated from philosophy and has become the science of psychology.... [Only those questions] to which, at present, no definite answer can be given, remain to form the residue which is called philosophy."[1]

Theology had also been separated, at the recommendation of Francis Bacon, the Lord Chancellor of England at the time of James I. In earlier centuries, philosophy and theology were often blended into the field known as scholasticism. Bacon, whose instincts were primarily those of a scientist, urged that theology should be divorced from philosophy. The philosophical remnant, or residue, as Russell called it, fell into a general obscurity. It became a place where storms were brewed in teacups, as Hoffer said, and where few laymen ventured. Most academic philosophy today is a closed book to non-specialists.

As a thinker, Hoffer sought insights more than the solution to philosophical "problems," most of which did not interest him. The problem of induction is one of the more famous and, in neglecting it, Hoffer no doubt showed the plain man's wisdom. The problem goes like this. We observe (to give a well-known example) that this, that, and thousands of other swans are white, and from this we infer that all swans are white. That last is the inductive step. But as the Scottish philosopher David Hume pointed out, there is no basis for believing that it is valid. Frequent past observations give no assurance that the observation will remain true in the future. In the case of swans this skepticism was justified. At about the time that Hume died, Europeans discovered black swans in Australia. However many times something has been observed, in other words, it does not follow that the next observation will agree. Therefore the universal law must remain unconfirmed.

We can't dismiss this as trivial either because all reasoning depends on inference by induction to general laws. If such inferences are themselves invalid, or at least insecure, then reasoning itself has an element of "faith" built into it. Bertrand Russell concluded that "every attempt to arrive at general scientific laws from particular observations is fallacious, and Hume's skepticism was inescapable." His challenge "still has not been met."[2]

Later in his own *Treatise of Human Nature*, nonetheless, Hume forgot his own doubts, and adopted the way out of the problem of induction that he recommended for others, that of "carelessness and inattention." His skepticism was directed at something so fundamental to the exercise of reason that he could not sustain that skepticism himself.

Hoffer, therefore, saved himself a lot of time by not bothering himself with questions of what we certainly know—the broad class of problems that has both obsessed and bedeviled modern philosophy. Hoffer's instinct more closely resembled that of Dr. Samuel

Johnson, who responded to philosophical doubts as to the reality of solid objects by kicking the stone at his foot, proclaiming, "I refute it thus."

Hoffer also had little patience for the philosophies of the system builders, in which categories, propositions, and postulates were manipulated for hundreds of pages, probably in the German language. He once wrote that "the trouble with the Germans is that they are trying to express in prose what could only be expressed in music." He quoted Kenneth Clark, the author of *Civilization*, as saying that "the non-existence of a clear, concrete German prose" had arguably been "one of the chief disasters of European civilization." The German-born Protestant theologian Paul Tillich pondered "the divine demonic conflict in nature," suggesting to Hoffer that such thinkers "think with their feelings."

There was "a German desire for murkiness," Hoffer argued, "a fear of the lucid and tangible." Worse, "the German disease of making things difficult" had conquered the world.

> In the words of Hegel: "Once the realm of notion is revolutionized, actuality does not hold out." Heine predicted that the words piled up by German philosophers would eventually bring about a revolution compared with which all other revolutions would seem a storm in a teacup.[3]

Hoffer thought that Hegel and "the ponderous professors of philosophy" had prepared the way for Hitler and Goebbels.

Late in life, still trying to come to grips with Hegel, Hoffer read Walter Kaufman's book on the German sage. But he found that after 154 pages, he still had no inkling of what Hegel was after.

> The time he lived in (1770–1831) was as eventful and unsettled as our own. No one knew what the next morning would bring. Yet here were a number of German professors, living practically on the battlefield (Jena) totally absorbed in producing thousands

of pages of abstruse philosophy, convinced that they alone had a hold on the ultimate truth. They were drunk with words."[4]

More to Hoffer's taste was the American (and Californian) philosopher Josiah Royce, who is considered a prominent American Hegelian and yet said of Hegel's philosophy: "Almost everybody has forgotten what it means and has therefore come to accept it as true."

Towering systems of abstract thought, such as Hegel's, have more or less collapsed, or at any rate are rarely read. And indubitable foundations for knowledge, sought since the time of Descartes, eventually turned into sand, and then into quicksand. An ever-widening skepticism turned into the opposite of enlightenment. Hoffer believed that "the purpose of philosophers is to show people what is right under their noses." The modern tendency has been for philosophers to doubt what is right in front of their eyes.

"Know Thyself"

Nonetheless it could be said that Hoffer did have a philosophy. He believed that a particular form of knowledge was essential, and that was self-knowledge. In fact, he responded to the oldest injunction of the philosophers, inscribed at the Temple of Apollo at Delphi: Know Thyself.

As Pascal put it in one of his *Pensees*: "One must know oneself. If this does not serve to discover truth, it at least serves as a rule of life."[5] Pascal, a Christian and a mathematician, was one of Hoffer's foremost guides to philosophy. Ludwig Wittgenstein, the eminent twentieth-century philosopher whose later thoughts and notebook entries sometimes resembled Hoffer's, said that "nothing is so difficult as not deceiving oneself."[6]

Hoffer often reflected on the difficulty of self-knowledge, for "we are the great unknown to ourselves." Indeed, "we know least about that which is nearest to us." He noted that the Bible says that no one can ever see God and live. But we "might say with less solemnity that no one can see himself as he really is and live." (In La Rochefoucauld's mordant assessment, "We are so accustomed to disguising ourselves to others that we end up being disguised to ourselves.")

We actively resist self-knowledge, said Hoffer. Our thoughts often involve concealing what we do not want to see. "Our resentments and intolerances are usually the watchdogs guarding forbidden ground within us." And those who tell us what we do not want to know about ourselves may become our sworn enemies.

Why is it so hard to tell the truth about ourselves? Because so often it is meager and unflattering. "By lying we as it were reform the world—arrange things as we would like them to be."

He thought that what we are looking for is not so much people who agree with us as people who think well of us and know how to say so effectively.

> We like them then, even though they disagree with us violently. For we think well of ourselves only in rare moments . . . We need people to bear witness against our inner judge who knows our innermost secrets and keeps score of all our trespassing and misdeeds.

He thought it vile and stupid to tell people the truth about themselves. We are often tempted to reform people or even change their attitude toward us by telling them what they are really like. But "if there is something no one must give us but we must discover for ourselves, it is the truth about ourselves."

It is equally difficult to discern our own motives.

> The less we know of motives, the better we are off. Worse than having unseemly motives is the conviction that our motives are all good. The proclamation of a noble motive can be an alibi for doing things that are not noble. Other people are much better judges of our motives than we are ourselves. And their judgment, however malicious, is probably correct. I would rather be judged

by my deeds than by my motives. It is indecent to read other people's minds. As for reading our own minds, its only worthwhile purpose is to fill us with humility.

Hoffer advised against wanting something—anything—with all one's heart. Any time we do so we are in a tough spot. "No dependence is so poignant and corrosive as the dependence of fervent desire." He also saw that most of us prefer to teach than to learn, and many people will learn only in order to teach. "Any time we are compelled to learn we become as children."

We must learn to appreciate what we have, he said, and doing so takes a special disposition. For we have a truer knowledge and a better appreciation of what we do not have. Nowhere is freedom more cherished than in a non-free society, for example. "An affluent free society invents imaginary grievances and decries plenty as a pig heaven."

As for deciphering others, the only real key is our self. And considering how obscure that is, "the use of it as a key in deciphering others is like using hieroglyphs to decipher hieroglyphs."

Thoughts about Thinking

Hoffer liked to propose informal rules for thinkers and how best to put thoughts on paper. The need for simplicity came first. "The essence of philosophy is the spirit of simplicity," he said. "To philosophize is a simple act." Originality in thought can scarcely be recognized if it is not expressed simply. Again, Wittgenstein thought along similar lines. "The aspect of things that are most important for us are hidden because of their simplicity and familiarity," he wrote.[7]

Hoffer also thought that we cannot have too much naiveté.

Sophistication is for juveniles and the birds. For the essence of naivety is to see the familiar as if it were new and maybe also the capacity to recognize the familiar in the unprecedentedly new.

There can be no genuine acceptance of the brotherhood of men without naivety.

A profusion of words dilutes and blurs thought. An idea has to be hacked out—which means that the emergence of the full idea is brought about by judicious elimination. Facility with words is not necessarily an aid in thinking; though a feel for words certainly is. There is a crucial difference between description—painting with words—and the bold delineation of an idea. Thinking is more like sculpting than painting. In the latter you have to splash on shadows, to add this or that. In thinking you chip away all the time.

How rare it is to come across a piece of writing that is unambiguous, unqualified and also un-blurred by understatement or subtleties, and yet at the same time urbane and tolerant. It is a vice of the scientific method when applied to human affairs that it fosters hemming and hawing and a scrupulousness which easily degenerates into obscurity and meaninglessness.

Exaggeration also has merit, a merit akin to that of simplicity. "It is impossible to think clearly in understatements," Hoffer would say. Thought itself was a process of exaggeration. "No thoughts ever fit an actual situation" and our truths are rarely more than half-truths anyway.

To think out a problem is not unlike drawing a caricature. You have to exaggerate the salient point and leave out that which is not typical. "To illustrate a principle," says Bagehot, "you must exaggerate much and you must omit much."

The more comprehensive and unobjectionable a thought became, "the more clumsy and unexciting it gets." He liked half-truths of a certain kind, because they are stimulating. There was no reason why "the profoundest thoughts should not make easy and exciting reading."

> A profound thought is an exciting thing, as exciting as a detective's deductions or hunches. The simpler the words in which a thought is expressed, the more stimulating its effect.

We also need self-confidence. We can't think when we are on the defensive; we can only quibble. Thinking "requires a readiness to let go of any supports, to venture forth and not to ward off. We cannot think when we are constantly afraid lest we expose an untenable position."

> The most intense insecurity comes from standing alone. We are not alone when we imitate. So, too, when we follow a trail blazed by others, even a deer trail.

There was also no substitute for patience where thinking was concerned. If he had a question in his mind, the only way he could find an answer was to "hang on long enough and keep groping." In many cases that meant allowing the mind to "stray from the task at hand." It must be free to be "elsewhere." And this took time.

When you do have the patience to hold on, it's as though "you are casting your net into the outside world." Sometimes the world seems to be bothered by your search and offers you new material to chew on. He was awed by what he had written in the past, because he could see the persistence that had gone into it. It was not the end product that impressed him so much as the "long, arduous effort needed to get at the ideas."

He had more time to think than most people because he didn't have a "multitude of responsibilities" and daily tasks. He also said he was "basically without ambition." That last comment was wrong, surely, and perhaps illustrated how obscure Hoffer was to himself, just as he said others were to themselves.

Sometimes he did feel harried or short of time. He noticed that when that happened it wasn't because he was too busy but because he was wasting his time.

> We are not at home in this world when we do not do the things that we really want to do—we are then on the run, constantly busy, constantly short on time.

At times he felt euphoric and he wondered how that arose. He came to believe that "the uninterrupted performance of some tasks" was the key to happiness. It was not the quality of the task, which could be trivial or even futile. "What counts is the completion of the circuit—the uninterrupted flow between conception and completion. Each such completion generates a sense of fulfillment."

But the search for happiness was not something that he recommended. It was often "the chief source of unhappiness," and happiness was not a right. "We ought to get our share of happiness when we are babes in arms." He believed that the search for happiness was a peculiarity of the modern era and "an after effect of the loss of millennial faith." It was a "search for heaven on earth—a substitute for faith in a kingdom of heaven." (Wittgenstein was quoted as saying: "I don't know why we are here but I'm pretty sure it is not in order to enjoy ourselves.")[8]

Man was not made for the "good" life, Hoffer believed:

> Whenever conditions are so favorable that struggle becomes meaningless man goes to the dogs. All through the ages there were wise men who had an inkling of this disconcerting truth. . . . There is apparently no correspondence between what man wants and what is good for him.

It did not take much to make him happy: a "new crumb of thought," the writing of a new paragraph, a well-written book to read; the evidence that someone thought well of him. He also found that when he got away from his writing table he grew less comfortable; his thoughts seemed trivial and uninteresting. The consolation was that the less he felt at home in the world, "the easier it will be to quit it."

Like many philosophers, ranging from St. Augustine to David Hume, Hoffer sought and polished his insights mainly because it gave him pleasure to do so. His belief that physical exercise also exercised the mind was hardly original, but he gave it an interesting twist:

> Flaubert and Nietzsche have emphasized the importance of stand-ing up and walking in the process of thinking. The peripatetics were perhaps motivated by the same awareness. Yet purposeful walking—what we call marching—is an enemy of thought and is used as a powerful instrument for the suppression of indepen-dent thought and the inculcation of unquestioned obedience.

He thought it essential to think alone. Peers who review one another and hold each other to a common standard are unlikely to create a productive milieu for thinkers. Anyway, solitude came naturally to Hoffer. Expecting others to help him think was like expecting them to help him digest his food. But he saw also that many people hated to be left alone and actively avoided it. They would rather be "pushed around and buffeted" than be left wholly to their own devices.

> What sort of people are they? People who have not and perhaps can never have business of their own. Their individual prospects, thoughts and affairs in general do not seem to them worth mind-ing. Such people will put up with a lot of abuse and unpleasantness so long as they are not forced to face their individual existence and see it for what it is.

He believed that some people have no original ideas not because they are incapable of them but because "they do not think well enough of themselves to consider their ideas worth noticing and developing." And for all of us, whatever our self-esteem, creativeness comes only in flashes. Here he conjured up some good metaphors from his gold mining days.

> Actual creativeness is a matter of moments. One has to piece together the minute grains to make a lump. And it is so easy to miss the momentary flashes. It is like sluicing in placer mining. He who lets the flakes float by has nothing to show for his trouble.

> Originality is not something continuous but something intermittent—a flash of the briefest duration. One must have the time and be watchful (be attuned) to catch the flash and fix it. One must know how to preserve these scant flakes of gold sluiced out of the sand and rocks of everyday life. Originality does not come nugget-size.

By his mid-sixties he found that he had to husband every grain of insight.

> I must continually sluice my mind for whatever gold there is in it. By sluicing I mean pouring it out on paper and trapping whatever has weight or color. I wonder what would happen if I sat down and wrote for a solid hour without stopping. It is something I must try soon.

Taking Things Too Seriously

Hoffer kept reminding himself not to take life too seriously.

> A deadly seriousness emanates from all other forms of life. The yell of pain and of fear man has in common with the beasts, but he alone smiles and laughs.

In trying to avoid solemnity Hoffer reminded us of Michel de Montaigne, the sixteenth-century French writer who was said to have originated the essay form. A major influence on Hoffer,

Montaigne adopted a tone of cheerful skepticism about almost everything. "The most certain sign of wisdom is cheerfulness," said Montaigne, who suffered great pain from gallstones and died at the age of 59. Like Hoffer, Montaigne almost never mentioned his mother, who came from a family of Sephardic Jews. Hoffer said that when he read Montaigne's essays in 1936 he felt "all the time that he was writing about me. I recognize myself on every page."[9]

Hoffer nonetheless did take himself seriously to the extent of working to develop his talents. He also knew he had something to contribute to our understanding of life. It's far from clear whether he really believed that life had no meaning (as he sometimes implied). He also compiled memorable quotations from his own wide reading. No one could do that without taking *something* about himself seriously. His injunction to avoid solemnity was really a way of reminding himself to keep things as simple as possible. Montaigne sounded like Hoffer when he said that "the greatest thing in the world is to know how to be self-sufficient."

A few times in his life Hoffer said that he "felt wise," but at such moments he knew that he was "but a hairsbreadth from the pompous." In such a mood he became convinced that taking life too seriously was "a frivolous thing":

> There is an affected self-dramatizing in the brooding over one's prospects and destiny. The trifling attitude of an Ecclesiastes is essentially sober and serious. It is in closer touch with the so-called eternal truths than are the most penetrating metaphysical probing and most sensitive poetic insights.

Friends urged him to read Albert Camus, the existentialist writer who was fashionable in the fifties. Hoffer did so, but was not bowled over. He quoted from Camus's *The Rebel*—"the encounter between human inquiry and the silence of the universe"—and commented:

> I have escaped a lot of grief by not being able to take myself seriously. It has never occurred to me that I had to have a philosophy;

that I was face to face with "the silence of the universe," that I had a duty to defend or denounce, etc. What I wanted was to think things through, to know the reason of things. I loathed Hitler and Stalin and Lenin and raged at the brazen hypocrisies of the Communists.

Self-dramatization was in fact a "falsification of reality." To feel desperate because life's meaning was elusive "was to wallow in specious feelings."

> There is no greater threat to sanity than the taking of one's life too seriously. No one will miss us long when we are gone. No one will lose his appetite because we are no more.

His thoughts on this were strongly shaped by his unbelief—by his refusal to accept the reality of an afterlife.

> The questions of immortality, of the meaninglessness of life, of absolute truth, do not exist for a man who knows that man is born to live and die and that is that.

Taking oneself too seriously was something that a child does.

> A child sees itself as the center of the world, it is serious in its needs, its games, its hurts and its joys. A child does not know that life is brief and vain.

Death

Hoffer linked the obscurity of much modern philosophizing to "the fact of death and nothingness at the end."

> [Death is] a certitude unsurpassed by any absolute truth ever discovered. Yet knowing this, people can be deadly serious

about their prospects, grievances, duties and trespassings. The only explanation which suggests itself is that seriousness is a means of camouflage: we conceal the triviality and nullity of our lives by taking things seriously. No opiate and no pleasure can so effectively mask the terrible truth about man's life as does seriousness.[10]

Like Montaigne, a practiced observer of his own thoughts, Hoffer gave lucid accounts of his (frequent) thoughts about death. He noted what man must forget if life is to be bearable:

There is but a heartbeat between him and eternal nothingness. His path is ever on the brink of a bottomless abyss. As he savors the sweetness of a beginning he must ward off the mordant fumes from the not distant end.

What seems most foreign to me is eternity—the eternity of death; the eternity of a limitless universe. It's a bottomless abyss at my feet and it follows me wherever I am. A misstep and down I plunge into the abyss. [I am] like the peasant who plants vineyards on the slopes of a potent volcano.

How many ambitions, hopes, dreams, plans and designs evaporate into thin air and come to naught? Each one of these strivings and stretchings of the soul is basically a reaching out for immortality—to achieve something that will endure and keep our memory alive after we are gone. Hence probably the strains and fears which beset us after we pass forty. We see the exit gate in the distance and realize that time is running out.

He saw that modern society and economic thought were promoting individualism (as opposed to the collectivism that was once prevalent and that Communism had tried to revive). But the universality of death discouraged individualism. Again, Hoffer's argument did not apply to believers, for whom individual actions, whether good or bad, influenced their future state.

> The difficulty of being an individual manifests itself in all eras. . . . In the past individualism was exclusively confined to a king and a few nobles, military or civil, whereas in the modern Occident practically a whole population feel themselves as individuals. Now, the greatest difficulty which confronts the individual, whether powerful or weak, exclusive or common—is the fact of death.

Echoing La Rochefoucauld, Hoffer wondered to what extent the deaths of people known to us, but who were not a part of our lives, really bother us.

> Surely the fact that they died while we are still alive registers strongly in our mind. For there is no superiority greater than that of the living over the dead. The death of others imparts a uniqueness to our being alive.

He learned early on "that it is much easier to do things for others than for oneself—good things and bad."

> It is easier to strive, to risk one's life and also to cheat, steal and murder for others. To some extent we partake of immortality when we strive for others because we step out of the limits of the perishable self. And we do feel self-righteous.

By the time he reached his sixties he found that thoughts of death often crowded in on his mind.

> The fact is that I have been dying by inches for several years. Leaves in autumn are still attached to the tree and are still green, yet they are dead—their sap and marrow is draining back into branches and trunk and it needs but a tug of wind to detach them from the tree of their life.

By his mid-sixties he found it "almost heartwarming to think that in a few years I shall be dead." He contemplated "total and eternal extinction without despair." For most of his adult life he had thought of himself as an old man and when old age really came he said that he hardly noticed it.

Overall, however, he found it remarkable "how little we worry about the things that are sure to happen to us, like old age and death, and how quick we are to worry ourselves sick about things which never come to pass." Montaigne said something very similar. His life had been full of "terrible misfortunes," he said, "most of which never happened."

Human Nature as Unreformable

Belief in the progress of human society was so influential in the nineteenth century that it was generally believed that human nature would advance, too. The Soviet Union was built on the doctrine of progress—an idea that endured in some quarters until the Second World War.

Hoffer had assumed as late as the 1950s that human nature was pliable. He had once believed that Communism could change people. Then he changed his mind. In August 1962, while sorting cargo at Pier 30, a "subdued excitement" possessed him. He was trying to outline "the theme of a return to Nature during the 19th century," when it dawned on him that "human nature is adamantly resistant to change—that human uniqueness in order to unfold and persist needs stability and continuity."

> Hence those who set their heart on a drastic transformation of man's existence must be hostile to human nature—to the superstructure of human uniqueness—and in a variety of ways they do all they can to strip man of his uniqueness and turn him into material, a puppet, an animal, an infant or a machine. This stripping process was pushed and promoted by all sorts of people in the 19th century.

Romantics, revolutionaries, social reformers, and economists were hacking away at man's essential humanity and blindly striving to press him back into the matrix of nature from which he has arisen.

> The preoccupation of the late 18th century was already that of the 19th; namely the retooling of man and his society. The Encyclopedists no less than Robert Owen and the scientific sociologists, anthropologists, economists, etc. had the conviction of a boundless human transformation and re-tooling. Montaigne and Pascal knew better.

The reformers of human nature also believed in its unlimited corruptibility, for perfectibility implied plasticity. What can be improved can also be degraded. Utopianists will therefore have a bias for censorship, supervision, and some sort of quarantine against evil influence.

> Any practice which bases itself on the assumption of human perfectibility is not only likely to end in failure but, by being hostile to human nature, runs counter to tolerance and benevolence to one's fellow men.

History itself showed that we have not changed. Not only was "all history contemporary, but anything worthwhile man wrought is contemporary." Anything that's good "is never out of date, and always has a vital bearing on the present."

> What Confucius, Ecclesiastes, Jesus, Aeschylus and Sophocles said about human nature is still fully valid today; and we still go back to them for knowledge of ourselves. But who will go back to the wise men of the ancient past for knowledge of nature and of things? What does this signify?

The idea of human perfectibility had surfaced only quite recently, Hoffer wrote, but its roots reached back to the distant past and probably started as a church heresy. In its recent incarnation it was conceived in the eighteenth century, at a time when man began to be equated with other living things "and even with inanimate matter."

The paradox, then, was that the belief in the perfectibility of man "arose when man was downgraded." If man really is "mere matter," then it became plausible to argue that this matter could be processed into whatever the reformers wanted.

> The powerful movement to perfect man and his society which has generated so much turmoil and strife since the end of the 18th century was born not of an exalted conception of man's uniqueness; but on the contrary of the assumption that man was nothing more than a physiochemical complex or a machine—that he can be experimented with the way the scientist experiments with matter. It was the downgrading of man by science that has emboldened self appointed soul engineers to operate on man with an ax.

He decided that the most fateful happenings of the twentieth century involved "the dissolution of illusions, the diminishing of dreams and visions, and the murder of orphic words." Just as the nineteenth century had seen "the raping of faith in God and in the kingdom of heaven so the 20th century saw the weakening of faith in man and the possibility of a heaven on earth."

Theorizing in the future, he predicted, would tend to regard humanity "as unchangeable and unreformable."

The Uniqueness of Man

Hoffer's insistence on the uniqueness of man was perhaps his most important venture into philosophy. It was also a bold departure from the conventional wisdom of his day. The widespread modern acceptance of man as an animal stemmed from the evolutionist views of Charles Darwin and his predecessors. Darwin saw the difference between man and "the higher animals" as "one of degree and not of kind."[11] Hoffer's insistence on a clear-cut distinction rather than a gradation therefore restored the earlier beliefs of both the philosophers and the theologians.

We saw that some fields of philosophy had been captured by science. Hoffer's disagreement on the status of man therefore amounted to an act of reclamation, restoring to philosophy what had been surrendered to science.

In his endless reading, Hoffer had encountered a remarkable quotation from Ferdinand Brunetière, a nineteenth-century French writer and critic who converted to Catholicism and became a member of l'Académie française. The great error of the nineteenth century, Brunetière said, had been "to mingle and confound man and nature" without pausing to consider that man is human "only insofar as he distinguishes himself from nature and makes himself an exception to it." Man had become good not by obeying nature but by resisting it.

Hoffer was impressed by that and could not think of "a single book or even an essay that makes the opposition between man and nature the cornerstone of a train of thought." His hunch was that that opposition was fundamental and should be revived.

Yet intellectuals had conceived it as their greatest challenge "to demonstrate that there is no basic difference between man and the rest of creation." This was a great irony, because their concerted effort to downgrade man had gone "hand in hand with an unprecedented increase of man's power over nature. Fantastic!"[12]

> The crucial paradox is that man's increased mastery over nature has not increased man's stature; it was not used as an instrument for the making of gods. By some blind, inexorable process, and without malice or viciousness, the great minds of the 19th century did all they could to denude the human entity of its uniqueness and demonstrate that man was but a link in a chain of creation not essentially distinct from other forms of life and subject to the same iron laws which dominate nature.

The invention and development of the machine was a second creation—man's way of fusing thought and will into inert
matter—yet this second creation has tended both in theory and
practice toward dehumanization. Practically every movement
and every intellectual system strived in one way or another to
reverse the ascent of man. In this Darwin, Marx, Nietzsche and
Freud worked toward a common goal. Nationalism, socialism,
and all movements of reform labored toward the absorption of a
unique individual into the predictable and manipulable group.

The original "humanization of man," as Hoffer called it, had
involved breaking away from nature. The great change came about
not because man was superior to other forms of life but because he
"came into being as a defective, unfinished and ill-equipped animal."
Animals could survive in forests in the winter. Man, lacking these
instincts, "had to finish himself," to equip himself with substitutes
for the animals' capacity to survive what would be impossible hardship for us.

The traits which distinguish man from animals, which constitute
human uniqueness, have their roots in man's deficiencies as an
animal. Man is a tool maker because he lacks specialized organs;
because unlike other animals he is not a born technician with a
built-in tool kit.

Nonetheless, in the nineteenth century, science had become "so
enamored with matter, so overwhelmed by the mathematical spirit
which permeated matter that it could not but expect man to be part
of nature, subject to the same beautiful laws."

It was a far-reaching chain of thought for Hoffer. The materialism that overtook science in the nineteenth century is still dominant today. Hoffer's dissent put him in immediate conflict with the
environmental movement that is riding high now but was then in
its infancy. "The wilderness boys are telling us that we must stand in

awe of nature" and reverence it, Hoffer wrote. "Why so? Pascal 300 years ago knew better."

Hoffer had experienced the environment up close as a migratory worker and placer miner, and from that perspective his views were decidedly unromantic. With Mother Nature breathing down his neck, he had "a distinct feeling that she didn't want to have me around." Poison oak, bugs, burrs, and interlocking manzanita tore at his clothes. Hard earth dug into his side when he lay down to rest. Dirt ate into every pore of his body. It all gave him "the unmistakable intimation that I pack up and be gone."

> The passionate partisanship for nature and the glorification of the wilderness is not basically different from an identification with holy causes in general. The wilderness boys are chauvinistic in temperament—ready to fight and die for immaculate, noble nature. Considering also their elitism, their contempt of the herd, their chauvinism borders on fascism.

The recent inclination of some "greens" has been not to identify humans with nature but to see us as the great enemy of nature—to insist once more on a separation, but this time as a product of our supposed recklessness. The publication of a bestselling book, *The World Without Us*, in which our disappearance from the earth is represented as a hopeful outcome, might have surprised Hoffer—or perhaps not.[13] For he concluded that we are more likely "to perish from the pollution and erosion of our cultural environment than from the pollution and destruction of our natural environment." He warned us to keep on guard against those who shed tears about what is happening to nature. In modern times, he said, back-to-nature movements had "set the stage for revolution and dictatorship."

EPILOGUE

"I shall not welcome death," Hoffer wrote. "But the passage to nothingness seems neither strange nor frightful. I shall be joining an endless and most ancient caravan. Death would be a weary thing had I believed in heaven and life beyond."

That was in 1977. A few years later he was less resigned about his prospects. He told Stacy Cole, who visited him regularly in the Children's Hospital in San Francisco, that he feared "the void." For public consumption he perhaps knew that he was expected to be "philosophical" about such things, so I believe he didn't write this down.

He said that Winston Churchill was the nearest thing to a hero he ever had. He mentioned "Montaigne and Dostoyevsky, [Menachem] Begin and [David] Ben-Gurion" as historical figures he greatly admired.

He worked on his "conversations with quotations." The preponderance of names early in the alphabet showed that that task was unfinished. He also worked on *Truth Imagined*. It consisted mostly of stories that he told to Gemma Kabitzke, a Dutch woman who had enrolled in Cole's community college in Fremont and had taken a court-reporting course. Through the efforts of James Koerner and the Sloan Foundation, a grant was made available to transcribe Hoffer's notebooks and Gemma was hired to do it. Over a two-year period she also recorded Hoffer's stories and typed them up. *Truth Imagined* was dedicated to her.

Hoffer continued to give interviews to journalists and at times his increasingly curmudgeonly disposition was unconcealed. To *People* magazine he said:

> I have always been retired. I am a solitary person, never in the stream of things. And I am not a writer. I never let them cast me in that role. I just shoot my mouth off. I am not good at doing my duty. That is why I never married.[1]

He told Camilla Snyder, a journalist with the *Los Angeles Herald Examiner*, that he lived on $5 a day. He shopped nearby, didn't cook, but made "very good salads." He had switched from Wild Turkey to Jack Daniels.[2] Recently he had stayed up all night reading Moshe Dayan's *Living with the Bible.*

He told another journalist that he was going blind. His eyesight would "probably last my life time, but there isn't much left." During that interview an old friend, George Knight, who had taken many photographs of Hoffer, including those published in Calvin Tomkins' book, returned with his clean laundry.[3]

Camilla Snyder returned in February 1980 for another interview, this one to help publicize Hoffer's new book *Before the Sabbath*. It was dedicated to Charlie Kittrell, an executive vice president of the Phillips Petroleum Company who once heard Hoffer speak at Stanford University. He told Hoffer that it was the best lecture he had ever heard on America and he invited him to Bartlesville, Oklahoma, to give a few speeches. Hoffer accepted. It was his last trip away from the Bay Area. Hoffer said of Kittrell:

> By some preference which I can't explain, we got attached to each other. He is probably the first friend I've ever made. I'm pushing 80 now and I don't make friends. I mean, I love people on the

waterfront and I've liked people all my life but I never stuck to friends. Lili, that's my girl, is about the only person I really got attached to.[4]

In this second interview with Snyder, Hoffer let fly with geopolitical views that even his latter-day neoconservative allies would have repudiated. He proposed that the United States occupy Saudi Arabia "and take away their oil fields, and put the Arab Sheiks in Switzerland with their belly dancers." Why not? "What are we afraid of? . . . There's nobody with daring in the Administration. We have become a nation of cowards."

He was outraged by "this disaster Carter" and called him the "Peanut Man." And he was indignant about the U.S. government's humiliation of the Shah, who had been driven from Iran and permitted only a brief stay in the United States.

Whom did Hoffer support in the approaching 1980 presidential primaries? He mentioned Senators Daniel Patrick Moynihan and Henry "Scoop" Jackson and ruled out Senator Edward Kennedy. As for Ronald Reagan, Hoffer failed to mention him.[5]

Freelance writer Gene Griessman interviewed Hoffer in February 1981. With the exception of my own interview when we were joined by Selden Osborne in April of that year, it was Hoffer's last press interview. It appeared after his death in the *Atlanta Weekly Magazine* published by the Atlanta newspapers.[6] By then Hoffer was tired and uninhibited enough to say more or less whatever came into his head.

He was "a sick man with emphysema," just out of the intensive care unit, he said. "I have the right to be left alone and I have nothing important to say any more." Ten days of intensive care had cost him a thousand dollars a day. If he had to do it again, "I'll be broke—a pauper." He "never wanted Social Security" and never applied for a union pension. They gave one to him anyway. "I've worked all my life, and now I'm reduced to this."

How about his book royalties?

"Nothing, nothing," said Hoffer. "The publisher has made thousands and thousands, and I've gotten virtually nothing."

How many copies of *The True Believer* were sold?

He didn't know. "I never read my books, except that recently I've begun to read *The Temper of Our Time*. You cannot imagine the clearness of the thoughts. I cannot believe that I wrote it. I will never be able to write that way again."

"Why not?"

"My memory. It scares me that I am losing my memory. There is not much left . . . I am discouraged. I've tried to commit suicide three or four times in my life. I don't know why they didn't let me die [in the hospital], why they spent so much time and effort keeping me alive. They should have let me die."

"There must have been some purpose," Griessman said.

"I don't believe in purpose. There is no purpose in life. Only chance. When I was in the hospital I was amazed that people cared about me. So many people who didn't even know me. Nurses, doctors, orderlies, students . . . I have a girl, she's been with me for thirty years. We've never married. I have told her I am not the marrying kind. She comes and picks me up at three o'clock every day and takes me to her place and gives me a drink. I get a little high and everything becomes blurry, and . . . then I come back and sleep again. The other day she asked me what I wanted written on my tombstone. I told her to write: 'He received much more than he deserved.'"

"But you've given so much yourself," Griessman said.

"I've always felt I owed much more than I have given. My students have taken my notebooks—you see that empty shelf? That's where they were. They're going to publish them in a book. It's going to be a beautiful book. My students are going to make an American of me. They bought a television set for me. I don't understand anything about sports, but I guess I'll have to learn. I never had a telephone, but they had one installed when I was in the hospital. The generosity of people is unbelievable. They care."

This talk of students was new. He was surely referring to Gemma Kabitzke, and perhaps also Stacy Cole, who qualified as a disciple and who had arranged for Kabitzke to be hired.

Hoffer was in and out of the hospital several times in the last four years of his life. His lungs would fill up and then have to be pumped out. Cole was his regular visitor, both in the Children's Hospital and later in his apartment. Hoffer's attending physician was Dr. Piero Mustacchi. "I would go over nearly every day from Fremont," Cole recalled. "He began to realize that he was in real trouble. It was getting harder and harder for him to get back on his feet and back to his apartment where he wanted to be." Hoffer also referred to his own death, but now with less equanimity.

"As one who claimed to be an atheist, he worried about what would happen with death," Cole said. "We all have that worry. But for someone with a mind as powerful, active and as constantly theoretical as his was? For him not to believe in any kind of after life, he worried about the void. And he talked to me about it several times. About disappearing into nothing.

"The last time we were there he raised the issue and Dr. Mustacchi was listening. He said: 'Mr. Hoffer, there won't be a void, because you will fill it.' He was one of the most distinguished physicians in San Francisco, an Italian who had been cited for the highest award that the Italian government gave for public service. It rendered Hoffer speechless and he loved it."[7]

Cole was himself "a backslidden Baptist, son of a Baptist preacher and the brother of two," but now he had ceased to be "a believer in such things." So he could not give Hoffer "adequate answers."

Hoffer also asked Cole several times if he thought that he would be remembered—if anything he had written would live after him.

"I was touched by that," Cole said, "and I assured him that what he had written would not only outlive him but that future generations would rediscover him, time and again."

Last Notebook

Beginning in September 1981, Hoffer kept a "Last Notebook, '81 to 82" (as Lili later labeled it). Entries show that, intermittently at least, his mind was still functioning well. Above the first entry below, Lili noted that "for the first time in his life, Eric agreed to a TV" in his room.

September 20, 1981

It is 1:20 a.m. I must have been sitting in the dark for hours. My mind seems littered with the shreds of TV stories. I am not alarmed. Had I had a topic to chew on the situation would have been more salubrious. Right now I seem to have run out of material for *Truth Imagined*.

The nature of obedience is a potent topic. The First World War marked the end of an age of obedience. Never again will millions march to slaughter at a word of command, nor will they automatically march to factories, mines, etc., day in day out, as they did in their millions through most of the 19th century...

It is unfair, and perhaps dangerous, to expect work prompted by noble motives. It is ignorant and hypocritical to maintain that money is the root of evil. There has been more oppression and injustice in moneyless than in moneyed societies. Non-idealistic mercenaries are more likely to be civilized than the idealists.

September 25, 1981

In all my life I never competed for fortune, for a woman or for fame. I learned to write in total isolation. My first work was also my best, and the first thing published. I never belonged to a circle or clique. I did not know I was writing a book until it was written. When my first book was published, there was no one near me, an acquaintance let alone a friend, to congratulate me. I have never savored triumph, never won a race.

I have written learnedly on the nature of creative milieus. Yet the milieu in which I did my best work was utterly coarse. Still, chances are I would never have written a thing had Hitler not existed.

In the past, the presence of the Jews in the Middle East coincided with earthshaking events. There are some who presage that the present return of the Jews from a long exile will coincide with the end of the world. During the Six-Day War I had a premonition that as it went with Israel, so it will go with all of us. Should Israel perish the holocaust will be upon us.

September 27, 1981

How does a man die? Does he know when death approaches? Friday night (25th) I vomited the first time in my life. The vomit was dark and bitter. The new experience of vomiting gave me the feeling that I was entering the realm of the unknown.

October 6, 1981

Anwar Sadat was assassinated this morning. The first impulse is to see this murder as the mark of a primitive, backward society. Actually, attempted murder of presidents was much more characteristic of American than of Egyptian society. And it is of course true that the murder of a president in Egypt must have far more weighty consequences than even the murder of a Lincoln. In short, the political and social stability of America depends little on the life and death of presidents.

Sadat's assassination made many things clear. The almost unemotional reaction of the Egyptian masses, so unlike that at the death of Nasser, suggests that the Egyptians are affected more deeply by the pride of Arabism cultivated by Nasser than by Egyptian nationalism and idealism, and the cosmopolitanism advanced by Sadat. Anti-Israeli policies will have a powerful appeal in the Middle East for the balance of the century. It will be suicidal for the Israelis to believe in the possibility of deep popular change.

Stacy Cole discussed with Lili what to do about Eric. With a two-story house in Fremont and a downstairs bed and bath, Cole offered that to Eric. But he knew it would take him out of his San Francisco surroundings and he doubted that Lili would agree. She was still going to work at her school in Redwood City, returning to the city and seeing Eric in the evenings.

Gemma Kabitzke would also go to Hoffer's apartment one day a week, as would Selden. By then Eric was "in a life threatening condition," said Cole. "Lili was looking at extended care places. We knew he shouldn't be alone and I hated the thought of his being with strangers."

At Lili's request, Mary Fabilli stayed with Eric one evening. Once again he surprised her. He asked: "Do you think Lili loves me? Deep down?" Mary had no doubt that she did but was amazed that Hoffer was unsure of what no one else had doubted.

"Eric's death came as a blessing because he was literally choking to death," said Cole. "I would go up there and he would be choking. I hated it, hated it, hated it. He had been so full of vitality, and to see him in this condition, with death staking its claim . . ." He didn't complete the sentence.

Stacy was at Eric's apartment on the penultimate night, a Thursday. It was his scheduled night to be there.

"I could see that his health was failing," he said. "Lili told me that Selden would be with him on Friday, and that she would be there, too."

He recalled, "On the Thursday night I knew that he was about to die. I put him to bed, but just before I left he turned over, faced the wall and said, 'I want to die.' Very simple. Matter of fact. No more fear of the void. No more 'Will people remember me?' Life had become too cumbersome for him to hold onto. Just 'I want to die.' I knew by the way he said it that he meant it. And because he meant it, I knew he was going to. He was going to let go. So I wasn't surprised to get the call."

On the Friday night, Selden was there. Lili had been held up, for some reason. Anyway she was reassured because she knew that Selden was reliable. Eric had also spoken to Stephen Osborne a few hours earlier by telephone. "I want to be able to go to sleep and that's it," he told Stephen, who had always been on good terms with Hoffer.

I had met Selden for the first time in 1981, but it wasn't until April 1987 that I was able to meet up with him again. I wanted to hear from him what had happened on the last night, the night when Hoffer had died. Selden was congenial, as always. But he had heard a report that my political views were in some ways not unlike Hoffer's. So before granting me the interview he had a question for me. It was in the nature of a test. If I passed it, well and good. If not, well, there would be no interview. I braced myself, but his little exam turned out to be simple in the extreme. He asked me: Was I in favor of a nuclear war with the Soviet Union?

"Definitely not!" I said. He was relieved that I had passed. Now we could be friends and I spent half the day with him. He showed me around the Embarcadero and the old longshoreman's hiring hall where he and Eric used to go to work. By then that part of the water-front had become a big tourist area. The freighters, and with them the longshoremen, had migrated to Oakland.

Selden told me that in his day a key union activity was opposing the introduction of new technology—the containerization of cargo in particular. In retrospect, he questioned whether that had been a wise policy. The containers came anyway, and Oakland rather than San Francisco was where the ships were now being unloaded, as they are today.

Selden, by then seventy-two, was in good health and still as radical as ever, going on peace marches and sometimes corresponding with Daniel Ellsberg, who leaked the Pentagon Papers to the press. Stopping the Strategic Defense Initiative missile defense system was by then Selden's overriding cause. I felt that his question for me was more than anything a test for himself—a way of reassuring himself that his old belief system was still intact.

So, what happened on that Friday night? Clearly Hoffer was near the end, Selden said. Lili had decided to move a cot into his apartment so that she could be with Eric in his last days.

Hoffer's mind was clear to the last, Selden said. He had been thinking of writing more about what had already become a favorite theme—the uniqueness of man: nature was predictable, but human nature is not (in Selden's admirable summary). "It was that notion that he wanted to explore."

Selden lay on a mattress not far from Eric's pull-down bed and turned out the lights. Eric's breathing was labored and distractingly audible. In the middle of the night he told Selden that he wanted to get up and go to the bathroom. Selden was ready to help but he worried that if Eric fell, he might not be strong enough to get him back onto his feet. But Eric made it back to his bed safely.

As they lay there in the dark, Selden once again heard Eric's heavy breathing. Reassured, Selden went back to sleep. But when he woke up again, perhaps an hour or two hours later, Eric's breathing could be heard no more. He was gone—you could say that he didn't say goodbye to anyone.

It is reckoned that he died early on Saturday morning, May 21, 1983.

Three months earlier, in February, President Reagan had awarded Hoffer the Presidential Medal of Freedom, the nation's highest civilian award. Hoffer had been unable to attend. Reagan recalled that when he was governor of California Hoffer came to see him and gave him "some pretty good, sound—and salty—advice."

The obituary in the *San Francisco Chronicle* called Hoffer, unflatteringly and inaccurately, "a primitive philosopher." Peter Worthington in the *Toronto Sun* said that Hoffer's mind was so clear and precise that "one cannot read a phrase of his without being mentally stimulated." He deserved a Nobel, said Worthington, whether for literature, peace or philosophy.[8]

Lili had already decided that Eric should be given a Catholic burial and he consented to the arrangement. A funeral Mass was celebrated at Most Holy Redeemer Church in San Francisco's Castro district. He was buried at the Holy Cross Cemetery in Colma, just outside San Francisco. Lili Osborne's grave is next to his.

A comment that Hoffer made in the course of John McGreevy's 1974 interview for the Canadian Broadcasting Corporation might serve as an epitaph:

> The individual has not changed. The individual cannot change. And maybe that's what we need. We have to return to the individual; to the genuine individual who knows that life is brief, that the joys are few, that what matters most in this universe is to have somebody to love and somebody who loves you. We are in an enormous waste land and it's the individual who has to confront all these things by himself. That has been the one thing closest to my understanding.[9]

Quotations and Comments

Over decades of reading, Hoffer would write down notable quotations on three-by-five-inch cards. He would take a handful with him to the University of California–Berkeley every week and discuss them with students.

"At the end of his life," Lili Osborne wrote in a note attached to his final manuscript, "Eric returned to these cards. He was struggling to write. His eyesight was failing, and his body, and his confidence in his own power of thinking."

A part of that manuscript follows.

"To Lili: My one and only. Eric"

....

Lord Acton: "It was from America that the plain ideas that men ought to mind their own business and the nation is responsible to Heaven for the acts of the state, ideas long locked away in the breasts of solitary thinkers and hidden away in Latin folios, burst forth like a conqueror upon the world they were destined to transform under the title of the Rights of Man."

Hoffer: Acton's mind and heart did not pull in the same direction. His mind championed liberty, but during the Civil War his heart sided with the slave-owning Confederates. "I broke my heart," he wrote, "over the surrender of Lee." Like most old European thinkers Acton found it offensive that the common people of Europe should have eloped with history to a New World and lived there in union with it, unhallowed by popes, princes and privileged elites.

....

Charles Babbage: "I cannot remember a single completely happy day in my life."

Hoffer: What would have made Babbage happy for a day? He was an early builder of calculating machines, prototypes of present-day computers. Would the discovery of a new way of doing things have kept him happy for a full day? One thing I know beyond doubt. Had he overheard someone he respected praise him highly it would have sweetened life for him for more than a day. We are starved for praise. It reconciles us with life. And people who have achieved much probably need praise more than people who have not distinguished themselves. When Wellington was asked what he would have done differently had he to live his life over again he replied promptly: "I would have praised people more."

> "In the prison of his days,
> teach the free man how to praise." [W. H. Auden]

Great persons had the need to borrow other men's opinions to think themselves happy, for if they judge by their own feeling they cannot find it. They are happy as it were by report. Self-doubt is at the core of our being. We need people who by their attitude and words will convince us that we are not as bad as we think we are. Hence the vital role of judicious praise. Charles Babbage must have had very little of it if he could not remember a single completely happy day in his life.

....

Francis Bacon: "It is regrettable and the origin of all evil that considerations of wealth have given way to considerations of power."

Hoffer: It is incredible how few foresaw that the coming of affluence would cause a shift from the pursuit of wealth to the pursuit of power, and that such a shift would be the origin of great evils. Where there is widespread plenty, common people will no longer be regulated and disciplined by the invisible hand of scarcity. Order and stability will have to be deliberately imposed by despotic power. At the same time, the well-off will no longer be able to derive a sense of uniqueness from riches. In an affluent society the rich and their children become radicalized. They decry the value of a materialist society and clamor for change. They will occupy positions of power in the universities, the media, and public life. In some affluent societies the children of the rich will savor power by forming bands of terrorists.

....

Francis Bacon: "There is little friendship in the world, and least of all between equals."

Hoffer: Equals are rivals. There are more limits to rivalry in a class-bound than in a classless society. There can be friendship only when there is a refuge from rivalry.

....

Francis Bacon: "Does any man doubt that if there were taken out of men's minds vain opinions, flattering hopes, false valuations and the like, but it would leave the minds of a number of men poor, shrunken things, full of melancholy and indispositions, and unpleasing to themselves?"

Hoffer: Can souls be purified? To Milton, "Good and evil we know in the world grow up together almost inseparably, and the knowledge of the good is so interwoven with the knowledge of evil that the two cannot be sorted apart."

Montaigne saw "our being so cemented by sickly qualities that whoever should divest men of them would destroy the fundamental condition of human life." Renan feared that we can get rid of the bad only at the sacrifice of what is excellent, remarkable, and extraordinary.

Bizet believed that a purified soul cannot make music. Frederick Meinecke was so disconcerted by the dark and impure origins of great cultural values that it seemed to him as if "God needed the devil to realize himself." The protagonists of reason, who set out to cleanse minds of the irrational, released demoniac forces beyond the control of reason.

Pascal, a scientist who saw it as his religious duty to study man, was staggered by the contrast between the simplicity of things and the fantastic complexity of man. He discovered that we do not remain virtuous by our own power, but by the counterpoise of two opposite vices: we remain standing as between two contrary winds. Take away one of these vices and we fall into the other. To Pascal, cleansing souls was, indeed, a risky undertaking.

....

Francis Bacon: "It was heathen opinion which had supposed the world to be the image of God, while sacred truth had denied the honor to the world and reserved it to man, declaring the world to be God's handiwork only and not His image."

Hoffer: Bacon touches upon two crucial differences between Judeo-Christianity and other religions. In a monotheistic universe nature is stripped of divine qualities—this is a downgrading of nature. At the same time, in a monotheistic universe, man is wholly unique, unlike any living thing.

It would have gone against Bacon's aristocratic grain to point out that the monotheistic God, unlike the God of other religions, is not an aristocrat but a worker, a skilled engineer. Bacon could have predicted the coming of a machine age by suggesting that if God made man in his own image, he made him in the image of a machine-making engineer.

....

Francis Bacon: "The delivering of knowledge in distinct and disjointed aphorisms leaves the wit of men more free to turn and toss."

Hoffer: An aphorism states a half truth and hints at a larger truth. To an aphorist all facts are perishable. His aim is to entertain and stimulate. Instruction means the stuffing of people with perishable facts. And since in human affairs the truthful is usually paradoxical, aphoristic writing is likely to prove helpful.

....

Walter Bagehot: "1848 demonstrated the intellectual's ineffectualness as a social builder."

Hoffer: The intellectual entered the 19th century convinced that it was going to be his century. Had he not launched the French Revolution? He saw himself as a member of the new ruling class, an aristocracy of the mind that would take the place of the hereditary aristocracy. However, it was soon clear that the 19th century was not the century of the intellectual but of the common man. The French Revolution and its Napoleonic aftermath were the first instances of history on a large scale made by nobodies.

One wonders what was going on in the minds of common men as they watched nobodies, people no better than themselves, outwit the most famous generals, topple kings, create new states and live in unimaginable splendor. The spectacle must have caused an explosion of confidence among nobodies everywhere which prompted them to try the untried and attempt the impossible. In this sense the industrial revolution, launched not by successful merchants but by venturesome nobodies, was the offspring of the French Revolution. So, too, the accelerated taming of the American continent had something to do with the release of the new confidence. Prior to the French Revolution both John Adams and Thomas Jefferson thought it would take a thousand years to settle the savage land.

And what happened to the intellectuals? They were kept out in the cold, eating their hearts out as they watched ignorant, vulgar nobodies making history. Their eyes strained for signs of failure, of the collapse of the common man's universe. Every financial crisis was seen as a herald of approaching doom, and every manifestation of social unrest as a harbinger of an impending upheaval.

It is against this background that the attitude of the European intellectual towards the American Civil War has to be seen in order to be understood. Europe's cultivated minds were offended by the sight of common people building and governing one of the largest and freest societies that ever existed. In America, common people were building cities, founding states, leading armies and doing effortlessly things which from the beginning of time were reserved for the privileged orders. It was therefore natural that when the civil war broke out most of Europe's intellectuals believed that America's days were numbered, and were glad of it. Here is how Walter Bagehot, as gentle and fair an intellectual as one could meet, saw it:

. . . .

Bagehot: "Europe at large and England especially have not grieved much at the close proximity of America's fall . . . A low vulgarity has deeply displeased the cultivated minds of Europe, and the American Union will fall little regretted even by those whose language is identical, whose weighted opinions are on most subjects the same as theirs. The unpleasantness of mob government has never before been exemplified as conspicuously, for it never before worked on so large a scale."

Hoffer: The simple truth is that intellectuals never found a democratic society acceptable. Bagehot himself was convinced: "If you once permit the ignorant class to rule you may bid farewell to deference forever." Why should deference be so vital? Will not poets sing, philosophers think, scientists discover where there is no deference?

In America there are tangible rewards—money, fame, power—but no deference. No one believes that people who accomplished great things are made of special clay. It is generally assumed that given the right condition almost anyone could write a great book, create a great work of art and so forth. And, so far, there is no way of telling whether lack of deference has hurt this country's powers.

....

Bagehot: "The characteristic dangers of great nations which have a long history of continuous creation is that they may at last fail from not comprehending the great institutions they have created."

Hoffer: How many nations comprehend their institutions? The United States is about the only country with a vivid, widespread awareness of the genesis and purpose of its institutions. Yet a mere economic depression caused F.D.R. to scorn the institutions which made America great and to proceed recklessly with harebrained experimentation. In retrospect, F.D.R. constitutes a fateful watershed in America's history. Before Roosevelt (B.R.) Americans usually blamed themselves for failure. After Roosevelt (A.R.) they blamed the system and the government, and nursed grievances against the world. America's decline began with F.D.R. and it is absurd to think of him as a great man.

....

James Baldwin: "Whatever white people do not know about Negroes reveals precisely and inexorably what they do not know about themselves. One is staggered by the incredible, abysmal and really cowardly obtuseness of white liberals."

Hoffer: To realize how unprecedented [is] the experience of the Negro in America during his emancipation in the second half of the twentieth century, one should read about the emancipation of the Jews in Western Europe during the first half of the nineteenth century. After centuries of discrimination the Jews were granted equality grudgingly—as a gift rather than a right. Both Gentiles and Jews took it for granted that the Jews still had to prove themselves worthy of equality. This assumption generated a creative ferment that pushed the Jews to the front rank in almost every field of human endeavor.

The Negro, on the other hand, is now entering the mainstream of American life as a creditor. He not only claims equality as a right but demands compensation for what he has been deprived of in the past. The fact that he has attained equality overnight has not allayed the Negro's grievances nor made his demands less clamorous.

The question is whether entering American life as a creditor will facilitate the Negro's integration. Would the Americanization of the 30 million immigrants who came to America before the First World War have proceeded so rapidly and smoothly, and their dormant energies released so fully, had they been given the benefit of affirmative action?

Baldwin's heavy handed rudeness is a symptom of his doubt that the Negro, bolstered by civil rights legislation, could recapitulate the performance of the unfavored millions of immigrants whose children now dominate America's economic, cultural and political life.

....

Balzac: "It has always been easier for men to bestir themselves, assemble in battalions, get themselves killed, than to produce an intellectual conception. Revolutions want noise and movement, but thought wants silence and peace."

Balzac: "Constant labor is the law of art."

Baudelaire: "L'inspiration c'est le travaille tout le jour."

Hoffer: It is only on rare occasions that people like Balzac or Baudelaire theorize about the nature of creativity. Most of the time the canons, techniques and prerequisites of the creative process have been formulated by non-creative people. It was the non-creative who harped through the ages on the primacy of inspiration, on the link between enthusiasm and great achievement, on the fructifying influence of experience and the deadening effect of routine. Strangely, most writers, artists etc., accepted these edicts unquestioningly, but without allowing them to interfere with the creative flow. Indeed, they sometimes manage to turn the wrong edicts into opportunities and advantages.

....

Luigi Barzini, Jr.: "The United States is, in my experience, the only country in the world where people will talk about themselves as 'average Americans.' In Italy everybody considers himself a unique person bordering on genius. That is why Italy does not function."

Hoffer: Is there a record of anyone going to the United States to become a great man the way Australians, New Zealanders, Canadians, Americans and even Germans went to England to become great scientists, writers, statesmen and so on? The tangible advantages of an average American's existence were such that he did not need illusions or delusions to make life bearable. The Italian immigrant who became an average American was too busy making the most of his opportunities to swagger as genius or Don Juan.

....

Saul Bellow: "During the 1960s the young of the well-off middle classes believed what their parents told them: that the parents were a lost generation, but they, the youth, were the meaning of it all; that society was corrupt, but they, the youth, were entitled to purity. The young really believed that there is no scarcity, that everything is present in abundance. And that therefore the solution to life's problems must also be there on demand."

Hoffer: Hardly an historian foresaw that widespread affluence would be a greater threat to social stability than widespread misery. Historians are almost without exception logicians and logic is useless and often misleading in interpreting man's past and in predicting the results of his actions. The record of professional historians as guides in human affairs has been as uniformly dismal as that of trained economists. It should be evident that there is little the behavioral sciences can teach us as long as they adopt the methods and attitudes of the natural sciences.

....

Saul Bellow: "When I say American I mean uncorrected by the main history of human suffering."

Hoffer: America's uniqueness is in its utter newness; it is the only truly new thing in the world. America has no roots in humanity's past nor does it shed light on humanity's future. It is a onetime thing, and like a work of art, chronically unfinished. America was built on a newly discovered continent by people who never had a hand in social building and who deliberately stripped themselves of ancient traditions, fears, habits and values.

....

Bizet: "As a musician, I declare that if you suppress adultery, fanaticism, crime, fallacy, the supernatural, there is no more means of writing a note."

Hoffer: Balzac and Baudelaire saw hard work as the soul of creative achievement. Bizet embraced the juvenile notion that excess releases a creative flow. But it is doubtful whether Bizet really needed a mess of absurdities to be able to write a note of music.

....

George Brandeis: "Ibsen seriously believed that a time will come when the intellectual minority in the Scandinavian countries will be forced to enlist chemistry and medicine in poisoning the proletariat to save themselves from being politically overwhelmed by the majority."

Hoffer: As it turned out, the masses, when given the vote, did not vote themselves but their "betters" into political office. Outside Europe, right now, the masses vote for intellectuals. Has this fact put an end to the intellectual's hysterical fear of the masses? The intellectuals loathe democracy because democracy creates a political climate without deference and worship. In a democracy the intellectual is without an unquestioned sense of superiority and a sense of social usefulness. He is not listened to and not taken seriously.

The sheer possession of power does not satisfy the intellectual. He wants to be worshipped.

....

F. Funck Brentano: In the Middle Ages, "architects, sculptors, glaziers, the composers of sacred music, and the authors of the mystery plays whose theater was the church porch all lived, thought and created as a body. Within the craft guilds, architects and master sculptors lived a life in common with their humbler fellows. Master craftsmen were paid like laborers by the day. This simple patriarchal system came to an end with the rise of Italian influence. The artist became a person of importance. He became a courtier and held a court post."

Hoffer: It is plain that the builders of great cathedrals in Germany and France did not need an exalted status in order to do their best. Pride in their work caused them to take great pains. It is significant that in Italy, too, during the early Renaissance artists considered themselves artisans and were treated as such. Things changed with the coming of the Medicis. Cosimo the Elder treated men of talent as superior beings and soon artists were courted by kings, ministers, prelates and so on. It was natural for artists to welcome the distinction conferred upon them, and their munificent prizes. They saw themselves members of an aristocracy of the spirit set apart from the rest of the population.

....

J. Bronowski: "A hundred and fifty years ago the working week in England was 80 hours for children. Cholera was more common than the flu. The country could hardly support ten million people, and not a million of them could read."

Hoffer: It is obvious that the greatest changes that have taken place during the past 150 years were changes in the fortune of little people. The United States, the French Revolution, the industrial revolution were to a considerable extent the result of history-making by nobodies. The modern era has been the creation of faceless people who never before had a hand in managing affairs. It can also be seen that the totalitarian regimes of our time are a reaction against this new type of history making, and a return to rule by elites. It would be fitting if the entrance of nobodies onto the stage of history should culminate in the release of the creative energies of common people in cultural fields.

. . . .

Arthur Bryant: "There has never been a time in history when the Jews have not been news. And the periods during which the Jews have occupied and dominated Palestine have been the most exciting and significant in man's sojourn on this planet."

Hoffer: Coming from the pen of a distinguished non-Jewish historian, this statement about the historical uniqueness of the Jews and their land is particularly impressive. Moreover, the truth of the statement is being strikingly demonstrated in our time. A hundred years ago, Palestine was a neglected backwater of the Ottoman Empire. As soon as the Jews started to return to their ancient homeland in the 20th century the place became a focus of international interest and international struggles. Of course, the mystery of why it should be so remains—the mystery of how a band of escaped slaves from Egypt became a peculiar people and made of a narrow strip of land on the eastern coast of the Mediterranean a peculiar country.

. . . .

Camus: "Marx overlooked the nation. The struggle between nations has been proved at least as important as a means of explaining history as the class struggle. But nations cannot be entirely explained by economics, therefore Marx ignored them."

Hoffer: Marx, a nineteenth century logician, knew very little of the inner logic of the human condition and human events. Not only did he not suspect that people will more readily die for a nation or race than for a class but he had not the least inkling that ever-increasing affluence is a greater threat to social stability than every increasing misery. Finally, Marx would have scorned any suggestion that the Right can be as genuinely revolutionary as the Left.

It is obvious that Marx's vast learning and his passionate preoccupation with the future did not make him a good prophet. Yet the fact that his predictions did not come true did not prevent Marx from becoming a fateful historical figure. The battle-cries of almost every revolution during the past hundred years were derived from Marx's wrong doctrines and prophecies.

....

Camus: "The dream of the revolutionary Slav Empire as [Russian anarchist Mikhail] Bakunin conjured it up before the eyes of Czar Alexander is exactly the same, down to the last detail of the frontiers, as that realized by Stalin."

Hoffer: Bakunin, ignorant, extravagant and irrational, was a far better prophet than Marx whose contemporary he was. Among his many startling prophecies was the one that "if any people attempts to realize Marxism in its own country it will be the most terrible tyranny which the world has ever seen."

....

Disraeli: "Something unpleasant is coming when men are anxious to tell the truth."

Hoffer: I used to think that only Russians are afraid of the truth, and see truth-tellers as traitors. Actually, we all see truth as a threat and do all we can to fortify ourselves against it. We consider truth tellers as unpleasant people.

....

Disraeli: "Those who want to lead must never hesitate about sacrificing their friends."

Hoffer: It seems to be true that the leader who can inspire fierce loyalty in his followers is without loyalty to anyone but himself. A great leader is a throwback to the pre-human monstrosity from which man evolved.

....

Goethe at 75: "Basically it has been nothing but toil and I may as well say that I have not had four weeks of real enjoyment in all my 75 years."

Hoffer: Pleasure does not mean happiness. Indulging the appetite does not still our anxiety about what we try to achieve. It is plausible that conquering ourselves prepares us for conquering the world.

....

E. H. Carr: "The world on which the First World War broke was on the whole a prosperous and orderly world. It was a world of contented and reasoned optimism—a world which, looking back on the past hundred years with pardonable self satisfaction, believed in progress as a normal condition of civilized human existence.

"After the war, the peoples of the victorious countries seemed to have abandoned their exalted ambitions for the future. Still obsessed with the idea of a return to the good old days, they thought of it no longer as a return to an uninterrupted path of effort and progress, but as the return to a static condition of automatic and effortless prosperity."

Hoffer: It is doubtful whether the fateful consequences of the First World War were due to the vast slaughter, particularly of the young, and the unprecedented waste of wealth. After all, the 23-year hemorrhage of the Revolutionary and Napoleonic Wars was a prelude to a hopeful and peaceful nineteenth century.

There were vital differences between the French wars and the First World War. The French wars were born of a revolution while the First World War gave rise to a revolution. To have acted as the midwife of Lenin's Revolution by destroying the Czarist regime was the First World War's most fateful role.

Secondly, the French wars ended with the defeat of France while at the end of the First World War a victorious, vengeful France dictated a Versailles peace treaty which readied Europe for the rise of Hitler.

Thirdly, the French wars were followed by a mass emigration of the poor and dissatisfied from Europe to the New World while the First World War marked the end of the fabulous *Volkerwanderung*.

Finally, though the slaughter of the French wars was as great as that of the First World War, death was less concentrated and visible. Never before has death seemed so tangible and inevitable as it did to Western Europeans during the four years of pauseless killing of the First World War. This tangibility of death created a climate inhospitable to illusion.

. . . .

G. K. Chesterton: "The artistic temperament is a disease that afflicts would-be artists."

Hoffer: The irony is that the would-be artists brainwash the genuine creators. Would-be artists set the tone. They not only dictate how the artist should dress and look but what they say when they speak about the nature of the creative. We find many distinguished artists maintain that enthusiasm, inspiration and an eventful life are vital to the creative flow. Actually, they know better and act differently. They know that what creation needs is hard work and eventless routine.

. . . .

Clemenceau: "When the phrases hang together neatly it is because your blood is circulating as it ought."

Hoffer: There was something wrong with Clemenceau's blood circulation every time he sat down to write a book. When he was criticized for the obscure style of his books he said: "What a shame that

I don't have three or more years to live. I might have rewritten the books for my cook."

....

Graham Greene in 1967: "If I had to choose between life in the Soviet Union and life in the United States of America I would certainly choose the Soviet Union. I speak out against the injustice done to some writers in the Soviet Union because the greater the affection one feels for a country the more one is driven to protest against failure of justice there."

Hoffer: What is it that Graham Greene prizes most? By choosing the Soviet Union over America it is evident that Greene does not prize intellectual freedom, truth and personal dignity. He chooses the Soviet Union because the writer's standing there is near the top. He lives in the finest houses and is better fed and clothed than the non-intellectual. If he sticks to the Communist line the royalties he is awarded are fabulous. He is taken seriously and made to feel socially useful. He doesn't mind crawling on his belly and licking the boots of the mighty.

....

Ibsen: "A man's gifts are not a property; they are a duty."

Hoffer: Talents do not come fully grown; they have to be developed. Do highly endowed people feel a duty to realize their potentialities? Sometimes a talent compels a person to develop. But it is probably true that from the beginning of time talents have been wasted on an enormous scale. It is the duty of a society to create a milieu optimal for the realization of talents. Such a society will preach self-development as a duty—a holy duty to finish God's work.

....

Ibsen: "Spiritual and intellectual freedom flourish best under absolutism; that was proved in France, then in Germany, and it is now being proved in Russia."

Hoffer: An absolutist government is evil when it makes the struggle for freedom hopeless, as is the case in Communist Russia. Under an inefficient Czarist tyranny spiritual and intellectual freedom flourished.

....

Kant: "The origin of the entire cosmos will be explained sooner than the mechanism of a plant or a caterpillar." [*Universal Natural History and the Theory of Heaven*]

Hoffer: The passage from inanimate to animate matter involved the introduction of elements which scientific logic cannot grasp. We must accept the presence of insoluble mysteries when we deal with the origin of life. Actually, the realm of the mysterious is infinitely greater: why should mathematical logic rule processes in inanimate nature? The origin of order is as great a mystery as the origin of life or the origin of man.

....

Louis XII, on his deathbed: "I have not loved God."

Hoffer: By accepting Christianity the warrior princes and peasants of Western Europe were saddled with a most uncongenial religion which galled and chafed on the backs of their souls. They could not love the pitiless Jehovah nor did they feel at ease with his Son. Yet it was this galling which made Europe the most energetic and enterprising part of the globe.

....

Marx: "Revolution is the locomotive of history."

Hoffer: It's truer of war than of revolution. Revolution is not the cause but the byproduct of change—the fumes emitted by a faulty engine. The twentieth century has shown us that revolutions do not revolutionize. When a revolution is over everything drops back to where it was before the revolution. Lenin thought his revolution would put an end to history and indeed Lenin's revolution marked the end of modern history and a return to the most ancient past. The nations that really made history—Britain, Germany, America, Japan, Israel—hardly had a revolution.

. . . .

Somerset Maugham: "The writer needs do nothing very much but he should do everything a little."

Hoffer: The writer must guard against being chewed up by experience. He should be able to know the taste of a loaf by swallowing a crumb. His creating consists in making much out of little. The writer creates to compensate himself for what he did not experience; for what he could not be.

. . . .

Francois Mauriac: "Sociability is the only pleasure after that of love which helps us tolerate life, and diverts us from thoughts of death."

Hoffer: Is being alone so terrible? I have lived alone most of my life. Sometimes I went for days without exchanging a word. But I cannot remember thoughts of death darkening my days. Things may be different in old age. Right now as I am approaching 80 [actually 84] death seems tangible and familiar. But by the sheer grace of God I am more cherished by friends than at any time in the past.

. . . .

Ortega: "Man is the only being who misses what he has never had."

Hoffer: It is probably true that man was made uniquely human by his imagination rather than by his intelligence. It is far more certain that animals lack imagination than that they lack intelligence.

. . . .

Pascal: "Revolutions change everything save the human heart."

Hoffer: More than any other century, the twentieth has seen fanatical soul engineers determined to change hearts. Perhaps the discovery of our time that revolutions are not revolutionary has generated the conviction that unless hearts are changed there can be no change.

A twentieth century Pascal would probably have written: "Revolutions change little, least of all the human heart."

....

Pasteur: "The more I contemplate the mysteries of nature the more my faith becomes that of a Breton peasant."

Hoffer: Nature is mindless yet works with ingenuity and precision. That blind chance working over long periods should accomplish what only the subtlest of minds could devise seems to us beyond belief. We would find it easier to believe in the crudest superstition. And the more we know of the inner working of nature the more strained our belief.

....

Renan (Speaking of the modern Jews): "This son of the prophets, this brother of zealots, this kinsman of Christ has become a finished worldling with little concern about a paradise the world has believed in on his word. How easily has he adapted to all fashions of modern civilization and contrives to enjoy the world he has not made, to gather the fruits of a field he never tilled. He supplants the idler who persecutes him, and makes himself necessary to the fool that scorns him."

Renan: "Judaism is a religion that obtains the most heroic sacrifice from its adherents though it be not of its essence to promise anything beyond this life."

[*These quotations illustrate Hoffer's long-time interest in Renan, but he didn't comment on them.*]

....

George Steiner: "We have no proof that a tradition of literary studies makes a man more humane. What is worse—a certain body of evidence points the other way. When barbarism came to twenti-eth century Europe the arts faculties in more than one university offered very little moral resistance. In a disturbing number of cases the literary imagination gave servile and ecstatic welcome to po-litical bestiality."

Hoffer: The creative individual is more uniquely human than the noncreative but not more uniquely humane. Malice is as uniquely human as compassion. Where the creative live together they live the lives of witches.

Increasing His Word-power

If he was unsure of the meaning of a word, Hoffer would look it up and write it down in a notebook. Here is a partial list:

From an early notebook, undated but 1930s

Concupiscence = sexual desire
Apposite = appropriate
Extenuation = excuse
Diffident = shy, modest
Factitious = artificial, sham
Animadversion = censure, stricture
Gratuitous = without provocation
Lapidary = as one who cuts and sets stones
Vitiate = to taint, deprave, annul
Vestigial = rudimentary
Otiose = functionless
Loath = unwilling
Loathe = despise

1941 Notebook: "I must fix in my mind the exact meaning of the following: invidious, mordant, ingenuousness, factitious, fustian, fecklessness, concupiscence, garrulous, gratuitous, venial, spurious, nugatory, ubiquitous, sedulous."

Ancillary	=	subordinate
Explicate	=	unfold the meaning of
Jejune	=	lacking interest or satisfaction; dry, barren
Temerarious	=	unreasonable, venturous, rash
Importunate	=	troublesomely urgent
Frenetic	=	frantic
Esoteric	=	secret
Mephitic	=	noxious, pestilential exhalation from the earth
Apodictic	=	absolutely certain
Saturnalia	=	general license and excess
Gelid	=	cold, frozen . . . "gelid old Rockefeller eliminating competitors like clay pigeons"
Vatic	=	prophetical
Histrionic	=	theatrical
Factitious	=	artificial
Perspicacious	=	of acute mental vision and discernment . . . "His cure was not as perspicacious as his analysis of the evil."
Placket	=	the opening of a woman's blouse
Repine	=	complain
Anodyne	=	soothing
Feral	=	wild, not domesticated
Venial	=	excusable
Venal	=	ready to sell honor
Perspicacity	=	keenness in mental penetration
Perspicuity	=	lucidity, clearness of expression or style
Elide	=	ignore, omit, annul
Advert	=	call attention, refer to

"Reflections," by Eric Hoffer

ISRAEL STANDS ALONE

Los Angeles Times, May 26, 1968.

The Jews are a peculiar people: things permitted to other nations are forbidden to the Jews.

Other nations drive out thousands, even millions of people and there is no refugee problem. Russia did it, Poland and Czechoslovakia did it. Turkey drove out a million Greeks and Algeria a million Frenchmen. Indonesia threw out heaven knows how many Chinese—and no one says a word about refugees.

But in the case of Israel, the displaced Arabs have become eternal refugees. Everyone insists that Israel must take back every single Arab. Arnold Toynbee calls the displacement of the Arabs an atrocity greater than any committed by the Nazis.

Other nations when victorious on the battlefield dictate peace terms. But when Israel is victorious, it must sue for peace. Everyone expects the Jews to be the only real Christians in this world.

Other nations, when they are defeated, survive and recover but should Israel be defeated it would be destroyed. Had Nasser triumphed last June [1967], he would have wiped Israel off the map, and no one would have lifted a finger to save the Jews.

No commitment to the Jews by any government, including our own, is worth the paper it is written on. There is a cry of outrage all over the world when people die in Vietnam or when two Negroes are executed in Rhodesia. But when Hitler slaughtered Jews no one remonstrated with him.

The Swedes, who are ready to break off diplomatic relations with America because of what we do in Vietnam, did not let out a peep when Hitler was slaughtering Jews. They sent Hitler choice iron ore, and ball bearings, and serviced his troop trains to Norway.

The Jews are alone in the world. If Israel survives, it will be solely because of Jewish efforts. And Jewish resources.

Yet at this moment, Israel is our only reliable and unconditional ally. We can rely more on Israel than Israel can rely on us. And one has only to imagine what would have happened last summer had the Arabs and their Russian backers won the war to realize how vital the survival of Israel is to America and the West in general.

I have a premonition that will not leave me; as it goes with Israel so will it go with all of us. Should Israel perish, the Holocaust will be upon us.

Israel must live!

NOTES

INTRODUCTION

1. Will and Ariel Durant, *The Story of Civilization,* Part VIII, "The Age of Louis XIV" (New York: Simon and Schuster, 1963), 630.
2. Durant, *The Story of Civilization,* Part X, "Rousseau and Revolution," 549.
3. Eric Hoffer, *Before the Sabbath* (New York: Harper & Row, 1979), entry from March 14, 1975.
4. Ibid., entry from April 20, 1975.
5. Eric Hoffer, *Reflections on the Human Condition* (New York: Harper & Row, 1973), dust jacket.
6. Calvin Tomkins, *Eric Hoffer: An American Odyssey* (New York: E.P. Dutton, January 1968), 54.

CHAPTER ONE   **The Enigma of Eric Hoffer**

1. James Koerner, *Hoffer's America* (La Salle, Ill.: Open Court Publishing, 1973), 6.
2. Ibid., 24.
3. Calvin Tomkins, *Eric Hoffer: An American Odyssey* (New York: E.P. Dutton, Perennial Library edition, 1970), 8.
4. James Day, sixth interview of Eric Hoffer, produced for National Educational Television by KQED, San Francisco, 1963. Transcript in Hoover Archives.
5. Tomkins, *An American Odyssey* (henceforth in these notes, all Tomkins pages refer to the Perennial Library edition), 8.

6. Ibid.

7. Ibid., 9–12.

8. Ibid., 10.

9. Ibid., 12.

10. Ibid., 11.

11. Talk of the Town column, "Literary Stevedore," *The New Yorker*, April 28, 1951.

12. Tomkins, *An American Odyssey*, 11.

13. Tomkins, *An American Odyssey*, 12.

14. Eric Hoffer, *Truth Imagined* (New York: Harper & Row, 1983), 4.

15. Tomkins, *An American Odyssey*, 13.

16. Ibid.

17. Ibid., 14–15.

18. Ibid.

19. Koerner, *Hoffer's America*, 16–17.

20. Tomkins, *An American Odyssey*, 15–16; and Hoffer, *Truth Imagined*, 8–9.

21. Tomkins, *An American Odyssey*, 16.

22. Hoffer, *Truth Imagined*, 11.

23. Ibid., 20.

24. Ibid., 21.

25. Tomkins, *An American Odyssey*, 17; Hoffer, *Truth Imagined*, 24.

26. Hoffer, *Truth Imagined*, 25.

27. Ibid.

28. Tomkins, *An American Odyssey*, 18.

29. Ibid.

30. Hoffer, *Truth Imagined*, 28.

31. Ibid., 33.

32. *Social Contract Journal,* vol. 20, no. 2, Winter 2009–2010.

33. Hoover Archives.

34. John McGreevy interview of Eric Hoffer for Canadian Broadcasting Corporation, 1974, Hoover Archives.

35. Eric Hoffer, "Chance and Mr. Kunze," Hoover Archives.

36. Eric Hoffer speech at College High, Bartlesville, Oklahoma, 1979, Hoover Archives.

37. Tomkins, *An American Odyssey*, 7–8.

38. Ibid., 10.

39. Hoover Archives.

40. Koerner, *Hoffer's America*, 2.

41. Ibid., 11.
42. Ibid., 3.
43. Ibid., 9.
44. Margaret Anderson letters, 1941, 1949.
45. Author's interview with Joe Gladstone, November 14, 2010.
46. Tomkins, *An American Odyssey*, 11–12.
47. Author's interview with Eric Osborne, October 2, 2010.
48. Calvin Tomkins, "Profiles," *The New Yorker*, January 7, 1967, 42.
49. Ibid., 43.
50. Tomkins, *An American Odyssey*, 12.
51. Koerner, *Hoffer's America*, 14.
52. Ibid., 14–15.
53. Calvin Tomkins to the author, October 27, 2009.
54. Batty thesis, Hoover Archives.

CHAPTER TWO   **The Migrant Worker**

1. Eric Hoffer, "Autobiographical Writings, 1934–1936," Hoover Archives.
2. Eric Hoffer, *The Ordeal of Change* (New York: Harper & Row, 1963).
3. Eric Hoffer, *Truth Imagined* (New York: Harper & Row, 1983).
4. Ibid., 33.
5. Kevin Starr, *Endangered Dreams, The Great Depression in California* (Oxford: Oxford University Press, 1996), 158.
6. Hoffer, "The Role of the Undesirables," *The Ordeal of Change*, 143–46.
7. Hoffer, *Truth Imagined*, 37.
8. Letter from Bob O'Brien to Eric Hoffer, July 4, 1951, Hoover Archives.
9. Joseph Henry Jackson, "Notes on the Margin," *San Francisco Chronicle*, December 14, 1952.
10. Starr, *Endangered Dreams*, 231.
11. Author's interview with Stacy Cole, 2010.
12. Starr, *Endangered Dreams*, chap. 8.
13. Eric Hoffer, "Reflections: A Free Society is a Skilled Society," *San Francisco Examiner*, February 23, 1969.
14. Hoffer, *Truth Imagined*, 43.
15. Hoffer, *The Ordeal of Change*, early draft, Hoover Archives.
16. Eric Hoffer, "Maintenance," *San Francisco Examiner*, April 27, 1969.
17. Calvin Tomkins, *Eric Hoffer: An American Odyssey* (Perennial Library edition, 1970), 2.
18. Hoffer, *The Ordeal of Change*, 117.

19. James Koerner, *Hoffer's America* (La Salle, Ill.: Open Court Publishing, 1973), 19.
20. Ibid., 20.
21. Hoffer, *Truth Imagined*, 64–65.
22. Koerner, *Hoffer's America*, 21.
23. This document on his 1937 Social Security application is the earliest physical evidence of Hoffer's existence. It was once in the Hoover Archives, but was returned to Lili Osborne in about 2004.
24. See Gerald Meyer, "The Cultural Pluralist Response to Americanization," *Socialism and Democracy*, November 2008; also, Tomkins, *American Odyssey*, 35.

CHAPTER THREE   **On the Waterfront**

1. *San Francisco Examiner*, March 14, 1968.
2. San Francisco Public Library 1948 notebook.
3. Eric Hoffer, *Truth Imagined* (New York: Harper & Row, 1983), 92.
4. Ibid., 93.
5. Kevin Starr, *Endangered Dreams: The Great Depression in California* (Oxford: Oxford University Press, 1996), 118.
6. Author's interview with Lewis Lapham, 2004.
7. Hoffer, *Truth Imagined*, 93.
8. Author's interview with Peter Duignan, 2003.
9. Eric Sevareid interview of Eric Hoffer for CBS-TV, "The Passionate State of Mind," broadcast September 17, 1967.
10. *The New Yorker*, April 28, 1951.
11. Calvin Tomkins, *Eric Hoffer: An American Odyssey* (Perennial Library edition, 1970), 40.
12. *Time*, March 14, 1955.
13. *The New Yorker*, January 7, 1967.
14. Ibid., 62.
15. "The Workingman Looks at the Boss," *Harper's*, March 1954.
16. Eric Hoffer, *Working and Thinking on the Waterfront; a journal, June 1958–May 1959* (New York: Harper & Row, 1969).
17. *The New Yorker*, January 7, 1967, 67.
18. Hoffer, *Working and Thinking*, entry of April 6, 1959.
19. *The New Yorker*, April 28, 1951.
20. Lili Osborne, letter to author, 2009.
21. Jack Fincher, "West" magazine, *Los Angeles Times*, July 11, 1967.

22. *The New Yorker,* January 7, 1967.

23. Hoffer, *Working and Thinking*, entry of December 2, 1958.

24. Selden Osborne's letter to *The Dispatcher* is in the ILWU's archives, 1188 Franklin St., San Francisco, California.

CHAPTER FOUR   Intimate Friendships

1. Leslie Fulbright, "Life at the Bottom: S.F.'s Sunnydale Housing Project," *San Francisco Chronicle*, February 3, 2008. See also C. W. Nevius in *San Francisco Chronicle*, November 5, 2011.

2. Eric Hoffer, *Working and Thinking on the Waterfront; a journal, June 1958–May 1959* (New York: Harper & Row, 1969), entry of February 19, 1959.

3. Author's interview with Joe Gladstone, October 7, 2010.

4. Author's interview with Rick Gladstone, May 2011.

5. Calvin Tomkins, *Eric Hoffer: An American Odyssey* (Perennial Library edition, 1970), 51.

6. Douglas M. Davis, "The Odds Say that Eric Hoffer Cannot Be," *National Observer*, December 11, 1967.

7. Author's interview of Eric Osborne, October 16, 2010.

8. Author's interview of Stephen Osborne, December 2010.

CHAPTER FIVE   The True Believer

1. Eric Hoffer, *Before the Sabbath* (New York: Harper & Row, 1979), p. 60.

2. Joe Gladstone, *Days of Pain and Pleasure*, unpublished memoir.

3. "Fanaticism Analysed," *Times Literary Supplement*, April 25, 1952.

4. Eric Hoffer, *The True Believer: Thoughts on the Nature of Mass Movements* (New York: Harper & Brothers, 1951), section 117.

5. Ibid., section 14.

6. Ibid., preface.

7. Ibid., section 15.

8. Ibid., section 104.

9. Ibid., section 106.

10. Ibid., section 105.

11. Ibid., section 104.

12. Ibid., preface.

13. Talk of the Town column, "Literary Stevedore," *The New Yorker*, April 28, 1951.
14. Orville Prescott, *New York Times*, March 16, 1951.
15. Johathan Randolph (Murray Rothbard), *Faith and Freedom*, September 1956.
16. *New York Post*, March 17, 1951.
17. James Koerner, *Hoffer's America* (La Salle, Ill.: Open Court Publishing), 51, 136.
18. Hoffer, *The True Believer*, section 1.
19. Ibid., section 7.
20. Ibid., section 8.
21. Ibid., section 43.
22. Ibid., section 111.
23. Ibid., section 7.
24. Ibid., section 7.
25. Ibid., section 26.
26. Hoffer, *The True Believer*, section 105, quoted in Bernard Theall, "When Does a Believer Become a Fanatic?" *Books on Trial*, April 1951.
27. Eric Hoffer, *In Our Time* (New York: Harper & Row, 1976), 66.
28. Hoffer, *The True Believer*, section 42.
29. Richard Pipes to author, July 30, 2003.
30. Eric Sevareid interview of Hoffer for CBS-TV, "The Passionate State of Mind," broadcast on September 17, 1967.
31. Eric Hoffer, "Scribe, Writer," in *The Ordeal of Change* (New York: Harper & Row, 1963), 88.
32. Hoffer, *The True Believer*, section 70.
33. Ibid., section 66.
34. Ibid., section 70. Also, see John McDonough, "Anatomy of Zealotry," *Wall Street Journal*, October 2, 2001.
35. Eric Hoffer, *Truth Imagined* (New York: Harper & Row, 1983), 88.
36. "President Urging A Book to Friends," *New York Times*, March 19, 1956.
37. Marguerite Higgins, "Eisenhower's Other Side," *New York Herald Tribune*, January 25, 1953.
38. Calvin Tomkins, *Eric Hoffer: An American Odyssey* (Perennial Library edition, 1970), 71.
39. Dick Pearce, "Longshoreman Writes Book About Philosophy," *San Francisco Examiner*, February 26, 1951.

CHAPTER SIX   Hoffer as a Public Figure

1. Eric Hoffer, "Automation Is Here To Liberate Us," *New York Times Magazine,* October 14, 1965.

2. Calvin Tomkins, *Eric Hoffer: An American Odyssey* (Perennial Library edition, 1970), 71.

3. Author's interview of Stanford Ph.D. researcher Bill Fredlund, 2003.

4. Eric Hoffer, *Working and Thinking on the Waterfront; a journal, June 1958–May 1959* (New York: Harper & Row, 1969). Entry from April 11, 1959.

5. Letter from Norman Jacobson to Eric Hoffer, October 16, 1963, Hoover Archives.

6. Author's interview with Tom Lorentzen, October 16, 2010.

7. Peter Collier, "Eric Hoffer: The Wizard of Was," *Ramparts*, December 1967.

8. Hoffer's second interview with Eric Sevareid, transcript in Hoover Archives.

9. Ibid.

10. First interview with Eric Sevareid, transcript in Hoover Archives.

11. Ibid.

12. Kenneth Crawford, "Passionate Believer," *Newsweek*, October 16, 1967, 38.

13. Second interview with Eric Sevareid, Hoover Archives.

14. Ibid.

15. *New York Times*, October 26, 1968.

16. UPI, "Hoffer, Negro Professor Blast Each Other in Violence Hearing," October 26, 1968.

17. Jerome Skolnick, "The Violence Commission: Internal Politics and Public Policy," *Transaction: Social Science and Modern Society,* 1970, 437.

18. Collier, "The Wizard of Was," *Ramparts,* December 1967, 65–69.

19. Tomkins, *American Odyssey*, 61.

20. Author's interview with Stacy Cole, 2007.

21. Mimi Jacobs, "The World of Eric Hoffer," *Pacific Sun,* September 13–19, 1973.

22. Eric Hoffer, *Before the Sabbath* (New York: Harper & Row, 1979), entry of February 12, 1975.

23. Thomas Eastham, "The Decision of Eric Hoffer," *San Francisco Examiner*, February 20, 1970.

24. Ibid.

CHAPTER SEVEN   The Literary Life

1. Calvin Tomkins, *Eric Hoffer: An American Odyssey* (Perennial Library edition, 1970), 53.
2. Eric Hoffer, *The Ordeal of Change* (New York: Harper & Row, 1963).
3. Eric Hoffer, *The Passionate State of Mind, And Other Aphorisms* (New York: Harper & Row, 1955).
4. Eric Hoffer, *Between the Devil and the Dragon* (New York: Harper & Row, 1982).
5. Murray Kempton, "The Cold Eye of Eric Hoffer," *New York Post*, March 6, 1955.
6. Eric Hoffer, *The True Believer: Thoughts on the Nature of Mass Movements* (New York: Harper & Brothers, 1951), section 125.
7. Eric Hoffer, "What Makes Nations Run Amuck?" *New York Herald Tribune*, December 2, 1951.
8. Ibid.
9. Eric Hoffer, "The Captive Peoples Revolt," *New York Times Magazine*, August 23, 1953; reprinted as "Popular Upheavals in Communist Countries" in *The Ordeal of Change*.
10. Eric Hoffer, *Working and Thinking on the Waterfront; a journal, June 1958–May 1959* (New York: Harper & Row, 1969), remarks dated February 6, March 12, and March 27, 1959.
11. Hoffer, *The True Believer*, section 122.
12. Eric Hoffer, *First Things, Last Things* (New York: Harper & Row, 1971), 116.
13. Hoffer, *The True Believer*, Section 125.
14. James Koerner, *Hoffer's America* (La Salle, Ill.: Open Court Publishing, 1973).
15. Eric Hoffer, *Reflections on the Human Condition* (New York: Harper & Row, 1973), 3.

CHAPTER EIGHT   America and the Intellectuals

1. Eric Hoffer, *First Things, Last Things* (New York: Harper & Row, 1971), 76.
2. Eric Hoffer, *Before the Sabbath* (New York: Harper & Row, 1979), 3.
3. Rebecca West, *The Meaning of Treason* (London: MacMillan & Company, 1949).
4. Eric Hoffer, *The Temper of Our Time* (New York: Harper & Row, 1967), 62.

5. Hoffer, *First Things, Last Things*, 123.

6. Eric Hoffer, *The True Believer: Thoughts on the Nature of Mass Movements* (New York: Harper & Brothers, 1951).

7. Hoffer, *The True Believer*, section 105.

8. Eric Hoffer, *The Ordeal of Change* (New York: Harper & Row, 1963), 18.

9. Eric Hoffer, *In Our Time* (New York: Harper & Row, 1976), 61.

10. Gene Griessman, "The Weariness of a True Believer: Eric Hoffer's Parting Words," *San Francisco Examiner* ("This World" section), July 10, 1983. The article was originally written for *The Atlanta Journal* and the *Atlanta Constitution*'s Atlanta Weekly Magazine.

CHAPTER NINE   God, Jehovah, and the Jews

1. Author's interview with Eric Osborne, September 22, 2010.

2. Author's interviews with Lili Osborne August 25, 2003, and August 14, 2010.

3. Eric Hoffer, *Working and Thinking on the Waterfront; a journal, June 1958–May 1959* (New York: Harper & Row, 1969), entry of February 9, 1959.

4. Hoover Archives, translation.

5. Eric Hoffer, *The True Believer: Thoughts on the Nature of Mass Movements* (New York: Harper & Brothers, 1951), section 62.

6. Hoffer, *The True Believer*, xi.

7. Author's interview with Mary Fabilli, January 2008.

8. Eric Hoffer, *Truth Imagined* (New York: Harper & Row, 1983).

9. Ibid., 16.

10. Eric Hoffer, *The Ordeal of Change* (New York: Harper & Row, 1963).

11. Eric Hoffer, *The Passionate State of Mind, And Other Aphorisms* (New York: Harper & Row, 1955), section 89.

12. Hoffer, *The Ordeal of Change*, Chapter 8.

13. Eric Hoffer, "Islam and Modernization," *The American Spectator*, June 1980.

CHAPTER TEN   The Longshoreman Philosopher

1. Bertrand Russell, *The Problems of Philosophy* (Oxford: Oxford University Press, 1959), 154–55.

2. Bertrand Russell, *A History of Western Philosophy*, (London: George Allen & Unwin Ltd., 1946), 663.

3. Eric Hoffer, *Before the Sabbath* (New York: Harper & Row, 1979), entry of January 19, 1975.

4. Ibid., entry of January 13, 1975.

5. Blaise Pascal, *Pensees* (New York: The Modern Library, Random House, 1941), section II, no. 6.

6. Ludwig Wittgenstein, *Culture and Value,* transl. Peter Winch, (Chicago: University of Chicago Press, 1980), 34e.

7. Wittgenstein, *Philosophical Investigations* (West Sussex, UK: Basil Blackwell Ltd., 1953), section 129.

8. Peter Hershey, *The Beginning of the End* (Virtualbookworm.com Publishing, 2004), 109.

9. Eric Hoffer, *Truth Imagined* (New York: Harper & Row, 1983), 52.

10. Eric Hoffer, *The Passionate State of Mind, And Other Aphorisms* (New York: Harper & Row, 1955), 93.

11. Charles Darwin, *Descent of Man*, 2nd ed. (London: John Murray, 1874), 126.

12. Eric Hoffer, *Working and Thinking on the Waterfront; a journal, June 1958–May 1959* (New York: Harper & Row, 1969), entry from April 5, 1959.

13. Alan Weisman, *The World Without Us*, 2007.

EPILOGUE

1. *People* magazine, January 16, 1978.

2. *Los Angeles Herald Examiner*, February 18, 1979.

3. Jane Dyer Abbot, *California Today*, March 4, 1979.

4. *Los Angeles Herald Examiner*, February 18, 1979.

5. Camilla Snyder, *Los Angeles Herald Examiner*, February 10, 1980.

6. Gene Griessman, "The Weariness of a True Believer," reprinted in the *San Francisco Examiner*'s weekend section. "This World," July 10, 1983.

7. Author's interview with Stacy Cole.

8. Peter Worthington, "Genius at Work," *The Toronto Sun*, November 23, 1982.

9. Hoover Archives.

ABOUT THE AUTHOR

TOM BETHELL is a journalist in Washington, D.C., where he is a senior editor of *The American Spectator*. He was Washington editor of *Harper's* magazine and before that an editor of the *Washington Monthly*. For twenty-five years he has been a visiting media fellow at the Hoover Institution, where Eric Hoffer's papers are now preserved. He interviewed Hoffer during reporting trips to San Francisco in 1980 and 1981 and was among the last journalists to do so.

A graduate of Oxford University, where he studied philosophy and psychology, Mr. Bethell emigrated to the United States in 1962 and became a U.S. citizen. He has published books about subjects ranging from the history of New Orleans jazz to the connection between wealth and private property. This is his sixth book.

INDEX